주한미군지위협정(SOFA)

서명 및 발효 19

주한미군지위협정(SOFA)

서명 및 발효 19

한국학술정보

| 머리말

미국은 오래전부터 우리나라 외교에 있어서 가장 긴밀하고 실질적인 우호 · 협력관계를 맺어 온 나라다. 6 · 25전쟁 정전 협정이 체결된 후 북한의 재침을 막기 위한 대책으로서 1953년 11월 한미 상호방위조약이 체결되었다. 이는 미군이 한국에 주둔하는 법적 근거였고, 그렇게 주둔하게 된 미군의 시설, 구역, 사업, 용역, 출입국, 통관과 관세, 재판권 등 포괄적인 법적 지위를 규정하는 것이 바로 주한미군지위협정(SOFA)이다. 그러나 이와 관련한 협상은 계속된 난항을 겪으며 한미 상호방위조약이 체결로부터 10년이 훌쩍 넘은 1967년이 돼서야 정식 발효에 이를 수 있었다. 그럼에도 당시 미군 범죄에 대한 한국의 재판권은 심한 제약을 받았으며, 1980년대 후반 민주화 운동과 함께 미군 범죄 문제가 사회적 이슈로 떠오르자 협정을 개정해야 한다는 목소리가 커지게 되었다. 이에 1991년 2월 주한미군지위협정 1차 개정이 진행되었고, 이후에도 여러 사건이 발생하며 2001년 4월 2차 개정이 진행되어 현재에 이르고 있다.

본 총서는 외교부에서 작성하여 최근 공개한 주한미군지위협정(SOFA) 관련 자료를 담고 있다. 1953년 한미 상호방위조약 체결 이후부터 1967년 발효가 이뤄지기까지의 자료와 더불어, 이후 한미 합동위원회를 비롯해 민 · 형사재판권, 시설, 노무, 교통 등 각 분과위원회의 회의록과 운영 자료, 한국인 고용인 문제와 관련한 자료, 기타 관련 분쟁 자료 등을 포함해 총 42권으로 구성되었다. 전체 분량은 약 2만 2천여 쪽에 이른다.

2024년 3월

한국학술정보(주)

| 일러두기

· 본 총서에 실린 자료는 2022년 4월과 2023년 4월에 각각 공개한 외교문서 4,827권, 76만 여 쪽 가운데 일부를 발췌한 것이다.

· 각 권의 제목과 순서는 공개된 원본을 최대한 반영하였으나, 주제에 따라 일부는 적절히 변경하였다.

· 원본 자료는 A4 판형에 맞게 축소하거나 원본 비율을 유지한 채 A4 페이지 안에 삽입하였다. 또한 현재 시점에선 공개되지 않아 '공란'이란 표기만 있는 페이지 역시 그대로 실었다.

· 외교부가 공개한 문서 각 권의 첫 페이지에는 '정리 보존 문서 목록'이란 이름으로 기록물 종류, 일자, 명칭, 간단한 내용 등의 정보가 수록되어 있으며, 이를 기준으로 0001번부터 번호가 매겨져 있다. 이는 삭제하지 않고 총서에 그대로 수록하였다.

· 보고서 내용에 관한 더 자세한 정보가 필요하다면, 외교부가 온라인상에 제공하는 『대한민국 외교사료요약집』 1991년과 1992년 자료를 참조할 수 있다.

| 차례

정/리/보/존/문/서/목/록

기록물종류	문서-일반공문서철	등록번호	947 9620	등록일자	2006-07-27
분류번호	741.12	국가코드	US	주제	
문서철명	한.미국 간의 상호방위조약 제4조에 의한 시설과 구역 및 한국에서의 미국군대의 지위에 관한 협정 (SOFA) 전59권. 1966.7.9 서울에서 서명 : 1967.2.9 발효 (조약 232호) *원본				
생산과	미주과/조약과	생산년도	1952 - 1967	보존기간	영구
담당과(그룹)	조약	조약	서가번호	--	
참조분류					
권차명	V.49 실무교섭회의 합의의사록, 제1-9차, 1962.9-12월				
내용목차	* 일지 : 1953.8.7 이승만 대통령-Dulles 미국 국무장관 공동성명 - 상호방위조약 발효 후 군대지위협정 교섭 약속 1954.12.2 정부, 주한 UN군의 관세업무협정 체결 제의 1955.1월, 5월 미국, 제의 거절 1955.4.28 정부, 군대지위협정 제의 (한국측 초안 제시) 1957.9.10 Hurter 미국 국무차관 방한 시 각서 수교 (한국측 제의 수락 요구) 1957.11.13, 26 정부, 개별 협정의 단계적 체결 제의 1958.9.18 Dawling 주한미국대사, 형사재판관할권 협정 제외 조건으로 행정협정 체결 의사 전달 1960.3.10 정부, 토지, 시설협정의 우선적 체결 강력 요구 1961.4.10 장면 국무총리-McConaughy 주한미국대사 공동성명으로 교섭 개시 합의 1961.4.15, 4.25 제1, 2차 한.미국 교섭회의 (서울) 1962.3.12 정부, 교섭 재개 촉구 공한 송부 1962.5.14 Burger 주한미국대사, 최규하 장관 면담 시 형사재판관할권 문제 제기 않는 조건으로 교섭 재개 통고 1962.9.6 한.미국 간 공동성명 발표 (9월 중 교섭 재개 합의) 1962.9.20~ 1965.6.7 제1-81차 실무 교섭회의 (서울) 1966.7.8 제82차 실무 교섭회의 (서울) 1966.7.9 서명 1967.2.9 발효 (조약 232호)					

마/이/크/로/필/름/사/항

촬영연도	*롤 번호	화일 번호	후레임 번호	보관함 번호
2006-11-24	I-06-0072	02	1-147	

0001

US-ROK STATUS OF FORCES AGREEMENT

Index of SOFA Articles as Negotiated in the 82 Negotiating Meetings

Herewith is an index of SOFA Articles in the US-ROK Status of Forces Agreement as contained in the Agreed Joint Summaries of the 82 SOFA negotiating session which resulted in the US-ROK Status of Forces Agreement. This index of the Summaries of the negotiating sessions indicates the negotiating meeting by number and date at which each individual Article was discussed. This tabulation has been prepared mainly to assist US Joint Committee and Subcommittee personnel in the use of the Agreed Joint Summaries. It should facilitate the use of these Summaries as a point-of-reference to obtain the US and ROK positions and points-of-view on various pertinent SOFA matters, as expressed at the formal SOFA negotiating meetings.

0002

INDEX OF US-ROK SOFA AGREED JOINT SUMMARIES

SOFA ARTICLE	Title	SOFA Negotiating Meeting No.	Date/Meeting Year	Day	Month
	Preamble	4	1962	19	Oct
		5	"	15	Nov
		7	"	26	Nov
		8	"	5	Dec - AGREED
	Definitions	4	1962	19	Oct
		5	"	1	Nov
		9	"	14	Dec
		10	1963	7	Jan
		15	"	25	Feb
		17	"	17	Mar
II	Facilities and Areas - Grant and Return	9	1962	14	Dec
		10	1963	7	Jan
		11	"	16	Jan
		16	"	8	Mar
		31	"	20	Sep
		32	"	4	Oct
		33	"	18	Oct - AGREED
III	Facilities and Areas-Security Measures in	9	1962	14	Dec
		11	1963	16	Jan
		18	"	29	Mar
		31	"	20	Sep
		32	"	4	Oct - AGREED
IV	Facilities and Areas - Improvement and Return	9	1962	14	Dec
		11	1963	16	Jan
		18	"	29	Mar
		19	"	11	Apr
		31	"	20	Sep
		32	"	4	Oct
		42	1964	14	Feb
		81	1965	7	Jun
		82	1966	-	- - AGREED

0003

No.	Article	Meeting No.	Year	Day	Month
V	Facilities and Areas - Compensation	9	1962	14	Dec
		11	1963	16	Jan
		15	"	25	Feb
		19	"	11	Apr
		81	1965	7	Jun -
				AGREED	
VI	Utilities and Services	11	1963	16	Jan
		12	"	24	Jan
		14	"	14	Feb
		20	"	24	Apr
		24	"	12	Jun
		35	"	14	Nov
		39	1964	17	Jan
		44	"	28	Feb
		45	"	6	Mar -
				AGREED	
VII	Respect for Local Law	12	1963	24	Jan
		13	"	5	Feb
		23	"	20	May
		24	"	12	Jun -
				AGREED	
VIII	Entry and Exit	4	1962	19	Oct
		5	"	1	Nov
		6	"	15	Nov -
				AGREED	
IX	Customs and Duties	6	1962	15	Nov
		7	"	26	Nov
		8	"	5	Dec
		12	1963	24	Jan
		13	"	5	Feb
		19	"	11	Apr
		34	"	30	Oct
		35	"	14	Nov
		36	"	3	Dec
		37	"	27	Dec
		38	1964	9	Jan
		39	"	17	Jan
		40	"	24	Jan
		41	"	6	Feb
		51	"	5	May

No.	Article	Meeting No.	Year	Day	Month
IX	Customs and Duties (cont'd)	53	1964	28	May
		54	"	9	Jun
		55	"	19	Jun
		56	"	26	Jur
		57	"	8	Ju: -
				AGREED	
X	Access of Vessels and Aircrafts	8	1962	5	Dec
		9	"	14	Dec
		10	1963	7	Jan -
				AGREED	
XI	Meteorological Services	12	1963	24	Jan
		20	"	24	Apr -
				AGREED	
XII	Air Traffic Control and Navigational Aids	8	1962	5	Dec
		9	"	14	Dec
		10	1963	7	Jan
		15	"	25	Feb
		16	"	8	Mar
		34	"	30	Oct -
				AGREED	
XIII	Non-appropriated Funds Organizations	20	1963	24	Apr
		21	"	3	May
		22	"	17	May
		36	"	3	Dec
		37	"	27	Dec
		38	1964	9	Jan
		40	"	24	Jan
		41	"	6	Feb
		58	"	16	Jul
		81	1965	7	Jun
		82	1966	-	--
				AGREED	
XIV	Taxation	24	1963	12	Jun
		25	"	26	Jun
		33	"	18	Oct
				AGREED	

No.	Article	Meeting No.	Year	Day	Month
XV	Invited Contractors	20	1963	24	Apr
		22	"	17	May
		23	"	20	May
		28	"	8	Aug
		32	"	4	Oct
		33	"	18	Oct
		41	1964	6	Feb
		42	"	14	Feb
		43	"	20	Feb
		48	"	3	Apr
		49	"	10	Apr
		56	"	26	Jun
		57	"	8	Jul
		81	1965	7	Jun
		82	1966	-	- -
				AGREED	
XVI	Local Procurement	25	1963	26	Jun
		26	"	10	Jul
		27	"	25	Jul
		31	"	20	Sep
		46	1964	13	Mar
		51	"	5	May
		53	"	28	May -
				AGREED	
XVII	Labor	41	1964	6	Feb
		42	"	14	Feb
		45	"	6	Mar
		46	"	13	Mar
		48	"	3	Apr
		64	"	16	Oct
		65	"	23	Oct
		68	"	23	Dec
		69	1965	25	Jan
		71	"	26	Feb
		72	"	2	Mar
		73	"	20	Apr
		75	"	28	Apr
		78	"	7	May
		79	"	12	May
		80	"	28	May
		81	"	7	Jun
		82	1966	-	- - -
				AGREED	

No.	Article	Meeting No.	Year	Day	Month
XVIII	Foreign Exchange Controls	14	1963	14	Feb
		15	"	25	Feb
		16	"	8	Mar
		17	"	19	Mar
		27	"	25	Jul
		53	1964	28	May
		54	"	9	Jun
		55	"	19	Jun
		81	1965	7	Jun - AGREED
XIX	Military Payment Certificates	16	1963	8	Mar
		17	"	19	Mar
		31	"	20	Sep
		53	1964	28	May
		54	"	9	Jun
		55	"	19	Jun
		81	1965	7	Jun - AGREED
XX	Military Post Offices	18	1963	29	Mar
		19	"	11	Apr
		35	"	14	Nov
		39	1964	17	Jan
		40	"	24	Jan - AGREED
XXI	Accounting Procedures	45	1964	6	Mar
		46	"	13	Mar - AGREED
XXII	Criminal Jurisdiction	23	1963	20	May
		42	1964	14	Feb
		44	"	28	Feb
		45	"	6	Mar
		46	"	13	Mar
		47	"	20	Mar
		49	"	10	Apr
		50	"	23	Apr
		52	"	20	May
		58	"	8	Jul
		59	"	28	Jul
		60	"	7	Aug
		61	"	14	Aug
		66	"	24	Nov
		67	"	16	Dec
		70	1965	12	Feb

No.	Article	Meeting No.	Year	Day	Month
XXII	Criminal Jurisdiction (contd)	71	1965	26	Feb
		74	"	23	Apr
		75	"	28	Apr
		77	"	6	May
		78	"	7	May
		80	"	28	May
		81	"	7	Jun
		82	1966	-	- - -
				AGREED	
XXIII	Claims	28	1963	8	Aug
		29	"	22	Aug
		30	"	5	Sep
		51	1964	5	May
		61	"	14	Aug
		62	"	28	Aug
		63	"	14	Sep
		66	"	24	Nov
		72	1965	2	Mar
		76	"	30	Apr
		79	"	12	May
		80	"	28	May
		81	"	7	Jun
		82	1966	-	-- -
				AGREED	
X[illegible]	Vehicle and Driver's Licenses	23	1963	20	May
		24	"	12	Jun
		28	"	8	Aug
		29	"	22	Aug -
				AGREED	
XXV	Security Measures	25	1963	26	Jun
		26	"	10	Jul
		43	1964	20	Feb
		46	"	13	Mar
		48	"	3	Apr
		55	"	19	Jun
		56	"	26	Jun
		62	"	28	Aug
		63	"	14	Sep
		81	1965	7	Jun -
				AGREED	

6

0008

No.	Article	Meeting No.	Year	Day	Month
XXVI	Health and Sanitation	25	1963	26	Jun
		26	"	10	Jul
		27	"	25	Jul-
				AGREED	
XXVII	Enrollment and Training of Reservists	12	1963	24	Jan
		13	"	5	Feb
		14	"	14	Feb
		15	"	25	Feb-
				AGREED	
XXVIII	Joint Committee	5	1962	1	Nov
		6	"	26	Nov
		9	"	14	Dec
		10	1963	7	Jan
		11	"	16	Jan
		15	"	25	Feb -
				AGREED	
XXIX	Entry into Force of Agreement	80	1965	28	May
		81	"	7	Jun
		82	1966	-	- - -
				AGREED	
XXX	Revision of Agreement	34	1963	30	Oct
		35	"	14	Nov
		36	"	3	Dec -
				AGREED	
XXXI	Duration of Agreement	80	1965	28	May
		81	"	7	Jun -
				AGREED	

Negotiations for the Status of Forces Agreement

Session	Date	Subject of Discussions
1st Session	September 20, 1962	Opening of the Negotiations.
2nd "	September 28, 1962	Scope and Content of a SOFA.
3rd "	October 10, 1962	Scope and Content of a SOFA.
4th "	October 19, 1962	1. Preamble 2. Definitions 3. Entry and Exit
5th "	November 1, 1962	1. Preamble 2. Definitions 3. Entry and Exit 4. Joint Committee
6th "	November 14, 1962	1. Entry and Exit 2. Customs and Duties.
7th "	November 26, 1962	1. Preamble 2. Customs and Duties.
8th "	December 4, 1962	1. Preamble 2. Customs and Duties 3. Access of Vessels and Aircraft 4. Air Traffic Control and Navigational Aids. 5. Meteorological Services
9th "	December 14, 1962	1. Definitions. 2. Joint Committee 3. Navigational Aids and Air Traffic Control. 4. Access of Vessels and Aircraft. 5. Facilities and Areas.
10th Session	January 7, 1963	1. Definitions. 2. Entry and Exit 3. Joint Committee. 4. Access of Aircraft and Vessels. 5. Air Traffic Control and Navigational Aids. 6. Facilities and Areas.

0010

Session	Date	Subject of Discussions
11th Session	January 16, 1963	1. Joint Committee 2. Facilities and Areas.
12th Session	January 24, 1963	1. Customs and Duties. ~~2. Meteorological Services.~~ 3. Respect for Local Law. 4. Enrollment and Training of Reservists.
13th Session	February 5, 1963	1. Respect for Local Law. 2. Enrollment and Training of Reservists. 3. Customs and Duties.
14th Session	February 14, 1963	1. Utilities and Services. 2. Enrollment and Training of Reservists. 3. Foreign Exchange Controls.
15th Session	February 25,1963	1. Foreign Exchange Controls. 2. Enrollment and Training of Reservists. 3. Joint Committee. 4. Definitions 5. Air Traffic Control and Navigational Aids.
16th Session	March 8, 1963	1. Air Traffic Control and Navigational Aids. 2. Foreign Exchange Controls. 3. Military Payment Certificates. 4. Facilities and Areas.
17th Session	March 19, 1963	1. Foreign Exchange Controls. 2. Military Payment Certificates. 3. Definitions
18th Session	March 29, 1963	1. Military Post Offices 2. Facilities and Areas.
19th Session	April 11, 1963	1. Military Post Offices. 2. Customs 3. Facilities and Areas.
20th Session	April 24, 1963	1. Utilities and Services. 2. Meteorological Services.

0011

Session	Date	Subjects of Discussions.
20th Session (cônt'd)		3. Invited Contractors. 4. Non-Appropriated Fund Organizations.
21st Session	May 3, 1963	1. Non-Appropriated Fuhd Organizations.
22nd Session	May 17, 1963	1. Non-Appropriated Fund Organizations. 2. Invited Contractors.
23rd Session	May 31, 1963	1. Invited Contractors. 2. Respect for Local Law. 3. Criminal Jurisdiction 4. Vehicle and Driver's Licenses.
24th Session	June 12, 1963	1. Respect for Local Law. 2. Vehicle and Driver's Licenses. 3. Utilities and Services. 4. Taxation.
25th Session	June 26, 1963	1. Taxation. 2. Health and Sanitation. 3. Local Procurement. 4. Security Measures.
26th Session	July 10, 1963	1. Health and Sanitation. 2. Local Procurement 3. Security Measures.
27th Session	July 25, 1963	1. Health and Sanitation 2. Local Procurement 3. Foreign Exchange Controls.
28th Session	August 8, 1963	1. Vehicle and Driver's Licenses. 2. Invited Contractors. 3. Claims.
29th Session	August 22, 1963	1. Vehicles and Drivers Licenses. 2. Claims.
30th Session	September 5,1963	1. Claims.
31st Session	September 20,1963	1. Facilities and Areas. 2. Military Payment Certificates. 3. Local Procurement.

0012

Session	Date	Subjects of Discusssions
32nd Session	October 4, 1963	1. Facilities and Areas. 2. Invited Contractors.
33rd Session	October 18,1963	1. Facilities and Areas. 2. Taxation 3. Invited Contractors.
34th Session	October 30,1963	1. Air Traffic Control and Navigational Aids. 2. Customs 3. Revision of the Agreement.
35th Session	November 14,1963	1. Customs 2. Military Post Offices. 3. Utilities and Services. 4. Revision of the Agreement.
36th Session	December 5,1963	1. Customs 2. Non-Appropriated Fund Organizations. 3. Revision of Agreement.
37th Session	December 27,1963	1. Non-Appropriated Fund Organizations. 2. Customs.
38th Session	January 9,1964	1. Non-Appropriated Fund Organizations 2. Customs.
39th Session	January 17,1964	1. Customs. 2. Utilities and Services. 3. Military Post Offices.
40th Session	January 24,1964	1. Military Post Offices. 2. Customs. 3. Non-Appropriated Fund Organizations.
41st Session	February 6, 1964	1. Customs. 2. Non-Appropriated Fund Organizations 3. Invited Contractors. 4. Labor
42nd Session	February 14,1964	1. Facilities and Areas. 2. Invited Contractors. 3. Criminal Jurisdiction. 4. Labor.

0013

Session	Date	Subjects of Discussions
43rd Session	February 20, 1964	1. Invited Contractors 2. Security Measures.
44th Session	February 28, 1964	1. Criminal Jurisdiction 2. Utilities and Services.
45th Session	March 6, 1964	1. Utilities and Services. 2. Accounting Procedures. 3. Labor. 4. Criminal Jurisdiction.
46th Session	March 13, 1964	1. Accounting Procedures. 2. Local Procurement 3. Security Measures. 4. Labor. 5. Criminal Jurisdiction.
47th Session	March 20, 1964	1. Criminal Jurisdiction
48th Session	April 3, 1964	1. Labor. 2. Invited Contractors. 3. Security Measures.
49th Session	April 10, 1964	1. Invited Contractors. 2. Criminal Jurisdiction.
50th Session	April 23, 1964	1. Criminal Jurisdiction.
51st Session	May 5, 1964	1. Local Procurement. 2. Customs. 3. Claims.
52nd Session	May 20, 1964	1. Criminal Jurisdiction.
53rd Session	May 28, 1964	1. Local Procurement. 2. Foreign Exchange Controls. 3. Military Payment Certificates. 4. Customs.
54th Session	June 9, 1964	1. Military Payment Certificates. 2. Foreign Exchange Controls. 3. Customs.

Session	Date	Subjects of Discussions
55th Session	June 19, 1964	1. Security Measures. 2. Military Payment Certificates. 3. Customs. 4. Foreign Exchange Controls.
56th Session	June 26, 1964	1. Invited Constractors. 2. Security Measures. 3. Customs.
57th Session	July 8, 1964	1. Customs. 2. Invited Contractors.
58th Session	July 16, 1964	1. Non-Appropriated Fund Organizations. 2. Criminal Jurisdiction.
59th Session	July 28, 1964	1. Criminal Jurisdiction.
60th Session	August 7, 1964	1. Criminal Jurisdiction.
61st Session	August 14, 1964	1. Claims. 2. Criminal Jurisdiction.
62nd Session	August 28, 1964	1. Claims. 2. Security Measures.
63rd Session	September 11, 1964	1. Claims. 2. Security Measures.
64th Session	October 16, 1964	1. Labor.
65th Session	October 23, 1964	1. Labor.
66th Session	November 24, 1964	1. Criminal Jurisdiction. 2. Claims.
67th Session	December 16, 1964	1. Criminal Jurisdiction.
68th Session.	December 23, 1964	1. Labor.
69th Session	January 25, 1965	1. Labor.
70th Session	February 12, 1965	1. Criminal Jurisdiction.
71st Session	February 26, 1965	1. Criminal Jurisdiction. 2. Labor.
72nd Session	March 2, 1965	1. Claims. 2. Labor.

0015

Session	Date	Subjects of Discussions
73rd Session	April 20, 1965	1. Labor.
74th Session	April 23, 1965	1. Criminal Jurisdiction.
75th Session	April 28, 1965	1. Labor. 2. Criminal Jurisdiction.
76th Session	April 30, 1965	1. Claims.
77th Session	May 6, 1965	1. Criminal Jurisdiction.
78th Session	May 7, 1965	1. Labor. 2. Criminal Jurisdiction.
79th Session	May 12, 1965	1. Labor. 2. Claims.
80th Session	May 28, 1965	1. Claim. 2. Criminal Jurisdiction. 3. Labor. 4. Duration of Agreement. 5. Ratification of Agreement.
81st Session	June 7, 1965	1. Duration of Agreement. 2. Security Measures. 3. Non-Appropriated Fund Organizations. 4. Foreign Exchange Controls. 5. Military Payment Certificates. 6. Facilities and Areas. 7. Claims. 8. Labor. 9. Ratification of Agreement. 10. Criminal Jurisdiction. 11. Invited Contractors.

0016

주둔군 지위협정교섭 제1차회의 요약기록

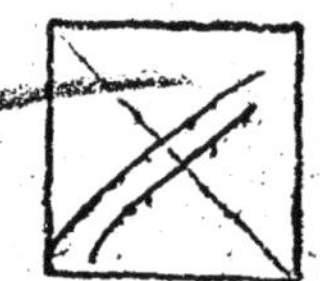

1962. 9. 20.

1. 시일 및 장소 : 1962. 9. 20. 하오 3시부터 4시 40분까지

   외무부 회의실

2. 참석자 :

한국측

최 덕 신	외무부장관
진 필 식	외무부 정무국장
신 관섭	재무부 세관국장
이 경 호	법무부 법무국장
박 근	외무부 미주과장
이 남 구 대령	국방부 군무과장
지 성 구 (공보관)	외무부 공보관
신 정 섭 (기록자)	외무부 2등서기관
이 창 범	외무부 3등서기관
강 석 재 (통역)	외무부 3등서기관

미국측 :

62-4-41P

사뮤엘 디. 버-거	주한미국대사
필립 씨. 하비브	주한미대사관 참사관
제이. 디. 로턴 준장	주한미8군 참모차장
윌리암 제이. 호드	주한미대사관 1등서기관
지.지. 오코나대령	주한미8군 참모차장
알.엠. 부론티대령	주한미해군참모부장
다불.에이. 쏠프대령	주한미8군법무참모

1 次

0017

62-4-R (5) 매방.음 87-1 Ø (12)

벤자민 에이. 후렘　　주한미대사관 1등서기관

로버트. 에이. 루이스　　주한미대사관 2등서기관겸 영사

지. 티. 스머멘중령　　주한미군 미사참모

알. 이. 밀러중령　　주한미8군 법무장교

3. 개회식사:

최 외무장관 및 버-거 주한미대사는 개회식사를 행하였다.

4. 소 개:

최 외무장관은 한국측 교섭자들을 소개하였고 버-거 주한미국 대사는 미국측 교섭자를 소개한후 회의장에서 퇴장하였다.

5. 회담 요지:

가. 인사교환

한국측 수석대표 "진" 씨는 미국대표단에 진심으로의 인사를 표하였으며 교섭이 양국간의 우호적 유대를 증진 하는데 기여하게될 협정의 성공적인 체결에 조속히 도달 하게되기를 원한다는 희망을 표명하였다. 미국대표단을 대신하여 "하비브" 씨는 "진"씨에 감사를 표하였으며 협정의 성공적인 체결을위한 후자의 희망에 동의하였다.

나. 공식언어 및 통역관 이용

공식언어로서 한국어 및 영어를 모두 사용하며 또한 각측이 자신의 통역관을 제공하도록 합의하였다.

다. 기 록

62-4-58

"하비브" 씨는 교섭회의 축어기록은 작성하지 말자고 제의하였다. 그는 1명의 기록자를 각측이 임명하여 2명의 기록자가 상호 협의하여 매회의의 요약 기록서를 작성할것을 제의하였다. 그는 또 언제든지 실질적 문제에 관하여

0019

2-4-2

미문 87-12

0020

합의가 이루어지면 합의의사록을 작성하여 차기회의에서 확인을 받도록 할것을 제의하였다. "진"씨는 이들제의에 대하여 원측적으로 동의하였다. 그는 한국측 기록자로서 "신정섭"씨를 지명하였고 "하비브"씨는 미국측을 위하여 "후렉" 씨를 지명하였다.

라. 회의 빈도

양측은 가능한 한 회의를 자주 가지도록 하자는 희망을 진술하였다. "진"씨는 최소매주 1회식 회의를 가지는 것을 원측으로 하는데 동의할것을 제의하였다. "하비브" 씨는 회의간에 어떠한 고정된 간격을두는것에 반대하였으며 매회의시에 다음 회의의 일자를 정할것을 제의하였다. "진"씨는 때때로 어느측에서 예를들면 특정문제에 관한 그의 견해를 설명할 목적으로 회의를 소집하고자 원할지 모른다고 제의함으로서 대답하였다. 그는 어느측이나 자진하여 언제든지 회의를 소집할수 있음에 합의토록 제의하였다. "하비브"씨는 미국측은 그러한 제안을 기꺼히 고려할것이나 어느측이던지 타방의 합의없이 회의를 소집할수 있다는 원측에 동의할수 없다고 응답하였다.

합의사항

1) 회의는 가능한 한 자주 개최할것임.

2) 매회의시에차기회의 일자를 결정할것임.

3) 회의간에 고정된 간격을 두지않을것임.

4) 어느 한쪽이 회의소집을 원할 경우에 타방은 그요청을 기꺼히 고려할것임.

마. 보도관계

"하비브"씨는 신문 발표문을 대중에 알리기 위하여 공동으로

62-4-51

0021

62-4-13

미문 87-1 ③

0022

작성하고 수시로 발표할것을 제안하였다. 그는 대표단의
각 대표들이 교섭내용을 기자들과 토의하지 말것을 지적
하였다. 그는 교섭자들이 발표하기를 원하는 그러한 공동
발표문을 작성하도록 각대표단에서 1명의 대표를 공보관으로
임명할것을 제안하였다. "진"씨는 이들 제안에 동의
하였으나 기자들은 매회의 말에 "뉴스"를 위하여 대기하고
있을것이라고 지적하였다. 그는 따라서 매회의가
끝나면 발표문을 기자에 발표토록 제안하였다. "하비브"
씨는 미국측은 신문이나 대중들에게 자격적인 표제를
성급히 기대하는 감을 일으키는 것은 바람직스러운 일이
아니라고 믿는다고 응답하였다. 어떠한 회의는 성질상
순수히 설명적인 것인만큼 신문에 발표할것이 반드시 있는
것이 아니다. 따라서 미국측은 매회의후에 발표문을 발표
할것이 요명되는것이 아니라고 믿는다. 어떤점에 관해서는
회의를 개최함이 없이 발표문을 발표할 경우가있을것임으로
융통성있는 정책이 요망된다. 교섭자들이 신문을 인도
해야하며 신문으로 하여금 이끌려서는 아니된다. "진"씨는
만약 아무런 발표문을 발하지 않는다면 신문은 공연한
억측을 하게될것이라고 응답하였다. 그러자 "하비브"씨는
당분간 매회의후에 발표문을 발표할것에 동의하였으나 후일
이문제를 제기할 권한을 보류하였다. "지"씨와 "후렐"
씨는 각기 대표단을 위한 공보관으로 임명되었다.

합의사항

1) 양측은 개개 교섭자가 교섭내용을 기자들과 토의하는
   것은 요망스러운 일이 아니라는데 합의하였다.

2) 당분간 2명의 공보관이 작성한 발표문을 매회의이후에
   발표할것이다. 미국측은 후일 이문제를 제기할권한을 보류한다.

0023

62-4-12

미문 87-1 ④

0024

바. 기타 사항

"하비브"씨는 각측은 사전에 타방에 이름과 전문분야를 통보하여 특수문제에 관한 필요한 추가적인 전문가들을 회의에 참석케할수 있을것을 제안하였다. "진"씨는 이에 동의하였다. "진"씨는 한국대표단원인 "로신영" 씨 및 "이경훈"씨는 공무로 해외출장 중이며 귀국하면 대표단에 참가할것이라고 발표하였다.

사. 차기회의 의제

"하비브" 씨는 차기회의의 의제는 그러한 검토가 확정적이 아니라는 양해하에 주둔군 지위협정의 범위와 내용에대한 일반적인 검토로 할것을 제안하였다. 제목사항은 일반적인 표제나 특수한 부제하에서 토의될수 있으며 추가적인 사항은 다음회의에서 제기될수 있다. "진"씨는 동의하였다.

다음 "하비브"씨는 한가지점을 명백히 해두고저 한다고 말하였다. 그는 현재의 교섭은 순전히 한미간의 협정에 관계한것이며 교섭자들은 비록 어느측이나 관계된다고 생각하는 문제는 무엇이든지 제기할수 있으나 다른 주둔군 지위협정 조항에 의하여 구애받지 아니한다는 점을 지적하였다.

"진"씨는 포괄적이며 모든것을 포함하는 가능한 최선의 주둔군지위 협정을 만드는일이 교섭자들의 목적이며 의도이어야 한다고 말하였다.

아. 차기회의 일자

차기회의는 9월 28일 하오 2시에 개최하도록 합의되었다.

자. 공동신문 발표

"지"씨 및 "후렘" 씨가 작성한 공동신문 발표문이 "진" 씨에 의하여 랑독되었으며 교섭자들에 의하여 승인되었다.

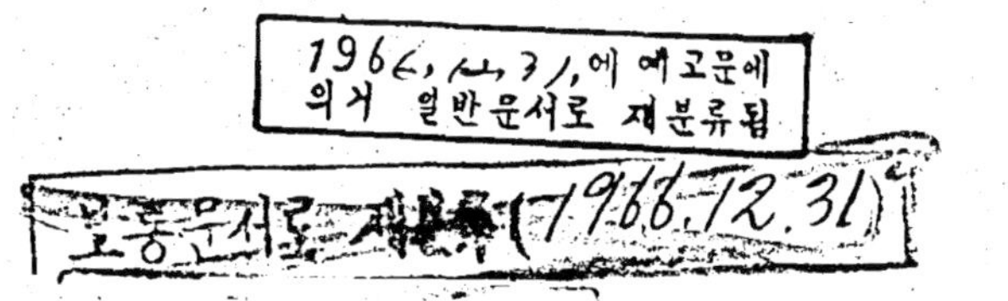

0025

62-4-12 (5)

미문 87-1 ⑤

0026

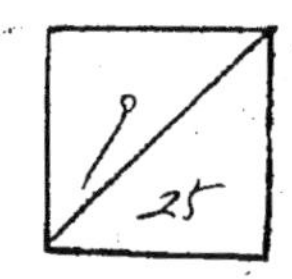

SUMMARY RECORD OF THE OPENING SESSION
STATUS FORCES NEGOTIATIONS

September 20, 1962

1. Time and Place: 3:00 to 4:40 p.m. on September 20, 1962 at Conference Room of the Ministry of Foreign Affairs

2. Present:

ROK Side:

H.E. Choi, Duk-Shin	Minister of Foreign Affairs
Mr. Chin, Pil Shik	Director Bureau of Political Affairs Ministry of Foreign Affairs
Mr. Shin, Kwan Sup	Director Bureau of Customs Ministry of Finance
Mr. Yi, Kyung Ho	Director Bureau of Legal Affairs Ministry of Justice
Mr. Pak, Kun	Chief, America Section Ministry of Foreign Affairs
Col. Lee, Nam Koo	Chief, Military Affairs Section Ministry of National Defense
Mr. Chi, Sung Koo (Press Officer)	Press Officer Ministry of Foreign Affairs
Mr. Shin, Chung Sup (Rapporteur)	2nd Secretary Ministry of Foreign Affairs
Mr. Lee, Chang Bum	3rd Secretary Ministry of Foreign Affairs
Mr. Kang, Suk Jae (Interpreter)	3rd Secretary Ministry of Foreign Affairs

0027

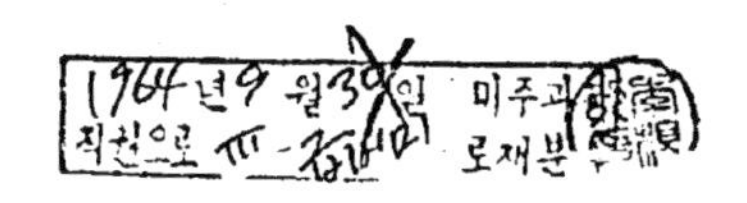

미문 87-1 ⓑ

0028

US Side:

H.E. Samuel D. Berger	Ambassador of the United States
Mr. Philip C. Habib	Counselor of the Embassy for Political Affairs
Brig. Gen. J.D. Lawlor	Deputy Chief of Staff 8th Army
Mr. William J. Ford	First Secretary of the Embassy
Col. G.G. O'Connor	Deputy Chief of Staff 8th Army
Capt. R.M. Brownlie	Assistant Chief of Staff USN/K
Col. W.A. Solf	Staff Judge Advocate 8th Army
Mr. Benjamin A. Fleck (Rapporteur and Press Officer)	First Secretary of the Embassy
Mr. Robert A. Lewis	Second Secretary and Consul of the Embassy
Lt. Col. G.T. Suderman	Staff Officer, J-5 USAF/K
Lt. Col. R.E. Miller	Staff Officer, JAG 8th Army

3. Opening Addresses:

Foreign Minister Choi and Ambassador Berger addressed the opening session.

4. Introduction:

Minister Choi introduced the negotiators of the ROK side; Ambassador Berger introduced the

0029

미문 87-1 ⑦

0030

U.S. negotiators; and then they withdrew from the conference site.

5. Gist of Talks:

a. Exchange of Greetings

The Chief delegate of the Korean side, Mr. Chin, extended heartfelt greetings to the American delegation and expressed the hope that the negotiations would soon lead to the successful conclusion of an agreement which would contribute to the promotion of friendly ties between the two countries. On behalf of the American delegation, Mr. Habib thanked Mr. Chin and concurred in the latter's hope for a successful conclusion of an agreement.

b. Official Languages and Use of Interpreters

It was agreed that both Korean and English would be used as official languages and that each side would provide its own interpreter.

c. Records

Mr. Habib suggested that no verbatim records of the negotiating sessions be kept. He suggested that a rapporteur be appointed by each side and that the two rapporteurs in consultation with each other prepare a summary record of each meeting. He further proposed that whenever agreement was reached on a substantive question that an agreed minute be made and referred to the following meeting for confirmation. Mr. Chin agreed in principle to these proposals. He then designated Mr. Shin Chung Sup as rapporteur for the Korean side and Mr. Habib designated Mr. Fleck for the American side.

미문 87-1⑧

0032

d. Frequency of Meetings

Both sides stated their desire to schedule meetings as frequently as possible. Mr. Chin proposed it be agreed in principle to have meetings at least once every week. Mr. Habib objected to the establishment of any fixed interval between meetings and suggested that at each meeting the date of the subsequent meeting be fixed. Mr. Chin responded with a suggestion that from time to time either side might wish to call a meeting, for instance, for the purpose of explaining its views on a specific subject. He suggested agreement that either side might call a meeting at any time on its initiative. Mr. Habib replied that the US side would willingly consider any such proposal but could not agree in principle that either side could call meeting without the agreement of the other side.

Points of Agreement:

1) Meetings will be held as frequently as possible.
2) At each meeting the date of the subsequent meeting will be fixed.
3) No fixed interval between meeting will be established.
4) When one side wishes to call a meeting, the other side will willingly consider the request.

e. Press Relations

Mr. Habib proposed that statements to the press prepared jointly and issued from time to time in order to keep the public informed. He pointed out the undesirability of individual members of either delegation discussing negotiations with the press. He proposed that one member of each delegation be designated as

미문 87-19

0034

press officer to draft such joint statements as the negotiators might wish to issue.
Mr. Chin agreed to these proposals but pointed out that the reporters will be waiting for news at the end of each session. He proposed, therefore, that a statement be issued to the press at the end of each meeting. Mr. Habib replied that the US side did not believe it desirable to create on the part of the press and the public a sense of urgent expectation of hot headlines. Inasmuch as some meetings may be purely explanatory in nature there would not necessarily be anything to report to the press. Therefore, the American side did not believe it desirable to issue a statement following every meeting. A policy of flexibility was desirable since there might be at some point occasion to issue a statement without even holding a meeting. The negotiators should lead the press and should not let the press lead them. Mr. Chin replied that if no statement were issued the press would indulge in undesirable speculation. Mr. Habib then agreed to the issuance of a statement after each meeting, for the time being, but reserved the right to reopen this question at a later date. Mr. Chi and Mr. Fleck were appointed press officers for their respective delegations.

Points of Agreement:

1) Both sides agreed on the undesirability of individual negotiators discussing the negotiations with the press.
2) For the time being a statement prepared by the two press officers will be issued after

미문 87-1 ⑩

0036

each meeting. The US side reserves the right to reopen this question at a later date.

f. Other Items

Mr. Habib proposed that each side be free to introduce additional experts on specific matters as required, with the names and fields of expertise to be notified to the other side in advance. Mr. Chin agreed.

Mr. Chin announced that Mr. Lho Shin Yong and Mr. Lee Kyung Hoon, members of the Korean delegation, were absent from the country on official business but would joint the delegation upon their return.

g. Agenda for Next Meeting

Mr. Habib proposed that the agenda for the next meeting consist of a general review of the scope and content of a status of forces agreement, with the understanding that such a review would not be definitive. Subject matter could be discussed under general headings and specific sub-titles, but additional matters could be raised at subsequent meetings. Mr. Chin agreed. Mr. Habib then stated that he would like to make one point clear. He pointed out that the present negotiations are concerned solely with an agreement between Korea and the United States and that the negotiators are not bound by the provisions of other status of forces agreements, although either side may introduce whatever material it believes relevant. Mr. Chin stated that it should be the purpose and intent of the negotiators to work out the best possible SOFA, which would be comprehensive and all-inclusive.

미윤87-1⑪

0038

h. Date of Next Meeting

It was agreed to hold the next meeting on September 28 at 2:00 p.m.

i. Joint Press Release

The joint press release prepared by Mr. Chi and Mr. Fleck was read by Mr. Chi and was approved by the negotiators.

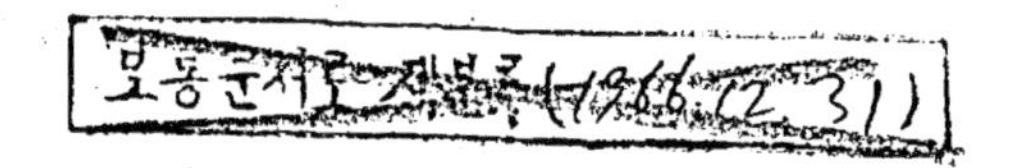

미북 87-1⑫ (12)

0040

주둔군 지위협정교섭 제2차회의 요약기록

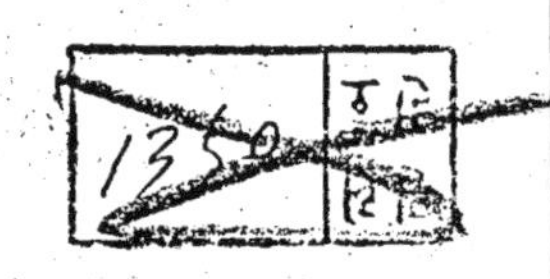

1962. 9. 28.

1. 시일 및 장소 : 1962. 9. 28. 하오 2시부터 4시 15분까지

   외무부 회의실

2. 참석자 :

   한국측

진 필 식	외무부 정무국장
신 관 섭	재무부 세관국장
이 경 호	법무부 법무국장
박 근	외무부 미주과장
이 남 구대령	국방부 군무과장
지 성 구 (공보관)	외무부 공보관
신 정 섭 (기록자)	외무부 2 등서기관
이 창 범	외무부 3 등서기관
강 석 재 (통역)	외무부 3 등서기관

   미국측 :

필립 씨. 하비브	주한미대사관 참사관
제이. 디. 로머준장	주한미8군 참모차장
윌리암 제이. 호드	주한미대사관 1등서기관
지. 지. 오코나 대령	주한미8군 참모차장
알. 엠. 부론리대령	주한미해군 참모부장
벤자민 에이. 후텍 (기록및 공보관)	주한미대사관 1등서기관
로버트 에이. 루이스	주한미대사관 2등서기관겸 영사
지. 티. 스머엔 중령	주한미군 민사참모
알. 이. 밀러 중령	주한미8군 법무장교

0041

62-4-13(4)

미주.문 87-2 ①(11)

0042

3. 회담요지 :

가. 교섭범위 및 내용에관한 미국측 견해발표

(1) 실질적 토의는 "밀러"중령에 의한 주둔군 지위협정의 범위와 내용에관한 미국측 견해 발표로 시작되었다. "밀러"는 그의 론평시초에 그의 해설은 어떠한 조항이나 특수협정에 관한 미국측 입장을 발표하는 것이 아니며 그의 론평은 결정적인것도 아니며 또한 후일 협정에 포함할 추가적 제목에대한 고려를 배제할것을 의도한것이 아님을 강조하였다.

(2) 그다음 "밀러"는 넓은의미에 있어서의 주둔군지위협정의 일반적 목적과 목표 이에이어 시설 및 토지, 공익물 및 용역, 관세업무, 그리고 조세, 노무, 현지조달, 청구권, 협정에 포함될 인원의 범주, 파견국 용역 및 시설의 이용 및 형사재판 관할권 문제를 포함한 특수제목에 관한 주둔군 지위협정을 검토하였다. (교섭범위와 내용에관한 미국측 및 한국측 입장 제시사본은 회의 말에 기록자에게 제공되었다)

나. 시설에대한 보상 및 형사재판 관할권에 관한미국측 성명

(3) "밀러"의 발표에 이어 "하비브"씨는 양측이 특정조문에 합의하게되면 미국측은 그합의의 최종 조문을 작성하기 전에 승인을 받기위하여 "와싱톤"에 합의된 문장을 제출할것이라고 진술하였다. 그는 한국측도 역시 잠정적으로 진행할것으로 추측하였다.

(4) "하비브"씨는 그는 또한 주둔군지위협정은 대한민국의 민정복귀를 기다려 체결될것이라는 미국측 기록자에 부항목을 포함한 완전한 게요가 제공되었다.

0043

62-4-B 미문 87-2

0044

라. 시설에대한 보상지불 및 형사재판관할권에 관한 미국측 성명에대한 한국측 응답

(9) "하비브"씨의 보충설명에 답하여:

(가) 교섭의 진행문제에 관해서 "진"씨는 "하비브" 씨가 제안한바와 같이 잠정적으로 진행하는데 합의하였다.

(나) 민정복귀후의 협정체결시기에 관해서 "진"씨는 교섭은 상당한 기간의 시간을요하며 따라서 양측은 다음 여름전에 대부분의 문제에 관한 교섭을 완료할목적으로 최선을 다해야하며 민정복귀후 가능한한 조속히 협정을 체결할 준비를 갖추어야 한다고 진술하였다.

(다) 시설 및 토지에대한 보상지불 및 미국과 비등한 사법기준에 관한 미국의 입장에 관해서 "진"씨는 "하비브"씨에게 한국정부도 또한 그의견해를 문서나 구두로서 미국정부에 과거 여러경우에 표시한바 있었다는 사실을 상기시켰다. "진"씨는 비록 양측이 다알고있는 견해의 차이가 있다고 하드래도 교섭을통하여 그러한 차이를 해결코져 하는것이 바로 이회의의 임무이라는 점을 강조하였다. 그는 또한 "하비브"씨에게 제의된 주둔군 지위 협정의 전반적인 범위와 내용을 다만 검토하는 이때에 그러한 문제에 관한 각정부의 특별한 입장을 토의하는것은 전혀 적절한일이 못된다고 말하였다. "하비브"씨도 이들 문제들은 교섭의 적절한 단계에서 토의될것이라는데 동의하였다.

0045

62-1-B  미문 87-200

0046

마. 기타사항

(10) "하비브"씨는 그의 부재시에는 "로버"준장이 미국측 교섭단을 인솔할것이라 하였다. "진"씨는 그의 부재시에는 "이경호"씨가 한국측 교섭단을 인솔할 것이라고 진술하였다.

바. 차기회의 의제 및 일자

(11) 차기회의에서는 교섭범위와 내용에 관하여 바로 행한바 있는 입장설명에 관한 의견교환으로 시작해서 이에 여러제목이 교섭될 순위를 고려하겠금 진행할것에 합의하였다. 차기회의는 10월 10일 오후 2시에 개최할 예정이다.

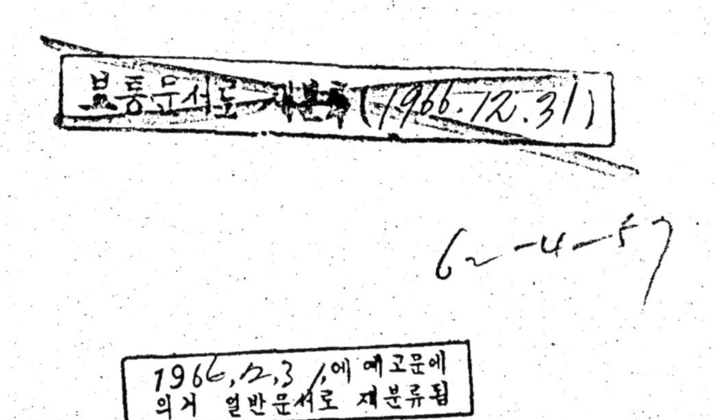

0047

62-4-13(4)

0048

SUMMARY RECORD OF THE SECOND SESSION
STATUS FORCES NEGOTIATIONS

September 28, 1962

I. Time and Place: 2:00 to 4:15 p.m. on September 28, 1962 at Conference Room of the Ministry of Foreign Affairs

II. Attendants:

ROK Side:

Mr. Chin, Pil Shik	Director Bureau of Political Affairs Ministry of Foreign Affairs
Mr. Shin, Kwan Sup	Director Bureau of Customs Ministry of Finance
Mr. Yi, Kyung Ho	Director Bureau of Legal Affairs Ministry of Justice
Mr. Pak, Kun	Chief, America Section Ministry of Foreign Affairs
Col. Lee, Nam Koo	Chief, Military Affairs Section Ministry of National Defense
Mr. Chi, Sung Koo	Press Officer Ministry of Foreign Affairs
Mr. Shin, Chung Sup (Rapporteur)	2nd Secretary Ministry of Foreign Affairs
Mr. Lee, Chang Bum	3rd Secretary Ministry of Foreign Affairs
Mr. Kang, Suk Jae (Interpreter)	3rd Secretary Ministry of Foreign Affairs

0049

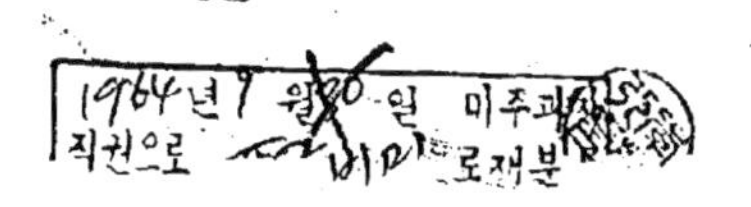

미문 87-2⑤

0050

US Side:

Mr. Philip C. Habib	Counselor of the Embassy for Political Affairs
Brig. Gen. J.D. Lawlor	Deputy Chief of Staff 8th Army
Mr. William J. Ford	First Secretary of the Embassy
Col. G.G. O'Connor	Deputy Chief of Staff 8th Army
Capt. R.M. Brownlie	Assistant Chief of Staff USN/K
Mr. Benjamin A. Fleck (Rapporteur and Press Officer)	First Secretary of the Embassy
Mr. Robert A. Lewis	Second Secretary and Consul of the Embassy
Lt. Col. G.T. Suderman	Staff Officer, J-5 USAF/K
Lt. Col. R.E. Miller	Staff Officer, JAG 8th Army

III. Gist of Talks:

a. U.S. Presentation of Views on Scope and Content

1. Substantive discussion began with the presentation by Lt. Colonel Miller, of the views of the U.S. side regarding the scope and content of a Status of Forces Agreement. At the beginning of his remarks Miller emphasized that his comments did not include a statement of the U.S. position in regard to any article or any particular agreement and that his remarks were not intended to be definitive nor to

0051

0052

exclude consideration at a later date of additional subjects for inclusion in an agreement.

2. Miller then reviewed the general purposes and objectives of a SOFA in broad terms, following this with reference to specific topics, including facilities and areas; utilities and services; customs duties; and taxes; labor; local procurement; claims; categories of persons to be included; use of sending state services and facilities; and criminal jurisdiction.

(Copies of the U.S. and Korean presentations on scope and content were made available to the rapporteurs at the end of the meeting.)

b. U.S. Statement on Payment for Facilities and Criminal Jurisdiction

3. Following Miller's presentation, Mr. Habib stated that whenever the two sides reached agreement on the text of specific articles, the U.S. side would submit the agreed language to Washington for approval before constructing the final text of the agreement. He presumed the Korean side would also proceed ad referendum.

4. Mr. Habib stated he also wished to reaffirm the understanding expressed in the joint press statement of September 6, 1962, that the conclusion of a SOFA will await the restoration of civilian government in the Republic of Korea.

5. Mr. Habib then referred to the position of the U.S. Government regarding payment for the use of facilities, as set forth prior to and at the time of negotiations held in April 1961, in the Aide Memoire submitted to the Foreign Minister on June 15, 1962, and in the various conversations between the

0053

미음 87-2⑦

0054

American Ambassador and the Foreign Minister before the latter date. Habib stated that the ROKG was aware thereby that the U.S. Government is not willing to pay compensation for the facilities used by U.S. Forces in Korea and shall continue to insist that the ROKG be responsible for all and any such claims, public or private. He added that the U.S. Government will, of course, cooperate to the maximum in releasing such facilities as may no longer be needed and in accepting satisfactory alternative facilities offered by the ROKG.

6. Turning to the subject of criminal jurisdiction, Habib stated that while detailed consideration of this subject would occur later in the negotiations, the U.S. side wished to make one basic observation at this time. In any agreement covering Status of Forces, he said, the U.S. Government is obligated to insist upon arrangements which will ensure that U.S. personnel will be guaranteed trials comparable to U.S. standards. He pointed out that this is a basic principle of particular concern to the U.S. Congress and is fundamental to the negotiation of all status of forces agreements.

c. Korean Presentation of Views on Scope and Content

7. Mr. Chin, the chief delegate of the Korean side, appreciated Col. Miller's presentation and said that the material would be of a great help in the course of their negotiations, for it was very comprehensive and all inclusive. Referring to the scope and content of SOFA as conceived by the Korean side, he said that the purpose of negotiations is to reconcile the need to grant facilities and privileges

미윤 817-2⑧

0056

to the armed forces of the sending state with the necessity to uphold the law and rights of the receiving state. Thus, he continued, "we have the difficult tasks of reconciling the two basic requisites." Mr. Chin further said "we have to discover an optimum equilibrium between the above two basic requisites with a view toward working out a best framework of coordination and cooperation in our joint struggle against the Communist threat."

8. Dr. Pak, on behalf of the Korean side, presented the views of the Republic of Korea on the scope and content of SOFA in the form of an outline, which contained the following principal subjects:

(1) Preamble and definition of terms
(2) Entry and exit
(3) Facilities and areas
(4) Access of vessels, aircraft, and traffic control and communication systems
(5) Criminal jurisdiction
(6) Civil jurisdiction and claims
(7) Customs
(8) Taxation
(9) Non-appropriated fund organization
(10) Purchase of goods, services and labour
(11) Armed forces contractors
(12) Foreign exchange control and use of MPC
(13) Joint Committee
(14) Military post office
(15) Miscellaneous items
(16) Final clause

(The complete outline, including sub-items, was made available to the rapporteur of the U.S. side.)

0057

미문87-2⑨

0058

d. <u>Korean Response to the U.S. statement on Payment for Facilities and Criminal Jurisdiction</u>

9. In response to Mr. Habib's supplementary explanation with respect to:

(1) procedural aspect of negotiations, Mr. Chin agreed to proceed <u>ad referendum</u> as proposed by Mr. Habib;

(2) the conclusion time of the agreement after the restoration of civil government, Mr. Chin stated that negotiations would require a considerable period of time, and therefore, both sides should do their utmost with a view to completing negotiations on most subjects before next summer and be ready for the conclusion of the agreement as soon as possible after civil government is restored;

(3) the U.S. position on compensation for facilities and areas and the judicial standard comparable to that of the United States, Mr. Chin reminded Mr. Habib of the fact that the Korean government had also expressed on many past occasions its views to the United States Government in written or oral form. Mr. Chin stressed that even though there are differences of views of which both sides were aware, it is the very task of the gathering to solve such differences through negotiations. He also told Mr. Habib that it was not quite relevant to discuss the specific position of each government on those subjects at that time, when they were only considering the overall scope and content of the proposed SOFA. Mr. Habib agreed that

0059

0060

these matters would be discussed at the appropriate stage of negotiations.

e. Other Business

10. Mr. Habib announced that in his absence, Brig. General Lawlor would lead the U.S. negotiating team. Mr. Chin stated that in his absence, Mr. Yi Kyung-ho would lead the Korean team.

f. Agenda and Date of Next Meeting

11. It was agreed that the next meeting begin with an exchange of views concerning the presentations just made on scope and content and that following such an exchange, the negotiators would proceed to consider the sequence in which the various subjects would be negotiated. The next meeting was scheduled for October 10 at 2:00 p.m.

미합.동 87-2⑪(11)

0062

주둔군 지위협정교섭 제3차회의 요약기록

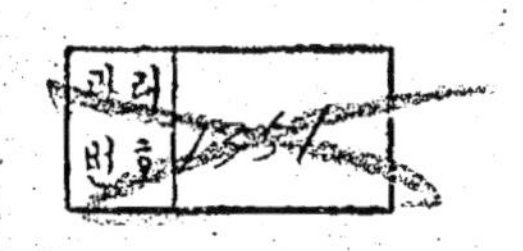

1962. 10. 10.

1. 시일 및 장소 : 1962. 10. 10. 하오 2시부터 3시 10분 까지
   외무부 회의실

2. 참석자 :

한국측 :

신 관 섭	재무부 세관국장
박 근	외무부 미주과장
이 남 구 대령	국방부 군무과장
지 성 구	외무부 공보관
신 정 섭 (기록자)	외무부 2 등서기관
이 참 범	외무부 3 등서기관
강 석 재 (통역)	외무부 3 등서기관

미국측 :

필립.씨.하비브	주한미대사관 참사관
제이.디.로머 준장	주한미8군 참모차장
윌리암.제이,포드	주한미대사관 1등서기관
지.지. 오코나 대령	주한미8군 참모차장
알.엠. 부른리 대령	주한미해군 참모부장
다불.에이.솔프대령	주한미8군 법무참모
벤자민 에이.후렉 (기록 및 공보관)	주한미대사관 1등서기관
로버트.에이.루이스	주한미대사관 2등서기관겸영사
지.티. 스드멘 중령	주한미군 민사참모
알.이. 밀러 중령	주한미8군 법무장교

62-11-58

0063

62-4-14 (6) 미조.윤 87-30 (13)

0064

3. 회담요지:

가. 교섭범위 및 내용에관한 추가적안 미국측 론평

(1) "진필식" 및 "이경호"씨의 부재로 사회를본 "신관섭" 씨는 전회의에서의 한국측의 교섭범위 및 내용에대한 입장 설명에관하여 미국측으로서 론평할것이 있는지의 여부를 문의하였다. "하비브"씨는 양측은 대체적으로 합의하고 있는것 같다고 대답하였다. 연이나 그는 한국측은 제시한 게요에 부표제를 포함하였으며 약간의 그부표제들은 관계된 특별한 문제에관한 입장을 밝히고 있는것으로 해석될수 있다고 주목하였다. 미국측은 교섭자들은 교섭의 현단계에서는 다만 협정에 포함되어야 할 중요한 제목만을 고려할것이지 실질적인 부표제를 고려해서는 않된다고 믿고있다.

(2) 전회의시에 "진"씨가 한 말에관하여 "하비브"씨는 미국측은 파견국 군대에대한 특권 및 면제의 부여와 접수국의 법률 및 예규 준수문제간에 약간의 모순이 있다는 "진"씨의 명백한 생각을 이해할수 없는바라고 진술하였다. "하비브"씨는 타국에 주둔하고있는 미국 군대의 정책은 항상 그나라 경부의 법률을 존중하는 것이었다고 지적하였다. 그는 특히 한국에있어서 미국 군대의 정책은 지방법률 렉행기관에 모든 가능한 협조를 제공하는것이었다고 지적하였다.

(3) "하비브"씨는 그다음 "밀러" 중령에게 발언권을 양도 하였으며 그는 중요제목 목록을 고려토록 제시하였다. "밀러"는 동목록은 한국측 게요에있는 16개 표제와 비교하여 26개 표제를 포함하고있음을 지적하였다.

0065

62-4-14 미본 8, -3

0066

그는 이것은 한국측 개요에있는 어떤항목을 2개 혹

그이상의 표제와 분리하였거나 어떤 한국측의 부표제를

중요제목의 지위로 향상시킨데 기인한다고 말하였다.

"밀터"는 한국측 개요에는 포함되지 않은 두가지

제목 즉 (ㄱ) 미국군대, 민간인 및 군인, 그들의 가족

및 재산의 안전을 제공하기 위하여 필요한 입법조치와

기타 조치를취해야 할 접수국의 의무 (제13항) 및

(ㄴ) 한국의 법률을 존중하고 협정의 정신에 합치되는

방법에서 행동해야할 파견국 인원의 의무 (제18항)이

미국측 목록에 포함되어 있다고 지적하였다.

나. 토 의

(4) "하비브"씨에 대한 답변으로 "신"씨는 파견국 군대에 대한 특권 및 면제의 부여는 한국정부의 현존법률과 예규의 수정 및 예외를 포함하는 것이라 진술하였다. 따라서 문제는 미묘한것으로서 한국측은 후일 이문제에 관한 견해를 상술할것이다. "밀터" 중령이제시한 목록에 대하여 "신"씨는 제13항을 명백히 하여달라고 부탁하였다.

(5) "밀터" 중령은 제13항은 주둔군지위협정에 의하여 필요한 입법조치나 기타 조치가 한국정부에 의하여 실행될것이라는 보장을 기본적으로 표시하는것이라 설명하였다. "하비브"씨는 이것은 주둔군지위 협정에 있어서 기본적인 특징이라고 부언하였다. 그것은 접수국측으로서의 의도와 파견국에 대한 입장에 대한 성명이다.

62-4-60

0067

62-4 미문 87-3

0068

(6) "신"씨는 그렇다면 제13항을 제26항에 통합할것을 제의하였다. "하비브"씨는 그들은 같은문제와 관련된 것이 아니라고 지적하였다. 그는 제 13 항은 주요한 실질적 제목을 포함하여 목록에있는 다른 항목은 반드시 특수조문을 나타내는것이 아니라고 말하였다. "신"씨는 제13항에서 의미하는 조치들은 한국측 계요의 3항(f) 로서 포함된다고 진술하였다. 그는 제13항의 입법은 대한민국 정부의 입법권한을 간섭하며 제한하는 함축성을 갖고있다고 말하였다. "박근" 박사는 이들조치는 기타 주요항목에대한 세부적 교섭시에 적절히 취급할것을 제의하였다.

(7) "하비브"씨는 제 13 항은 중요제목을 형성한다는 미국측의 생각을 강조하였다. 연이나 그는 동항목을 취급할 방법은 다음 교섭시에 결정할것에 동의하였으며 그시에 그는 미국측은 이항목의 관련성과 중요성에 대하여 한국측을 이해시킬수 있을것이라 확신하였다.

(8) 그러자 "신"씨는 한국측 계요의 16항(d)(주둔군지위협정에 배치되는 현존 제협정의 파기를 위한조항)이 미국측 목록에 포함되어 있지 않음을 지적하였다. "하비브"씨는 주둔군지위협정은 물론 종래의 관계협정에 우위할것이라 답변하였다. "신"씨는 양대표단은 한국측으로서 그입장을 보류하기를 원하는 제 13 항을 제외하고는 미국측 목록에 포함되어있는 중요제목들에 관하여 합의하고 있는것같다고 진술하였다. "하비브"씨는 동의하였다.

(9) "신"씨는 그다음 전회의시 "밀러" 중령이 대한민국과

0069

0070

미국군대간의 현존하는 제협정에 관하여 말한바 있는 입장설명에 언급하였다. "신"씨는 이들 제협정들은 현재는 존재하지 않는 과거의 특수환경하에서 이루어 졌으며 한국측 견해로서는 사정변경으로 말미암아 주둔군 지위협정에 의하여 대체되어야 할것이라고 진술하였다. "하비브"씨는 주둔군지위협정은 다만 주둔군지위협정에 관련된 제협정만을 대체할것이라고 답변하였다. 그는 교섭중에있는 주둔군지위협정은 (타국에서 파견된 유엔사령부군대와 달리) 미국군대에 관하여 관계될것이라고 설명하였다. 그는 이문제를 후일 더욱 충분히 토의될것이라고 말하였다. "신"씨는 이에동의하고 한국측은 특수조항에 대한 토의가 시작될 때까지 교섭범위 및 내용에관한 미국측 견해에 대하여 이상 논평하기를 고려할것이라 시사하였다.

다. 차기회의 의제

(10) "하비브"씨는 특수조항에 관한 교섭을 차기회의에서 시작할것을 제의하였다. 그는 적절한 시작으로서 서문, 정의조항 및 시간이 허용한다면 합동위원회 설치에 관한 조항을 고려하도록 제의하였다. "신"씨는 서문은 교섭의 완료단계까지 남겨두도록 제의하였다. 그는 한국측은 정의조항에 토의에는 합의하나 합동위원회 조항보다 오히려 인원의 출입국관리 조항을 토의할것을 바라는 바라고 말하였다. 62-11-62

(11) "하비브"씨는 서문은 결코 보통서문이 아니다 즉 그것은 주둔군지위협정이 이루어질 기본적인 근거이라고 지적하였다. 서문은 전체 협정에대한 성격을 마련하며

62-4-14 미문 87-3⑤

0072

주둔군지위협정이 양국정부간의 상호방위 조약에
근거하여 교섭되었음을 명백히 하는것이다. 그는
한국측이 재고해줄것을 요구하였다. 그는 미국측은
출입국관리 문제를 토의하는데 반대하지 않으나
합동위원회가 주둔군지위협정을 통하여 언급되고 있으며
교섭자들은 특수조항에 관련하여 합동위원회의 기능에
토의할때 무엇에 언급하고 있는지를 알아야 할것임으로
합동위원회 조항을 제일먼저 적절하다고 생각하는바라고
말하였다. "신"씨는 서문토의에는 동의하였으나
뒤에 이를수있는 합동위원회 조항대산에 출입국관리
문제를 취급하도록 요구하였다. 그러한다음 차기회의
의제는 다음과같이 할것으로 합의하였다.

(ㄱ) 서문

(ㄴ) 정의

(ㄷ) 출입국 관리

(12) 차기회의는 10월19일 하오 2시에 개최키로 되었다.

62-4-63

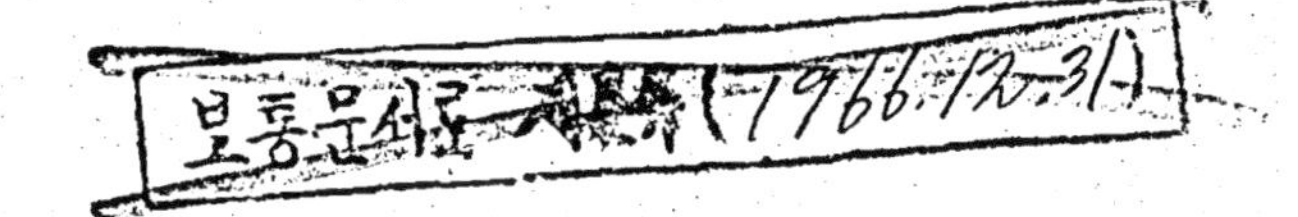

1966.12.31.에 예고문에 의거 일반문서로 재분류됨

0073

62-4-14 (6)　　미론 87-3 ⑥

0074

SUMMARY RECORD OF THE THIRD SESSION
STATUS FORCES NEGOTIATIONS

October 10, 1962

I. Time and Place: 2:00 to 3:10 p.m. on October 10, 1962 at Conference Room of the Ministry of Foreign Affairs

II. Attendants:

ROK Side:

Mr. Shin, Kwan Sup	Director Bureau of Customs Ministry of Finance
Mr. Pak, Kun	Chief, America Section Ministry of Foreign Affairs
Col. Lee, Nam Koo	Chief, Military Affairs Section Ministry of National Defense
Mr. Chi, Sung Koo	Press Officer Ministry of Foreign Affairs
Mr. Shin, Chung Sup (Rapporteur)	2nd Secretary Ministry of Foreign Affairs
Mr. Lee, Chang Bum	3rd Secretary Ministry of Foreign Affairs
Mr. Kang Suk Jae (Interpreter)	3rd Secretary Ministry of Foreign Affairs

0075

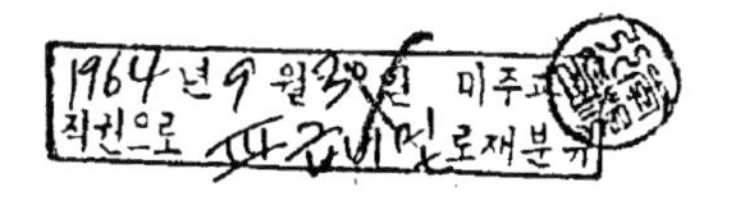

미문 87-3①

0076

US Side:

Mr. Philip C. Habib	Counselor of the Embassy for Political Affairs
Brig. Gen. J.D. Lawlor	Deputy Chief of Staff 8th Army
Mr. William J. Ford	First Secretary of the Embassy
Col. G.G. O'Connor	Deputy Chief of Staff 8th Army
Capt. R.M. Brownlie	Assistant Chief of Staff USN/K
Col. W.A. Solf	Staff Judge Advocate 8th Army
Mr. Benjamin A. Fleck (Rapporteur and Press Officer)	First Secretary of the Embassy
Mr. Robert A. Lewis	Second Secretary and Consul of the Embassy
Lt. Col. G.T. Suderman	Staff Officer, J-5 USAF/K
Lt. Col. R.E. Miller	Staff Officer, JAG 8th Army

III. Gist of Talks:

a. Further U.S. Comments on Scope and Content

1. Mr. Shin Kwan-sup, presiding in the absence of Messrs. Chin Pil-shik and Yi Kyung-ho, asked whether the U.S. side had any comments to make on the Korean side's presentation of scope and content at the previous meeting. Mr. Habib replied that the two sides appeared to be in general agreement. However, he

0077

0078

noted that the Korean side had included sub-headings in the outline which it had presented, some of which might be construed as setting forth a position in regard to the particular subjects to which they pertained. The U.S. side believed that at this stage in the negotiations, the negotiators should be considering only the major topics which should be included in the agreement and should not be considering substantive sub-headings.

2. With regard to the remarks made by Mr. Chin at the previous meeting, Mr. Habib stated the U.S. side was puzzled by Mr. Chin's apparent belief that some conflict exists between the granting of privileges and immunities to the sending state's forces and the upholding of the laws and regulations of the receiving state. Mr. Habib pointed out that it has always been the policy of U.S. forces stationed in another country to respect the laws of that government. In Korea particularly, he pointed out, the policy of the U.S. forces has been to render all possible assistance to the local law enforcement agencies.

3. Mr. Habib then relinquished the floor to Lt. Colonel Miller, who presented a list of major topics for consideration. Miller pointed out that the list contained 28 headings, compared with 16 headings in the Korean outline. This, he said, was due to the separation of certain of the items in the Korean outline into two or more separate headings and the elevation of certain of the Korean sub-headings to the status of major topics. Miller pointed out that two topics not included in the Korean outline were included in the U.S. list:

(a) the obligation of the receiving state to enact such legislation, and take such other action as may be

미문 87-3⑨

0080

necessary, to provide for the security and safety of the U.S. armed forces, their civilian and military members, their dependents and their property (Item 13), and (b) the obligation of sending state personnel to respect the laws of Korea and to conduct themselves in a manner consistent with the spirit of the agreement (Item 18).

b. Discussion

4. Replying to Mr. Habib, Mr. Shin stated that the granting of privileges and immunities to the sending state's forces involved modification and exceptions in the existing laws and regulations of the Korean government. The problem, therefore, was a delicate one on which the Korean side would elaborate its views on this matter at a later date. Turning to the list presented by Lt. Col. Miller, Mr. Shin asked for clarification of Item 13.

5. Lt. Col. Miller explained that basically Item 13 represented an assurance that the necessary legislation or other actions required by the SOFA would be carried out by the ROKG. Mr. Habib added that this was a standard feature in status of forces agreements. It was a statement of intent on the part of the receiving state and an assurance to the sending state.

6. Mr. Shin then suggested that Item 13 be incorporated with Item 26. Mr. Habib pointed out that they were not concerned with the same subject. He said Item 13 covered a major substantive topic and, the other items on the list, did not necessarily represent a specif: article. Mr. Shin stated that the measures implied in Item 13 were covered by Item 3(f) of the Korean outline. He said that the phrasing of Item 13 carried an implication of interfering with and limiting the legislative

0081

미본 81-3 ⑲

0082

authority of the ROKG. Dr. Pak Kun suggested that these measures be dealt with as appropriate during the detailed negotiation of other major items.

7. Mr. Habib emphasized the belief of the U.S. side that Item 13 constituted a major subject. He agreed, howecer, that the manner in which it would be handled would be determined in the subsequent negotiations, during which he was certain that the U.S. side would be able to convince the Korean side of the relevance and importance of this item.

8. Mr. Shin then pointed out that Item 16(d) of the Korean outline (provision for abrogation of existing agreements incompatible with the SOFA) was not included in the U.S. list. Mr. Habib replied that the SOFA would, of course, take precedence over previous relevant agreements. Mr. Shin stated that the two delegations appeared to be in agreement with regard to the major topics included in the U.S. list, with the exception of Item 13, regarding which the Korean side wished to reserve its position. Mr. Habib agreed.

9. Mr. Shin then referred to the presentation made at the previous meeting by Lt. Col. Miller, in which Miller had referred to existing agreements between the Republic of Korea and the U.S. Armed Forces. These agreements, Mr. Shin stated, were reached under specific circumstances existing in the past which no longer exist and, in the view of the Korean side, will be superseded by the SOFA because of changed conditions. Mr. Habib replied that the SOFA may supersede only those agreements which are relevant to the SOFA. He explained that the SOFA being negotiated would pertain to, and be relevant to, United States armed forces (as distinct from UNC forces

미운 87-3 ⑪

0084

from other countries). He said this subject would be discussed more fully at a later date. Mr. Shin agreed, and indicated that the Korean side would reserve further comment on the views of the U.S. side regarding scope and content until detailed discussion of specific articles is begun.

c. Agenda for Next Meeting

10. Mr. Habib suggested that negotiation of specific articles be commenced at the next meeting. As an appropriate beginning, he suggested consideration of the preamble, definitions article, and if time should permit, the article regarding the establishment of a joint committee. Mr. Shin suggested that the preamble might be left until the concluding stage of the negotiations. He said the Korean side agreed to a discussion of the definitions article but would prefer to discuss the article governing entry and exit of persons rather than the joint committee article.

11. Mr. Habib pointed out that the preamble was not just an ordinary preamble; it is the fundamental basis on which the SOFA is erected. It sets the tone for the entire agreement and makes clear that the SOFA was negotiated on the basis of the Mutual Security Treaty between the two governments. He requested the Korean side to reconsider. He said that the U.S. side had no objection to discussing entry and exit but felt it appropriate to consider the joint committee article first, inasmuch as the joint committee is referred to throughout a SOFA and the negotiators should know to what they are referring when discussing the activities of the joint committee in regard to specific articles.

0085

0086

Mr. Shin agreed to a discussion of the preamble but requested that entry and exit should be taken up instead of the joint committee article, which could come later. It was then agreed that the agenda for the next meeting should be as follows:

a. Preamble

b. Definitions

c. Entry and Exit

12. The next meeting was scheduled for October 19 at 2:00 p.m.

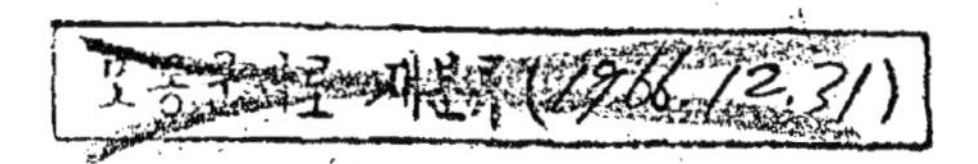

0088

주둔군 지위협정교섭 제4차회의 요약기록

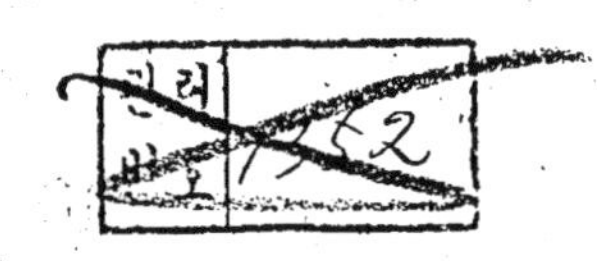

1962. 10. 19.

1. 시일 및 장소 : 1962. 10. 19. 하오 3시부터 4시 50분까지

   외무부 회의실

2. 참석자 :

   한국측 :

진 필 식	외무부 정무국장
신 관 섭	재무부 세관국장
이 경 호	법무부 법무국장
박 근	외무부 미주과장
이 남 구 대령	국방부 군무과장
신 정 섭 (기록자)	외무부 2 등서기관
이 창 범	외무부 3 등서기관
강 석 재 (통역)	외무부 3 등서기관

   미국측 :

필립 씨.하비브	주한미대사관 참사관
제이.디.로머 준장	주한미8군 참모차장
윌리암 제이. 호드	주한미대사관 1등서기관
지.지. 호코나 대령	주한미8군 참모차장
알.엠. 부론리 대령	주한미해군 참모부장
다불.에이.솔프 대령	주한미8군 법무참모
벤자민 에이. 후렉 (기록및 공보관)	주한미대사관 1등서기관
로버트 에이.루이스	주한미대사관 2등서기관겸영사
지.티 스드멘 중령	주한미군 민사참모
알.이. 밀러 중령	주한미8군 법무장교

62-4-64

0089

62-4-13 (7)

0090

3. 회담요지 :

가. 교섭범위 및 내용에관한 한국측 추가론평

(1) 합의된 의제에 따라 진행하기 전에 "진"씨는 미국측의 중요제목 목록에있는 제13항에관한 전회의에서의 토의에 언급하기 원한다고 진술하였다. 그는 양측이 완전합의에 이루지못한 미국측 목록에 제13항을 포함하는데 합의함을 말하고저 한다고 말하였음. 미국측은 이성명을 환영하였음.

나. 서 문

(2) 그후 양측은 서문의 초안을 제출하였다. 각측이타방의 초안을 검토할 기회를 가진후 다음회의에서 이를토의 할것에 합의하였다.

다. 정의조항

(3) "샬프"대령은 미국측의 정의조항 초안을 제출한였다. "진"씨는 한국측 초안과 미국측 초안간의차이가 적음으로 미국측 초안이 토의기초로하기를 제의하였다.

(4) "진"씨는 세항의 "따로이 그지위가 규정된자를 제외한" 이란 구절을 해명해줄것을 요청하였다. "샬프"대령은 이구절은 특정한 미국군대 인원 즉 대사관 무관 및 군사고문단원들은 주둔군지위협정의 규정에 포함되지 않는다는 사실을 명백히 하기위하여 포함된것이라고 답변하였다. 그는 군사고문단 인원들은 1950년 1월 26일 의 군사고문단 협정의 규정하에서 들어왔음을 지적하였다. "진"씨는 한국측은 이문제를 검토하여 차기회의에서 토의할것이라고 진술하였다. 62-4-65

(5) 그다음에는 2중국적 문제에관하여 토의하였다.

0091

62-4-15 미문81-40

0092

"샐프"대령은 미국측 초안은 국적보다 거주지를
기준으로하였기 때문에 2중국적 문제가 상세히 기술되지
않았다고 지적하였다. 미국측 초안은 통상 한국에
거주하고 있는자를 제외할것을 규정하고 있다. "샐프"
대령은 또한 대한민국이나 미국의 국적법은 국민이
자진하여 타국국적을 취득하는 경우에는 국적상실을
규정하고 있음을 첨언하였다. 따라서 이협정의 내용에
2중국적 문제를 포함하는것은 필요한것같지 않다
"진"씨는 미국군인의 한국인 부인은 세항(c)의 의미에
있어서의 가족인 까닭으로 문제를 제기하지 않을것이라
지적하였다. "진"씨는 그는 토의결과 2중국적 문제는
곤란한 문제가 아니라는것이 밝혀졌다고 생각한다고
진술하였다.

(6) "진"씨는 그다음 한국측은 군속을 미국시민에게만
제한하도록 요망한다는 것을 표시하였다. 그는 세항(b)
의 첫줄의 "민간인"이란 말바로 뒤에 "미국국적을 가진"
이란 구절을 삽입할것을 제안하였다.

(7) "샐프" 대령은 토의중에있는 조항은 다만 정의의 한가지이며
어떠한 권리나 특권을 양도하는것은 아니라고 답변하였다.
또한 고용을위한 필요요건을 두는것도 아니다. 그는
이문제에 관하여 한국측에서 가질지 모르는 대부분의
문제는 다른조항과 관련하여 매우 적절히 토의될수 있을
것이라고 제의하였다. 그는 주한미국군대는 과거와
달리 얻을수없는 특수기술을 가졌기 때문에 비교적
소수의 제3국 국민을 고용하였다는 점을 지적하였다. 그는
이것은 미국군대와 대한민국 정부의 이익을 위하여 행한

62-11-66

0093

62-4-15 미공 87-4③

0094

것이라고 진술하였다. 그는 이러한 사람들의 경우에 있어서 특권이나 권리에관하여 하등의 차별이 있어서 안된다고 부언하였다.

(8) "진"씨는 한국측은 군속을 미국국민으로 제한하고저 원하며 또한 한국에 거주하는 외국인들로 하여금 미국 군대에 부여한 특권과 면제를 향유하지 않도록 원한다고 응답하였다. "하비브"씨는 토의중에 있는 조항은 군속의 고용조건을 포함하는 다음조항과는 관계가없다는 것이라 되풀이 말하였다. 그는 만약 제3국 국민이 미국군대에 의하여 고용된다면 그들은 군속의 정의속에 포함되어야 한다는 것이 미국입장이라고 말하였다. 그는 한국에 거주하는 외국인은 미국초안 조건에의하여 제외되고 있다고 지적하였다. "샤프"대령은 그는 한국측의 고려를 위하여 한가지점을 더 첨가하고저 한다고 말하였다. 비율빈과의 주둔군지위협정 "나토" 주둔군지위협정 ("나토"의타국 국민에관한) 및 일본주둔군지위 협정하에 운영하는 합동위원회에 의한 행정조치는 모두 제3국 국민의 군속으로의 인정을 규정하고 있다. "하비브"씨는 이것은 실제적 문제와 하나이며 그기술이 미국이나 한국에서 얻을수없는 자들은 특권이나 면제에관하여 차별대우 되어서는 안된다고 부언하였다. "진"씨는 한국측은 모든 필요한 기술은 미국국민이나 혹은 한국국민으로부터 얻을수있다고 믿었다고 답변하였다. "하비브"씨는 중요한 말한 "얻을수 있는것"이라고 말하였다. 그다음에 차기 회의에서 그문제를 더욱 토의할것이 합의되었다.

62-11-67

0095

62-4-15

미문 87-4

0096

다. 가족의 정의 (세항 c)

(9) 세항 (c)로 옮겨서 "진"씨는 한국측은 그초안에서 "기타 친척" 이라는 언급을 포함치않았다고 진술하였다. "하비브"씨는 이것은 또하나의 실제 문제이며 사실상 동구절은 가족단위의 정의이라고 답변하였다. "솔프"대령은 이경우에서 의도한바는 가족단위의 불필요한 파괴를 피하는데 있다고 설명하였다. 장인, 장모, 시부모와 부양형제 혹은 자매는 제외되지 않아야 한다. 그는 미국측 초안에 있어서의 기준은 미국조세법의 기준에 흡사하다 즉 부양가족이라 함은 생계비의 50% 이상을 부양자에 의자하지 않으면 않된다고 부언하였다. "진"씨는 그는 미국입장을 이해하며 대체적으로 합의한다고 답변하였다. 연이나 그는 이항에대한 토의를 차기회의에서 계속하기를 제의하였다.

라. 출입국 관리

(10)"하비브"씨는 출입국 조항에관한 미국측 초안을 간략히 소개하고 교섭자에게 배부하였다. 한국측은 초안을 읽어본후 론평을 하지않고 제 1,2,3,5 및 6항 조문에 동의하였다.

(11) 제3항에 관하여 "하비브"씨는 합동위원회는 문서면에서 해야할일이 많을것이라고 지적하였다. 그는 교섭자들에게 모든 주둔군지위협정에 경우에 있어서 이와 같았다고 다짐하였다. 그것은 어떤때에는 협정에 대한 합의의사록에 의하여 어떤때에는 합동위원회에 의한 행정조치를 통하여 취급되었다. 그는 세항(a)에 언급하여 미국측은 다음과같은 사항을 규정할 조치를 기대한다고 말하였다.

62-V-68

0097

62-4-15 대문 87-4⑤

0098

(ㄱ) 미국 법규집행인원 (헌병, 경비원등)은 공무집행 중 요구에따라 제시할 양국어로된 신분증을 소지 해야한다.

(ㄴ) 미국군대는 요청에따라 한국당국에 주한미국 군인이 착용하는 각종군복에 대한 설명서와 신분증의 견본은 제공할것이다.

제3항의 최종절에 관하여 "하비브"씨는 교섭자들은 신분증을 요구에따라 제시되나 양도되지 않는다는 양해에 도달할것을 제안하였다. 그는 그러한 양해의 형식은 다음교섭시에 결정할수 있다고 제의하였다.

(12) "진"씨는 한국측은 제1 및 3항을 이행하기위한 기술적 조치의 필요성을 충분히 이해한다고 답변하였다. 그는 합의의사록이나 합동위원회에 의한 조치나 한국측에 수락될수 있다고 표시하였다.

(13) 제4항에 언급하여 "진"씨는 동항에서 말하고 있는 사람들은 군인보다 오히려 민간인인고로 "적절한 문서" 라는 말대신에 "여권"이라는 말이 삽입되어야 한다고 제의하였다. "하비브"씨는 미국측은 이제의를 검토하여 차기회의에서 대답하겠다고 답변하였다.

(14) 제6항에 관하여 "하비브"씨는 교섭자들은 제5항에 의거한 지위의 변경통고가 있은후 제6항하의 미국의 책임은 제5항에 의거 통고된후 (퇴거명령이) 상당한 기간내에 발해진 경우에만 발생한다는 양해의 도달하도록 제의하였다. "진"씨는 그조건은 후일 정할수있는 그러한 양해에 동의하였다.

바. 차기회의 의제

62-u-6p

(15) "진"씨는 그의 의견으로는 교섭자들이 그날회의에서

0099

62-4-15

미농 87-4⑥

0100

많은 진전을 하였다고 진술하였다. 그는 합의된 특정 사항을 밝히는 합의의사록을 작성할것을 제의하였다. "하비브"씨는 미국측은 항별보다 조문별로 합의사항을 기록하는것이 요망스러운것으로 생각한다고 답변하였다. "진"씨는 이에 동의하였다.

(16) "하비브"씨는 교섭자들은 차기회의에서 그들의 성과 있는 토의를 계속하여 완전합의에 도달하도록 모색하기를 제안하였다. 그런다음 만약 시간이 허용한다면 합동 위원회 설치 조항의 검토에 들어갈수 있을것이다. "진"씨는 이미 ㅈ 안된 3개 조항에관한 토의의 계속에 동의하였으나 한국측은 합동위원회 조항의 트의에관한 입장을 보류하기를 바란다고 진술하였다.

(17) 차기회의는 11월 1일 하오 2시에 개최키로 합의되었다.

62-4-70

0101

62-4-15(17)

미문 87-4 ⑪

0102

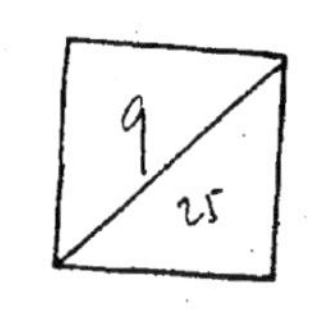

SUMMARY RECORD OF THE FOURTH SESSION
STATUS FORCES NEGOTIATIONS

October 19, 1962

I. Time and Place: 3:00 to 4:50 p.m. on October 19, 1962 at Conference Room of the Ministry of Foreign Affairs

II. Attendants:

ROK Side:

Mr. Chin, Pil Shik	Director Bureau of Political Affairs Ministry of Foreign Affairs
Mr. Shin, Kwan Sup	Director Bureau of Customs Ministry of Finance
Mr. Yi, Kyung Ho	Director Bureau of Legal Affairs Ministry of Justice
Mr. Pak, Kun (press officer)	Chief, America Section Ministry of Foreign Affairs
Col. Lee, Nam Koo	Chief, Military Affairs Section Ministry of National Defense
~~Mr. Chi, Sung Koo~~	~~Press Officer~~ ~~Ministry of Foreign Affairs~~
Mr. Shin Chung Sup (Rapporteur)	2nd Secretary Ministry of Foreign Affairs
Mr. Lee, Chang Bum	3rd Secretary Ministry of Foreign Affairs
Mr. Kang, Suk Jae (Interpreter)	3rd Secretary Ministry of Foreign Affairs

0103

미문 87-40

0104

US Side:

Mr. Philip C. Habib	Counselor of the Embassy for Political Affairs
Brig. Gen. J.D. Lawlor	Deputy Chief of Staff 8th Army
Mr. William J. Ford	First Secretary of the Embassy
Col. G.G. O'Connor	Deputy Chief of Staff 8th Army
Capt. R.M. Brownlie	Assistant Chief of Staff USN/K
Mr. Benjamin A. Fleck (Rapporteur and Press Officer)	First Secretary of the Embassy
Mr. Robert A. Lewis	Second Secretaty and Consul of the Embassy
Lt. Col. G.T. Suderman	Staff Officer, J-5 USAF/K
Lt. Col. R.E. Miller	Staff Officer, JAG 8th Army

III. Gist of Talks:

a. Further ROK Comment on Scope and Content

1. Before proceeding to the agreed agenda, Mr. Chin stated that he wished to refer to the discussion at the previous meeting concerning Item 13 on the U.S. list of major topics. He said the Korean side wished to state its agreement to the inclusion of Item 13 in the U.S. list, in regard to which both sides were now in complete agreement. The U.S. side welcomed this statement.

0105

미분 89-4 ⑨

0106

b. Preamble

2. Both sides then tabled drafts of the Preamble. It was agreed that these would be discussed at the next meeting, after each side had the opportunity to study the other's draft.

c. Definitions Article

3. Colonel Solf introduced the U.S. draft of the definitions article. Mr. Chin suggested that, since the difference was small between the Korean draft and the U.S. draft, the U.S. draft serve as the basis for discussion.

4. Mr. Chin asked for clarification of the phrase "except for those for whom status has otherwise been provided" in sub-paragraph (a). Colonel Solf replied that this phrase was included in order to clarify the fact that certain U.S. military personnel, i.e. the military attaches at the Embassy and the members of the Military Assistance Advisory Group, were not covered by the provisions of the SOFA. He pointed out that the MAAG personnel came under the provisions of the MAAG Agreement of January 26, 1950. Mr. Chin stated that the Korean side would study this matter and discuss at the next meeting.

5. There followed a discussion of the question of dual nationality. Colonel Solf pointed out that dual nationality was not specifically mentioned in the U.S. draft because this draft was based on the criterion of residence rather than of nationality. It provided for the exclusion of persons ordinarily resident in the Republic of Korea. Also, Colonel Solf added, the nationality laws of both the Republic of Korea and the United States provide for the loss

0107

미들 81-4⑩

0108

of nationality when a national voluntarily acquires another nationality. Therefore, it did not seem necessary to introduce the question of dual nationality in the context of this agreement.
Mr. Chin pointed out that Korean wives of U.S. military personnel would pose no problem since they are dependents within the meaning of subparagraph (c). Mr. Chin stated that he believed the discussion showed that the question of dual nationality was not a problem.

6. Mr. Chin then indicated that the Korean side desired to confine the civilian component to American citizens. He proposed the insertion of the phrase "of U.S. nationality" immediately after the words "civilian persons" in the first line of subparagraph (b).

7. Colonel Solf replied that the article under discussion is solely one of definitions; it does not convey any rights or privileges. Nor does it establish pre-requisites for employment. He suggested that many of the questions which the Korean side might have concerning this matter might more appropriately be discussed in connection with other articles.
He pointed out that in the past, the U.S. armed forces in Korea have hired a relatively small number of third state nationals because they had specific skills not otherwise available. He stated that this had been done in the interests of both the U.S. forces and the ROKG. In the case of these people, he added, there should be no discrimination in regard to privileges or rights.

8. Mr. Chin replied that the Korean side wished to limit the civilian component to U.S. nationals and

0109

0110

wished to preclude aliens residing in Korea from enjoying the privileges and immunities granted to the U.S. forces. Mr. Habib reiterated that the article under discussion had no relation to later articles covering the terms of employment of members of the civilian component. He said that the U.S. position was that if third state nationals are employed by the U.S. forces, they should be included in the definition of the civilian component. He pointed out that aliens resident in Korea are excluded by the terms of the U.S. draft. Colonel Solf said he wished to add one further point for the consideration of the Korean side. The SOFA with the Philippines, the NATO SOFA (with respect to nationals of other NATO countries), and an administrative arrangement by the Joint Committee operating under the Japanese SOFA, all provide for the admission of third state nationals as members of the civilian component. Mr. Habib added that this was a practical matter; that persons whose skills were not available either in the U.S. or in Korea should not be discriminated against in regard to privileges and immunities. Mr. Chin replied that the Korean side believed all the necessary skills were available either among U.S. nationals or Korean nationals. Mr. Habib said the key word was "availability". It was then agreed to discuss the matter further at the next meeting.

d. Definition of Dependents (subparagraph (c))

9. Moving on to subparagraph (c), Mr. Chin stated that the Korean side had not included in its draft any mention of "other relatives". Mr. Habib replied that this was another practical matter and that, in effect, the paragraph was a definition of the family unit.

0111

미문 81-4⑫

0112

Colonel Solf explained that the intention in this instance was to avoid any unnecessary breaking up of the family unit. Parents-in-law and dependent brothers or sisters should not be excluded. He added that the criterion in the U.S. draft was very similar to that found in the U.S. tax laws, i.e. the dependent must rely for more than 50% of his support on the sponsor. Mr. Chin replied that he understood the U.S. position and was in general agreement. However, he suggested that discussion of this paragraph be continued at the next meeting.

e. Entry and Exit

10. Mr. Habib then briefly introduced the U.S. draft of the entry and exit article, which was distributed to the negotiators. After reading the draft, the Korean side, without comment, agreed to the text of paragraphs 1, 2, 3, 5, and 6.

11. With regard to paragraph 3, Mr. Habib pointed out that there would be much work for the Joint Committee in the field of documentation. This, he assured the negotiators, was the case in all status of forces agreements. It was handled sometimes by an Agreed Minute to the agreement, sometimes through administrative arrangements made by the Joint Committee. Referring to subparagraph (a), he said the U.S. would expect action which would provide that:

a. U.S. law enforcement personnel(MPs, SPs, etc.) should carry bilingual identity cards to be shown on request when the bearer is in the performance of his duty;

b. the U.S. armed forces would furnish to the

0113

0114

Korean authorities, on request, a description of the various uniforms worn by members of the U.S. forces in Korea and sample copies of the identification cards.

With regard to the last sentence of paragraph 3, Mr. Habib proposed that the negotiators reach an understanding that the identity cards be displayed upon request but not surrendered. He suggested that the form of such an understanding could be determined during subsequent negotiations.

12. Mr. Chin replied that the Korean side fully understood the necessity for technical arrangements to implement paragraphs 1 and 3. He indicated that either an Agreed Minute or action by the Joint Committee would be acceptable to the Korean side.

13. Referring to paragraph 4, Mr. Chin suggested that since the persons referred to in the paragraph are civilians rather than military personnel, the word "passports" should be inserted in place of the words "appropriate documentation". Mr. Habib replied that the U.S. side would study this suggestion and reply at the next meeting.

14. With respect to paragraph 6, Mr. Habib suggested that the negotiators reach an understanding that following a notice of change of status pursuant to paragraph 5, the responsibilities of the U.S. under paragraph 6 shall arise only if the expulsion order is issued within a reasonable time after the notice under paragraph 5 is given. Mr. Chin agreed to such an understanding, the terms of which could be worked out later on.

0115

기본 87-4(上)

0116

f. Agenda for Next Meeting

15. Mr. Chin stated that in his opinion the negotiators had made great progress in that day's meeting. He suggested that an Agreed Minute be prepared, setting forth the specific items agreed upon. Mr. Habib replied that the U.S. side believed it would be preferable to record agreement article by article rather than paragraph by paragraph. Mr. Chin agreed.

16. Mr. Habib proposed that the negotiators continue their fruitful discussion at the next meeting and seek to reach full agreement. Then, if time permitted, they might go on to consider the article establishing the Joint Committee. Mr. Chin agreed to continuation of discussion on the three articles already tabled but stated that the Korean side wished to reserve its position with regard to discussion of the Joint Committee article.

17. It was agreed to hold the next meeting on November 1 at 2:00 p.m.

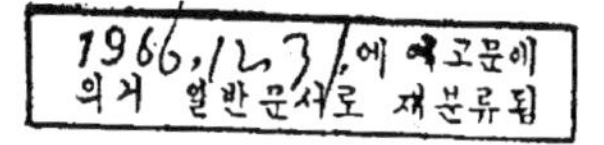

0117

0118

관리번호 1353

주둔군 지위협정교섭 제5차회의 요약기록

1962. 11. 1.

1. 시일 및 장소 : 1962. 11. 1. 하오 2시부터 3시 10분까지

   외무부 회의실

2. 참석자 :

   한국측 :

이 경 호	법무부 법무국장
박 근	외무부 미주과장
오 원 용	외무부 조약과장
이 남 구	국방부 군무과장
지 성 구 (공보관)	외무부 공보관
이 경 훈 (기록자)	외무부 2등서기관
신 정 섭	외무부 2등서기관
강 석 재 (통역)	외무부 3등서기관

   미국측 :

필립 씨.하비브	주한미대사관 참사관
제이.디.토마 준장	주한미8군 참모차장
윌리암.제이.오드	주한미대사관 1등서기관
지.지. 오코나 대령	주한미8군 참모차장
알.엠 부론티 대령	주한미해군 참모부장
다블.에이.실프대령	주한미8군 법무참모
벤자민.에이. 후텔 (기록 및 공보관)	주한미대사관 1등서기관
로버트 에이.루이스	주한미대사관 2등서기관겸영사
지.티. 스트멘 중령	주한미군 민사참모
알.이. 밀러 중령	주한미8군 법무장교

62-4-71

0119

62-4-16 (6)　　미주문 87-5 ① (14)

0120

3. 회담요지 :

가. 한국측 참가자 소개

(1) 실질적 토의에 들어가기전에 한국측 수석교섭자를 대리하여 "이경호" 씨는 새로 임명된 외무부 방교국 조약과장 "오원용"씨와 정무국 미주과 2 등서기관 "이경훈"씨를 소개하였다.

나. 서 문

(2) 지난회의에서 토의된 제목에 대하여 "이"씨는 2개의 서문초안에 있어서 중요한 상의점은 한국측 초안은 유엔결의에 언급하였으나 미국측 초안에는 그러한 언급이 없다는데 있다고 말하였다. "하비브"씨는 동의하였으나 미국측이 "와싱톤"으로부터 지시를 기다리고 있는만큼 서문에관한 이이상의 토의는 다음회의까지 연기할것을 제의하였다. "이"씨는 이에 동의하였다.

(3) "하비브"씨는 한국측이 역사적 배경을 제공하는 목적외에 유엔결의에 대한 언급을 제안하는데 어떠한 목적이 있는지를 문의하였다. "이"씨는 그목적은 미국군대가 미국 군대로서 또는 유엔사령부의 일부로서 활동하든간에 주둔군 지위협정의 규정에 복종한다는 것을 명백히 하기위한 것이라고 답변하였다. "하비브"씨는 미국측은 차기 회의에서 토의하기 위하여 이입장을 고려하겠다고 진술하였다.

다. 정 의

62-4-72

(4) "이"씨는 정의조문에 관한 미국측안의 세항 (a)에 언급하여 "그지위가 달리 규정된자를 제외한" 이란 구절은 너무 애매하며 한국측은 그문제를 다른 방식으로 아마 합의의사록의 방법으로 취급토록 하는것을 원한다고

0121

62-4-16

[illegible]

[illegible]

[illegible]

[illegible]

[illegible]

0122

말하였다. "하비브"씨는 교섭자들은 비록 이경우뿐만 아니라 다른사항에 관해서도 합의의사록의 이용을 유의하고 요망스러운것으로 알지 모른다고 응답하였다. 그는 한국측은 특별히 제의할 말이 있느냐고 물었다. "이"씨는 현재 특별히 제의할 말은없으나 그구절을 합의의사록의 형식으로 더욱 정확히 하도록 제의하였다. 그러한다음 정의에관한 그 이상의 토의는 다음회의까지 연기하는데 합의하였다.

62-V-73

타. 출입국 관리

(5) 출입국 조문에관하여 "이"씨는 제 4 항에있는 "적절한 문서"를 낱말 "여권"으로 대체하도록 하는 한국측 제의에 관하여 미국측의 논평을 구하였다. "하비브"씨는 한국측이 동 제안을 재고하여 줄것을 요구하였다. 그는 "적절한 문서"라는 말은 "여권"이라는것 보다 훨씬넓은 말이라고 지적하였다. 그말은 "여권"이 "적절한 문서"를 포함치않는데 반하여 후자를 포함한다. 미국측 초안에있는 말은 한국측의 필요에 적응할것이며 미국 당국으로 하여금 미국여권을 받지못할자들에 관하여 야기될지 모르는 어떠한 예기치 못한사태를 처리하게금 할것이다. 그는 실제에 있어서 이와관련하여 일어날 어떠한 문제도 아마 합동위원회에 의하여 해결될것이라고 말하였다. 그는 또한 미국인의 한국인 가족은 미국여권이 발급될수 없다는 점을 지적하였다.

(6) "이"씨는 양측이 군속에게는 여권이 발급되어야하며 예외적 경우는 합동위원회에 의하여 고려된다는 원칙에 합의하도록 제의하였다. "하비브"씨는 미국당국이 외국인들에게 여권을 발급할수 없음으로 합동위원회가

62-4-16

미문 87-7 ③

[illegible]

[illegible]

0124

합일이 거의 없을것이라고 답변하였다. 그는 매우 일반적인 말인 "적절한 문서"가 매우 유용하며 주둔군 지위협정의 이조항을 시행하는데 매우 용이하게 할 것임으로 채택하도록 제의하였다. 각측의 그의 입장을 밝힌 의견교환후에 이문제에 관한 더이상의 토의를 다음 회의까지 연기하도록 결정하였다.

(7) "하비브"씨는 그다음 이전회의에서 원측에 있어서 합의를 본 여러사항을 명백히 밝히는 출입국 조문에 대한 4개항의 합의의사록의 초안을 제출하였다. "이"씨는 동 합의의사록은 수락할수 있을것 같으나 한국측은 그들을 특히 (동 조문의 제 5 및 6 항에 의거한 미국 및 한국 정부의 책임에 대하여 언급하는) 네재번것을 고려할 시간을 갖고저 한다고 말하였다.

마. 합동위원회

(8) 그다음 "하비브"씨는 교섭자들은 다음 합동위원회 설치에 관한 조문을 토의하자고 제의하였다. "이"씨는 이 조문은 다음회의에서 관세업무 조문과함께 고려할것을 제의하였다. "하비브"씨는 미국측은 다음회의시에 관세조문을 토의할 준비가 전혀 안될지 모르겠다고 시사하고 그대신 토지시설 조문의 토의를 제의하였다. "이"씨가 한국측은 토지 및 시설문제를 토의할 준비가 되지않을 것이라고 답변하자 양교섭단의 장이 의제를 결정하기 위하여 차기회의 전에 개인적으로 회합하도록 합의를 보았다.

(9) 그후 합동위원회 조문을 고려하도록 결정보았으며 양측은 초안을 제출하였다. "하비브"씨는 용어상에 있어서의 다음과같은 차이점을 지적하였다: 62-11-74

0125

62-4-16

미도87-5(4)

[illegible]

[illegible]

[illegible]

[illegible]

[illegible]

0126

ㄱ. 2 항에 있어서 양정부에대한 언급이 한국측 초안의
첫문장에서 전도되어 있으며 최종문장에서는
간략히 되어있다.

ㄴ. 미국측초안의 제 1 항의 첫문장 말에 있는 추가적인
구절은 통신시설을 다룰 아직 제출되지 아니한 다른
조문에대하여 언급하는 것이다. 그는 이구절의
관련성은 시설 및 토지조문이 토의될시 한국측에게
명백히 될것이라고 부언하였다. 그는 이것은 순수히
기술적 문제이며 다른 관련성은 없다고 말하였다.

ㄷ. 한국초안은 제3항에서 "적절한" 계통보다 "외교적"
계통을 말하고있다. "하비브"씨는 미국측은 "적절한"
이란말이 매우 좋으며 유익한말로 생각한다고 말하였다.

ㄹ. 한국초안은 시설 및 토지문제에 관련한 합동위원회
의 특수한 기능에관한 미국초안의 제 1 항의 최종문장을
포함치않고 있다.

(10) "이"씨는 양 초안사이에는 다만 적은 차이점이 있을뿐
대체적으로 일치하는것 같다고 논평하였다. 그는 한국측
초안은 제 1 항의 최초문장에 있는 "시행"이란 말 바로
앞에 "해석"과"라는 말이 삽입되고 있다고 지적하였다.
"하비브"씨는 합동위원회는 주둔군지위 협정을 "해석"할
권한을 갖지않는다 다시말하면 합동위원회는 협의하고
협정은 "시행"하나 해석하지는 않는다고 답변하였다.
"이"씨는 이문제의 토의는 다음회의에서 계속하도록
제의하였다.

62-4-75

(11) "이"씨는 그는 미국측 초안에있는 추가적 구절 (상기
(9)ㄴ. 참조)에 대한 필요성을 이해할수 없다고 말하였다.

0127

62-4-16 미본 87-5 ⑤

0128

"하비브"씨는 그것은 통신문제를 포함한 특별한 조치를 위한 필요성이 나타나게될 시설 및 토지조문을 토의할때 명백히 될것이라고 답변하였다. 그는 한국측이 그때까지 이점에관한 론평을 보류하도록 요구하였다. "이"씨는 이에 동의하였다.

(12) "하비브"씨는 한국측 초안에 나타나지 않은 미국측 초안 제 1 항의 최종문장에 대한 한국측 견해를 요구하였다. "이"씨는 합동위원회 기능중 이면에대한 특별한 규정을둔 필요성을 질문하였다. "하비브"씨는 미국측은 이문장은 합동위원회의 가장 중요한 기능의 하나에대하여 언급하는 것이며 따라서 포함되어야 한다고 믿는다고 말하였다. 그는 그점에대하여 한국측으로서 합동위원회에 대한 그들의 견해와 상치되는 점이 있는지를 문의하였다. "이"씨는 동 위원회의 기능은 시설 및 토지 조문에서 규정될것이며 여기에서 반복할 필요가없다고 답변하였다.

62-4-76

(13) "이"씨는 그다음 "적절한" 계통에반하여 "외교적" 계통의 이용에 관하여 언급하였다. 그는 한국측은 외교 계통이라는 정확하고 명확한 언급을 의도한것이라 말하였다. 그는 "적절한" 이란말이 무엇을 의미하는지를 문의하였다. "하비브"씨는 합동위원회는 어떠한 계통이 사용될것인지를 결정토록 허용되어야 한다고 제의하였다. 아마도 대사관이나 외무부가 항상 반드시 좋은 계통이라고는 할수없다. 아마 그들은 주둔군 지위협정의 집행에 있어서 모든 세부사항에 관계되어서는 안될것이다. 따라서 "적절한"이란 말의 사용이 더욱 적합할것이다. "이"씨는이점에관하여 다음회의에서 더욱 토의할것을 제의하였다.

(14) 차기회의는 11월 13일 하오 2시에 개최키로 결정되었다.

62-4-16(6)

[illegible]

0130

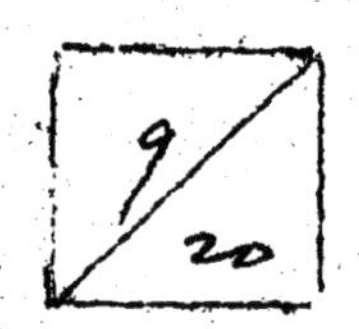

SUMMARY RECORD OF THE FIFTH SESSION
STATUS FORCES NEGOTIATIONS

November 1, 1962

I. Time and Place : 2:00 to 3:10 p.m. on November 1, 1962 at Conference Room of the Ministry of Foreign Affairs

II. Attendants:

ROK Side:

Mr. Yi, Kyung Ho	Director Bureau of Legal Affairs Ministry of Justice
Mr. Pak, Kun	Chief, America Section Ministry of Foreign Affairs
Mr. O, Won Yong	Chief, Treaty Section Ministry of Foreign Affairs
Col. Lee, Nam Koo	Chief, Military Affairs Section Ministry of National Defense
Mr. Chi, Sung Koo	Press Officer Ministry of Foreign Affairs
Mr. Lee, Kyung Hoon (Rapporteur)	2nd Secretary Ministry of Foreign Affairs
Mr. Shin, Chung Sup	2nd Secretary Ministry of Foreign Affairs
Mr. Kang, Suk Jae (Interpreter)	3rd Secretary Ministry of Foreign Affairs

0131

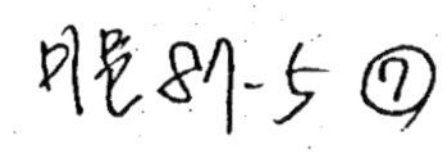

0132

US Side:

Mr. Philip C. Habib	Counselor of the Embassy for Political Affairs
Brig. Gen. J.D. Lawlor	Deputy Chief of Staff 8th Army
Mr. William J. Ford	First Secretary of the Embassy
Col. G.G. O'Connor	Deputy Chief of Staff 8th Army
Capt. R.M. Brownlie	Assistane Chief of Staff USN/K
Col. W.A. Solf	Staff Judge Advocate 8th Army
Mr. Benjamin A. Fleck (Rapporteur and Press Officer)	First Secretary of the Embassy
Mr. Robert A. Lewis	Second Secretary and Consul of the Embassy
Lt. Col. G.T. Suderman	Staff Officer, J-5 USAF/K
Lt. Col. R.E. Miller	Staff Officer, JAG 8th Army

III. Gist of Talks:

a. <u>Introduction of New Korean Participants</u>

1. Before beginning substantive discussion, Mr. Yi Kyung-ho, acting as Chief Negotiator for the Korean side, introduced Mr. O Won-yong, newly appointed Chief of the Treaty Section in the International Relations Bureau of the Foreign Ministry, and Mr. Lee Kyung Hoon, Second Secretary in the America Section of the Ministry's Political Affairs Bureau.

0133

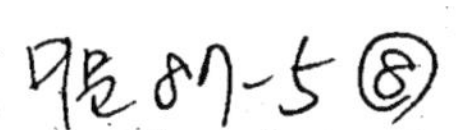

0134

b. Preamble

2. Turning to the topics discussed at the last meeting, Mr. Yi said that the principal difference in the two drafts of the Preamble was that the Korean draft referred to the UN Resolutions and the U.S. draft omitted any such reference. Mr. Habib agreed but suggested that further discussion regarding the Preamble be deferred until the following meeting, in as much as the U.S. side was awaiting word from Washington. Mr. Yi agreed.

3. Mr. Habib asked whether the Korean side had any purpose on proposing the reference to the UN Resolutions other than that of providing historical background. Mr. Yi replied that the purpose was to make clear that the U.S. forces, whether operating as U.S. forces or as members of the United Nations Command, would come under the provisions of the SOFA. Mr. Habib stated that the U.S. side would consider this position for discussion at the next meeting.

c. Definitions

4. Mr. Yi referring to subparagraph (a) of the U.S. draft of the definitions article, said that the phrase "except those for whom status has otherwise been provided" was too vague and that the Korean side would prefer that the matter be handled in some other fashion, perhaps by means of an agreed minute. Mr. Habib replied that the negotiators might find the use of agreed minutes advantageous and desirable,

0136

not only in this case but also in regard to other items. He asked whether the Korean side had any specific language to suggest. Mr. Yi replied he did not have any specific language to suggest at the moment, but suggested that the phrase be worded more precisely in the form of an agreed minute. It was then agreed to defer further discussion of the definitions article until the next meeting.

d. Entry and Exit.

5. Turning to the entry and exit article, Mr. Yi asked for comment by the U.S. side on the Korean suggestion that the word "passports" be substituted for "appropriate documentation" in paragraph 4. Mr. Habib asked the Korean side to reconsider its proposal. He pointed out that the term "appropriate documentation" is a much broader term than "passports". It would include the latter whereas "passports" would not include "appropriate documentation". The language in the U.S. draft would meet the Korean needs and would permit the U.S. authorities to take care of any contingencies that might arise with respect to people not entitled to a U.S. passport. In practice, he said, any problem arising in this connection would probably be settled by the Joint Committee. He also pointed out that Korean dependents of U.S. personnel could not be issued U.S. passports.

0137

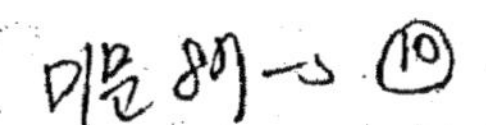

0138

6. Mr. Yi suggested that both sides agree in principle that passports should be issued to members of the civilian component and that exceptional cases should be considered by the Joint Committee. Mr. Habib replied that there would be little the Joint Committee could do, since the U.S. authorities could not issue passports to aliens. He suggested that the more general phrasing "appropriate documentation" be adopted because it would be more useful and would make this article of the SOFA easier to administer. After several more exchanges in which each side reiterated its position, it was decided to postpone further discussion of this question until the next meeting.

7. Mr. Habib then tabled the draft texts of four Agreed Minutes to the entry and exit article, setting forth explicitly the various matters agreed to in principle at the previous meeting. Mr. Yi said the Agreed Minutes appeared to be acceptable but the Korean side would like to have time to consider them, particularly the fourth one (which refers to the responsibilities of the U.S. and Korean governments under paragraphs 5 and 6 of the article).

e. Joint Committee

8. Mr. Habib then suggested that the negotiators next consider the article establishing the Joint Committee. Mr Yi suggested that this article be

0139

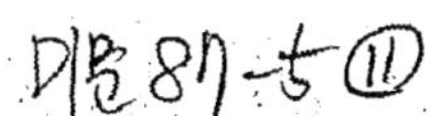

0140

considered along with the customs and duties article at the next meeting. Mr. Habib indicated that the U.S. side might not be quite ready to discuss the customs article at the next meeting and suggested instead discussion of the areas and facilities articles. When Mr. Yi replied that the Korean side would not be ready to discuss areas and facilities, it was agreed that the chairmen of the two negotiating teams should meet privately before the next meeting in order to draw up an agenda.

9. It was then decided to go ahead with consideration of the Joint Committee article and both sides tabled drafts. Mr. Habib pointed out the following differences in language:

a. In paragraph 2, the references to the two governments are reversed in the first sentence and simplified in the final sentence of the Korean draft.

b. The additional phrase at the end of the first sentence in paragraph 1 of the U.S. draft refers to another article not yet tabled which will deal with communications facilities. The relevance of this phrase will become clear to the Korean side, he added, when the facilities and areas articles are discussed. He said this was a purely technical matter and had no other relevance.

c. The Korean draft speaks of "diplomatic" channels in paragraph 3 rather than "appropriate" channels. The U.S. side, Mr. Habib indicated, believes that "appropriate" is a better and more useful word.

d. The Korean draft does not include the final sentence of paragraph 1 of the U.S. draft relating to the particular functions of the Joint Committee in connection with facilities and areas.

0141

미은 87-5 ⑫

0142

10. Mr. Yi commented that there appeared to be general agreement between the two drafts, with only minor points of difference. He pointed out that the Korean draft contained the insertion of the words "interpretation and" immediately before the word "implementation" in the first sentence of paragraph 1. Mr. Habib replied that the Joint Committee has nor power to "interpret" the SOFA; it consults and "implements" the agreement but it does not interpret. The two governments are the interpreting agencies. Mr. Yi suggested that discussion of this matter be continued at the next meeting.

11. Mr. Yi said he did not understand the necessity for the additional phrase in the U.S. draft (see para. 9b above). Mr. Habib replied that it would become clear when the facilities and areas articles are discussed, at which time the necessity for special arrangements covering communications would emerge. He asked the Korean side to reserve their comments on this point until that time. Mr. Yi agreed.

12. Mr. Habib asked for Korean views on the final sentence of Paragraph 1 in the U.S. draft which did not appear in the Korean draft. Mr. Yi replied that the Korean side questioned the necessity for specific stipulation of this aspect of the Joint Committee's functions. Mr. Habib said the

0143

미문 87-5 (B)

0144

U.S. side believed this sentence referred to one of the most important of the Joint Committee's functions and should therefore be included. He asked if the Korean side found anything in it which was inconsistent with their view of the Joint Committee. Mr. Yi replied that this function of the Committee would be spelled out in the facilities and areas articles and that there was no need to repeat it here.

13. Mr. Yi then referred to the use of "diplomatic" as opposed to "appropriate" channels. He said the Korean side intended a precise and specific reference to diplomatic channels. He asked what the term "appropriate" meant. Mr. Habib suggested that the Joint Committee should be permitted to decide what channels should be used. Perhaps the Embassy and the Ministry of Foreign Affairs would not necessarily always be the right channel. Perhaps they should not be involved in every little detail of SOFA implementation. Therefore, use of the word "appropriate" would be more suitable. Mr. Yi suggested further discussion of this point at the next meeting.

14. It was decided to hold the next meeting on November 13 at 2:00 p.m.

0145

미일.문 87-5 ⑭ (14)

0146

주둔군 지위협정교섭 제6차회의 요약기록

1962. 12. 14.

1. 시일 및 장소 : 1962. 12. 14. 하오 3시 30분부터 4시 40분까지

   외무부 회의실

2. 참석자 :

   한국측 :

진 필 식	외무부 정무국장
이 남 구 대령	국방부 군무과장
주 문 기	법무부 법무과장
박 봉 진	재무부 관세과장
채 의 석 (기록및공보관)	외무부 2등서기관
신 정 섭	"
강 석 재	외무부 3 등서기관
이 창 범	"

   미국측 :

필립 시. 하비브	주한미대사관 참사관
제이.디.로버 준장	주한미8군 참모차장
윌리암 제이.포드	주한미대사관 1등서기관
지.지.오코나 대령	주한미8군 참모차장
알.엠 부톤티 대령	주한미해군 참모부장
다불.에이.살프 대령	주한미8군 법무참모
벤자민 에이.후펠 (기록및공보관)	주한미대사관 1등서기관
로버트 에이.루이스	주한미대사관 2등서기관겸영사
알.이. 밀러 중령	주한미8군 법무장교

62-4-77

0147

62-4-17 (6)　　미국.윤 87-6 ①(13)

0148

3. 회담요록 :

가. 한국측 참석자 소개

(1) 실질적 토의를 시작하기전에 "진"씨는 회의에 처음으로 참석하고 있는 한국측 대표를 소개하였다. 그들은 "이경호"씨를 대신하여 나온 법무부 법무국 법무과장 "주문기"씨, "신관섭"씨를 대신하여 나온 재무부 세관국 관세과장 "박봉진"씨와 기록자 "이경훈"씨 및 공보관 "지성구"씨를 대신하여 나온 외무부 정무국 미주과 2등서기관 "채의석" 씨이다.

(2) 본회의에서 어느쪽도 서문과 정의조항에 관하여 추가적 론평을 하지 않았음으로 이조문들에 대한 토의를 차기회의 까지 연기하기로 합의하였다.

나. 출입국 관리

(3) 출입국 관리조문에 대해서 "하비브"씨는 지난회의에서 미국측이 제출한 합의의사록 초안에 관하여 한국측으로서 론평할것이 있는지를 문의하였다. "진"씨는 첫 3개 의사록에 관하여서는 의의가 없으나 넷째의사록의 "상당한 시간내에"라는 구절에대한 해명을 요청하였다. "하비브"씨는 주둔군지위협정은 일반적인 원측만 수립하고 그러한 원측의 세부적 시행은 합동위원회에 맡겨야한다고 제의하면서 답변하였다. 이와같이 "상당한 시간"이라는 것은 원측이며 그 에대한 시행은 합동위원회에 의하여 상세히 규제될것이다. 그는 "상당한 시간"은 양측이 상당하다고 믿는 기간일것이라고 지적하였다. "진"씨는 한국측은 합동위원회가 넷째 의사록의 "상당한 시간내에" 라는 구절의 정확한 의미를 결정한다는 양해 하에 동합의의사록을 수락한다고 진술하였다. 62-4-78

0149

62-11-17

[illegible]

[illegible]

[illegible]

0150

합동회의 요록은 이양해사항을 합동위원회의 지침을 위하여 기록할것에 합의하였다.

(4) "하비브"씨는 그다음에 미국초안 제 4 항의 "적절한 문서"라는 구절에 관하여 지난회의에서 교환된 견해 차이를 교섭자들에게 회상시켰다. 그는 미국측은 상금도 그구절이 한국측이 사용할것을 바라는 "여권" 말보다 더욱 적절하고 유용하다고 생각한다고 말하였다. 미국당국은 미국시민의 한국인 가족들과 또한 주둔군 지위협정의 규정하에 한국에 입국이 허용될 미국 국적 소유자가 아닌 다른사람들에게 여권을 발급할수 없는 단순한 이유 까닭으로 이조문의 목적을 위하여 또한 다른 조문의 어떠면 특수한말에 관계없이 "적절한 문서" 라는말이 더좋다. 그는 이말이 결코 협정의 다른조문에 영향을 미치거나 혹은 훼손케하는것이 아니라고 계속하였다.

(5) "진"씨는 한국측은 그문제를 고려하여 왔으나 여전히 본조문의 규정하에 한국에 입국하는자의 대다수는 미국 여권의 소지자이며 다만 소수자만이 미국여권을 소지하지 않을것임으로 "여권"이라는 말을 사용하고 예외적 경우를 다루도록 합의의사록을 작성해야 한다는 견해를 가지고 있다고 진술하였다.

(6) "하비브"씨는 여권 그자체는 소지자의 신분을 확인하는데 충분한 사항을 반드시 포함하지는 않는다고 지적하였다. 여권이 그소지자가 미국시민이라는 것을 증명하나 군속의 일원이나 혹은 가족인 그의 신분을 표시하기 위해서는 기타의 문서가 필요할것이다. 따라서 "적절한 문서"가 문서상의 확인을위하여 한국측의 필요를 더욱 만족스럽게 충족할것이다. 그는 이것은 주둔군지위 협정이

62-4-17

[illegible]

[illegible]

[illegible]

0152

기본적인 원측을 수립하고 세부사항은 합동위원회에 의하여 규정되도록 맡겨두게되는 경우의 한 좋은 예이라고 지적하였다.

(7) "하비브"씨는 만약 발급된 문서가 소지자들의 신분을 한국당국에 만족스러운 방법으로 증명치 못한다면 합동위원회는 명백히 그문제를 고려할수 있다는것을 지적하였다. "진"씨의 질문에 답하여 "하비브"씨는 제 4 항의 규정에 속하는 미국적 보유자들은 통상 여권과 신분증명서 혹은 명령서와 같은 기타 증명서를 포함하는 문서를 소지할것이라고 진술하였다. 이문서는 한국정부 당국으로 하여금 신분을 확인케할수 있도록 충분히 명기될것이다. "진"씨는 한국측은 그러한 문서는 한국정부 당국으로 하여금 소지자의 신분을 확인할수 있도록 충분한 정보를 포함하여야만 한다는 양해밑에서 "적절한 문서"라는 말의 사용에 동의한다고 진술하였다. 그리하여 최종적인 협정으로 통합될 원문으로서 4개의 합의의사록과 함께 출입국 관리조문의 미국측 초안을 수락하는데 동의하였다. 그리하여 상호 축하를 교환하였다.

다. 합동위원회

62-4-80

(8) 지난회의에서 제출된 합동위원회 조문의 미국측 초안에 언급하여 "하비브"씨는 제 1 항의 첫째문장의 조그마한 문법상의 착오를 지적하였다. 그는 동문장의 최종구절은 "따라 규정하지 않는한" 대신에"따라 규정할 경우를 제외하고"로 정정토록 한다고 말하였다. 미국측으로서는 현재 실질적인 논평을할것이 없다는 "하비브"씨의 말이 있자 이조문의 그이상의 토의는 연기할것에 합의하였다.

0153

62-4-17 미문 87-0④

0154

다. 관세업무

(9) "호드"씨에 의하여 관세업무 조문의 미국측 초안이 제출되었으며 그는 교섭자들은 인원의 출입국관리에 대한 토의를 완료하고 이제 물품 출입문제에 관심을 돌리게되었다고 지적하였다. 그는 미국측 초안은 그규정에 속하는 자들은 약간의 특별한 예외가 있으나 한국의 관세법 및 규정에 복종해야함은 명백히 기술하고 있다는 사실에 주의를 환기시켰다.

(10) "호드"씨는 동조문이 파견국의 임무의 성공적인 수행을 돕기위한 여건을 마련하고 있음을 강조하면서 아마 동 조문의 가장 중요한 특징은 그조문이 부여하는 특혜와 면제가 그 혜택을 받는 군대 및 피파 인원의 사기에 상당한 영향을 주는것이라 진술하였다. 그는 동조문은 미국 군대 및 그기관에의하여 수입되었거나 사용될 물자 장비 및 보급물의 무세통관을 규정한다고 지적하였다. 연이나 동조문에 의하여 포함된 개인에 탁송되었거나 사용( )을 위한 물건은, (ㄱ) 개인이 처음 한국에 도착할때 수입된 가구, 가정용품 기타 개인용품과, (ㄴ) 사용을위한 자동차 및 부속품 및 (ㄷ) 미국 군사 우편국을 통하여 수입된 사용을위한 적당한 량의 개인용품 및 가정용품을 제외하고 통관세를 내야한다.

(11) "호드"씨는 또한 동조문 초안은 공문서, 우편물 및 군사하물에 대해서는 세관검사를 할수없다고 규정하고 있음을 지적하였다. 동 조문은 추가하여 한국으로 수입된 물자는 한국과 미국정부당국 간에 합의된 조건에 따라서만 처분될수 있음을 규정하고있다. 62-4-81

0155

62-4-19 미몰 87-6⑤

0156

그는 또한 통관세 및 기타 수수료 면제로 수입된 물자를 통관세 혹은 기타 수수료를 면제하고 한국밖으로 재수출될수 있다는 규정에 언급하였다.

(12) "호드"씨는 조문초안의 소개를 끝맺으면서 동조문에서 부여된 특권의 남용방지를 위한 필요성을 말하였다. 그는 동초안은 미국군대는 한국정부 당국과의 협조하에 그러한 남용을 방지하기 위한 필요한 조치를 취해야 함을 규정하고 있다. 그러한 협조는 혐의가 있는 남용에 대한 조사를 실시하는데 있어서의 상호협조 및 통관세와 기타 수수료의 지불을 기하기위한 협조제공이다.

(13) "호드"씨의 말을맺고 동조문 및 관계된 합의의사록의 미국측 초안이 제출되었다. 미국측 초안을 읽은다음 "진"씨는 미국측의 것과 한국측 초안은 비슷한 원측에 근거하고 있으며 물자의 분류에관하여 약간의 차이가 있다고 말하였다. 그는 그다음 한국측 초안을 제출하고 양측이 두개의 초안을 검토하여 다음회의에서 항별로 토의할 준비를 하도록 제의하였다.

(14) 한국측 초안을 잠시 검토한후 "하비브"씨는 최초의 검토결과 넓은분야가 합의하고 있는것같다고 말하였다. 그러나 그는 실질적 중요성을 가진 몇가지의 차이점을 발견하였다. 다음회의에서 본조문을 항별로 토의하기로 합의하였다.

(15) 다음회의는 12월 26일 하오 2시에 개최키로 합의되었다.

0157

62-4-17 (6)

미문81-6⑥

0158

0160

SUMMARY RECORD OF THE SIXTH SESSION
STATUS FORCES NEGOTIATION

November 14, 1962

I. Time and Place: 3:00 to 4:40 p.m. November 14, 1962 at Conference Room of the Ministry of Foreign Affairs

II. Attendants:

ROK Side:

Mr. Chin, Pil Shik	Director Bureau of Political Affairs Ministry of Foreign Affairs
Col. Lee, Nam Koo	Chief, Military Affairs Section Ministry of National Defense
Mr. Chu, Mun Ki	Chief, Legal Affairs Section Ministry of Justice
Mr. Pak, Pong Chin	Chief, Customs Duty Section Ministry of Finance
Mr. Chai, Eui Sok	2nd Secretary Ministry of Foreign Affairs
Mr. Shin, Chung Sup	2nd Secretary Ministry of Foreign Affairs
Mr. Kang, Suk Jae	3rd Secretary Ministry of Foreign Affairs
Mr. Lee, Chang Bum	3rd Secretary Ministry of Foreign Affairs

U.S. Side:

Mr. Philip C. Habib	Counselor of the Embassy for Political Affairs
Brig. Gen. J.D. Miller	Deputy Chief of Staff 8th Army
Mr. William J. Ford	First Secretary of the Embassy
Col. G.G. O'Connor	Deputy Chief of Staff 8th Army
Capt. R.M. Brownlie	Assistance Chief of Staff USN/K
Col. W.A. Solf	Staff Judge Advocate 8th Army

0159

Mr. Benjamin A. Fleck (Rapporteur and Press Officer)	First Secretary of the Embassy
Mr. Robert A. Lewis	Second Secretary and Consul of the Embassy
Lt. Col. R.E. Miller	Staff Officer, JAG 8th Army

0165

III. Gist of Talks:

a. Introduction of New Korean Participants

1. Before beginning substantive discussion, Mr. Chin introduced several members of the Korean side participating in the negotiations for the first time. They were: Mr. CHU Mun-ki, Chief of the Legal Affairs Section of the Justice Ministry's Bureau of Legal Affairs, substituting for Mr. YI Kyung-ho; Mr. PAK Pong-chin, Chief of the Customs Duty Section of the Finance Ministry's Bureau of Customs, substituting for Mr. SIN Kwan-sop; and Mr. CHAE Eui-sok, Second Secretary in the America Section of the Foreign Ministry's Political Affairs Bureau, substituting as Rapporteur for Mr. YI Kyung-hun and as Press Officer for Mr. CHI Sung-ku.

2. As neither side wished to make additional comments at this meeting regarding the Preamble or the Definitions article, it was agreed to postpone further discussion of these articles until the next meeting.

b. Entry and Exit

3. Turning to the entry and exit article, Mr. Habib asked if the Korean side had any comment to make on the draft agreed minutes tabled by the U.S. side at the previous meeting. Mr. Chin replied that there was no disagreement regarding the first three minutes but requested

0161

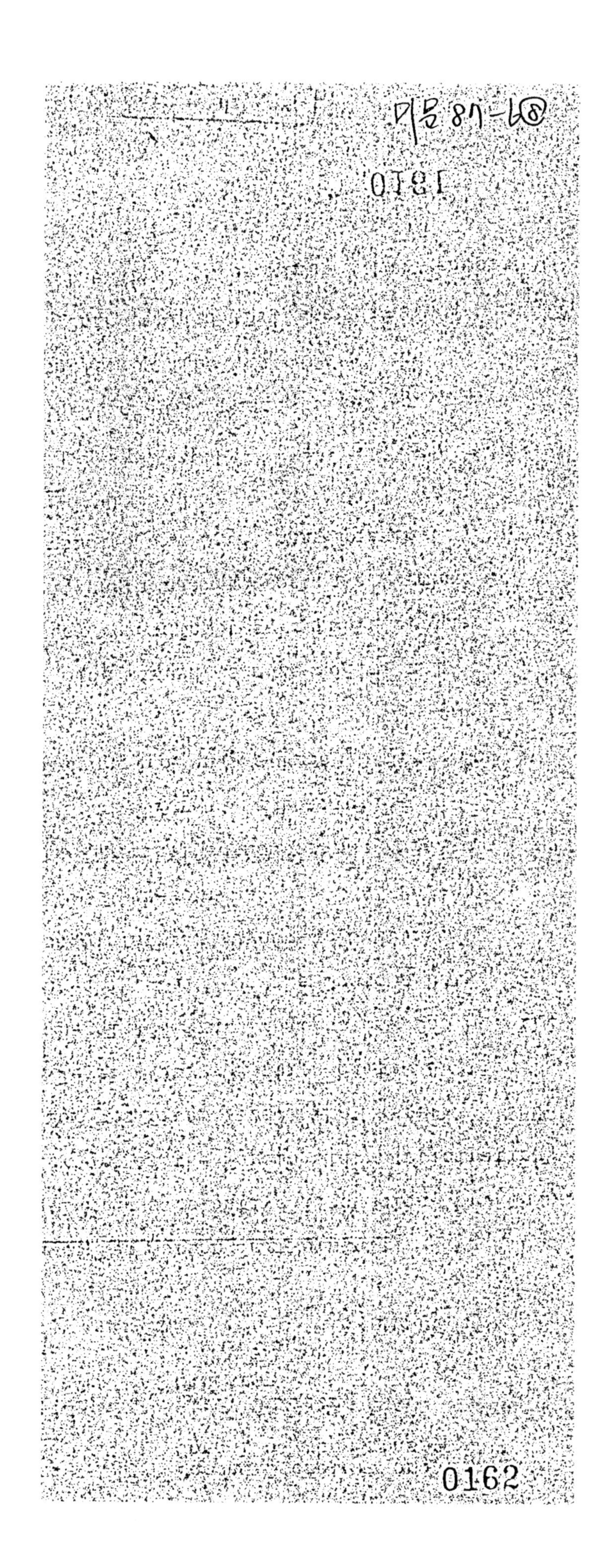

clarification of the phrase "within a reasonable time" in the fourth minute. Mr. Habib replied by suggesting that the SOFA should establish general principles, leaving to the Joint Committee the detailed implementation of those principles. Thus "a reasonable time" is a principle the implementation of which should be worked out in detail by the Joint Committee. He pointed out that "a reasonable time" would be a period of time which both sides believe to be reasonable. Mr. Chin stated that the Korean side accepted the agreed minutes, with the understanding that the Joint Committee will decide the exact meaning of the phrase "within a reasonable time" in the fouth minute. It was agreed that the joint agreed summary of the meeting should record this understanding for the guidance of the Joint Committee.

4. Mr. Habib then reminded the negotiators of the difference of opinion which had developed at the previous meeting regarding the phrase "appropriate documentation" in paragraph 4 of the U.S. draft article. He said the U.S. side still believed that this phrase was more appropriate and more useful than the word "passports" which the Korean side wished to use. For the purposes of this article, and irrespective of any specific wording in any other article, "appropriate documentation" was better, for the simple reason that the United States authorities cannot issue passports to Korean dependents of U.S. citizens or to other persons of non-U.S. nationality who would be permitted enty into Korea under the provisions of the SOFA. In no way, he

미문 87-69

0164

continued, would this language affect or detract from anything said in any other article of the agreement.

5. Mr. Chin stated that the Korean side had considered the matter but still held the view that since the majority of persons entering Korea under the provisions of this article could be U.S. passport bearers and only a small minority would not have U.S. passports, the word "passports" should be used and an agreed minute drafted to cover the exceptional cases.

6. Mr. Habib pointed out that a passport by itself does not necessarily contain sufficient information to verify the status of the bearer. While the passport indicates the bearer to be a U.S. citizen, other documentation would be necessary to indicate his status as a member of the civilian component or as a dependent. Therefore, "appropriate documentation" would more satisfactorily meet the need of the Korean side for documentary verification. He pointed out that this was another good example of a case in which the SOFA should establish a basic principle and leave the details to be worked out by the Joint Committee.

7. Mr. Habib pointed out that if the documentation issued did not verify the status of the bearers in a manner satisfactory to the Korean authorities, the Joint Committee obviously would consider the matter. In answer to questions by Mr. Chin, Mr. Habib stated that persons of U.S. nationality falling under the provisions of paragraph 4 would ordinarily carry documentation including passports and other identifying papers such as indentity cards or written orders. This documentation would be sufficiently detailed to permit the Korean authorities to verify their status. Mr. Chin stated that the Korean side agreed to the

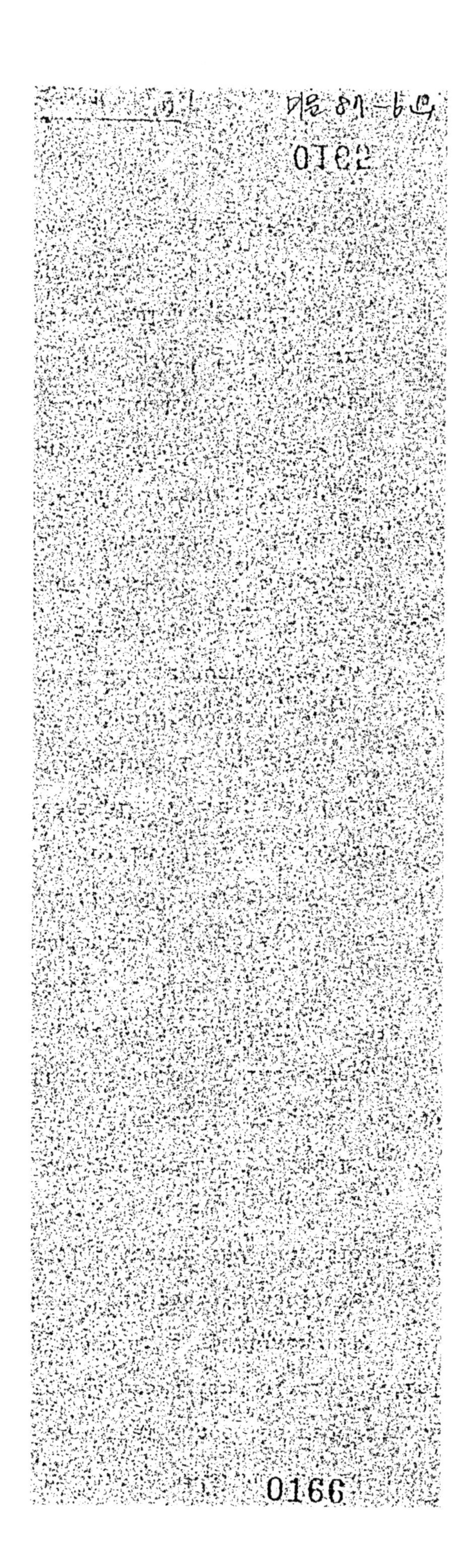

0166

use of "appropriate documentation", with the understanding that such documentation must include sufficient information to permit the Korean authorities to verify the status of the bearer. It was then agreed to accept the U.S. draft of the entry and exit article, together with the four agreed minutes, as the text to be incorporated into the final SOFA. Mutual congratulations were thereupon exchanged.

c. Joint Committee

8. Referring to the U.S. draft of the Joint Committee article tabled at the previous meeting, Mr. Habib reported a slight grammatical error in the first sentence of paragraph 1. He said the final phrase of the sentence should read "except where otherwise provided" instead of "unless otherwise provided for". Upon Mr. Habib's statement that the U.S. side had no substantive comment to make at this time, it was agreed to defer further discussion of this article.

d. Customs and Duties

9. The U.S. draft of the customs and duties article was introduced by Mr. Ford, who pointed out that the negotiators, having just completed consideration of the entry and exit of persons, were now turning their attention to the entry and exist of things. He called attention to the fact that the U.S. draft explicitly states that the persons subject to its provisions shall be subject to the customs laws and regulations of Korea, with certain specific exceptions.

10. Emphasizing that the article provides the basis for facilitating the successful accomplishment of the sending state's mission, Mr. Ford stated that perhaps the most important feature of the article is that the privileges and immunities which it confers have a considerable impact upon the morale of the troops and other persons who share

0167

[illegible]

0168

its benefits. He pointed out that the article provides for the entry free of customs duties of materials, equipment, and supplies imported by and for the use of the U.S. armed forces and their agencies. However, property consigned to, and for the personal use of individuals covered by the article would be subject to duties, with the exception of: (a) furniture, household goods, and personal effects imported when the individuals first arrive in Korea; (b) vehicles and parts for private use; and (c) reasonable quantities of personal effects and household goods for private use imported through U.S. military post offices.

11. Mr. Ford also pointed out that the draft article provides that customs examination shall not be made in the case of official documents, mail, and military cargo. In addition, the article provides that any disposal of goods imported into Korea shall be effected only in accordance with conditions agreed upon between the authorities of Korea and the United States. He also referred to the provision that goods imported free from customs duties and similar charges may be re-exported from Korea free of any customs or similar charges.

12. Concluding his introduction of the draft article, Mr. Ford mentioned the necessity for prevention of the abuse of privileges granted therein. He pointed out that the draft provides that the U.S. armed forces, in cooperation with the Korean authorities, shall take necessary steps to prevent such abuse. Such cooperation extends to mutual assistance in conducting investigations of suspected abuses, and the rendering of assistance to ensure payment of duties and other fees.

0169

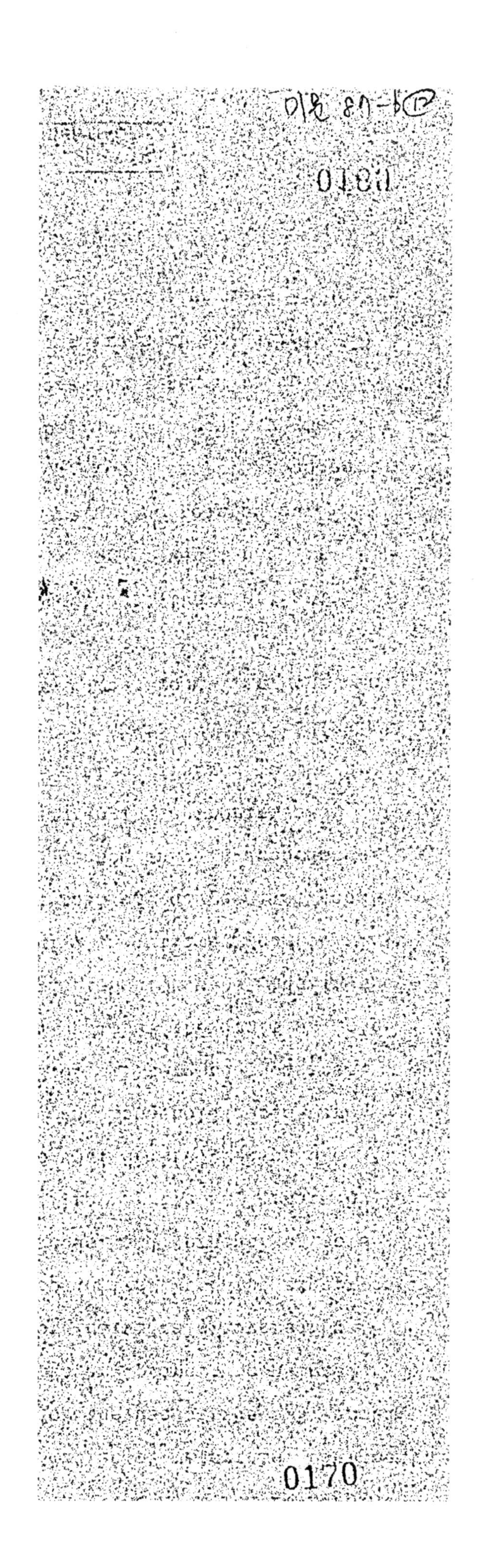

13. At the conclusion of Mr. Ford's remarks, the U.S. draft of the article and related agreed minutes was tabled. After reading the U.S. draft, Mr. Chin remarked that it and the Korean draft were based on similar principles, with perhaps some minor points of difference with regard to the classification of goods. He then tabled the Korean draft and suggested that both sides consider the two drafts and be prepared to discuss them, paragraph by paragraph, at the next meeting.

14. After a quick persual of the Korean draft, Mr. Habib remarked that upon first examination, there did appear to be broad areas of agreement. However, he detected a number of differences of substantial importance. It was agreed to discuss this article, paragraph by paragraph, at the next meeting.

15. It was agreed to hold the next meeting on November 26 at 2:00 p.m.

0171

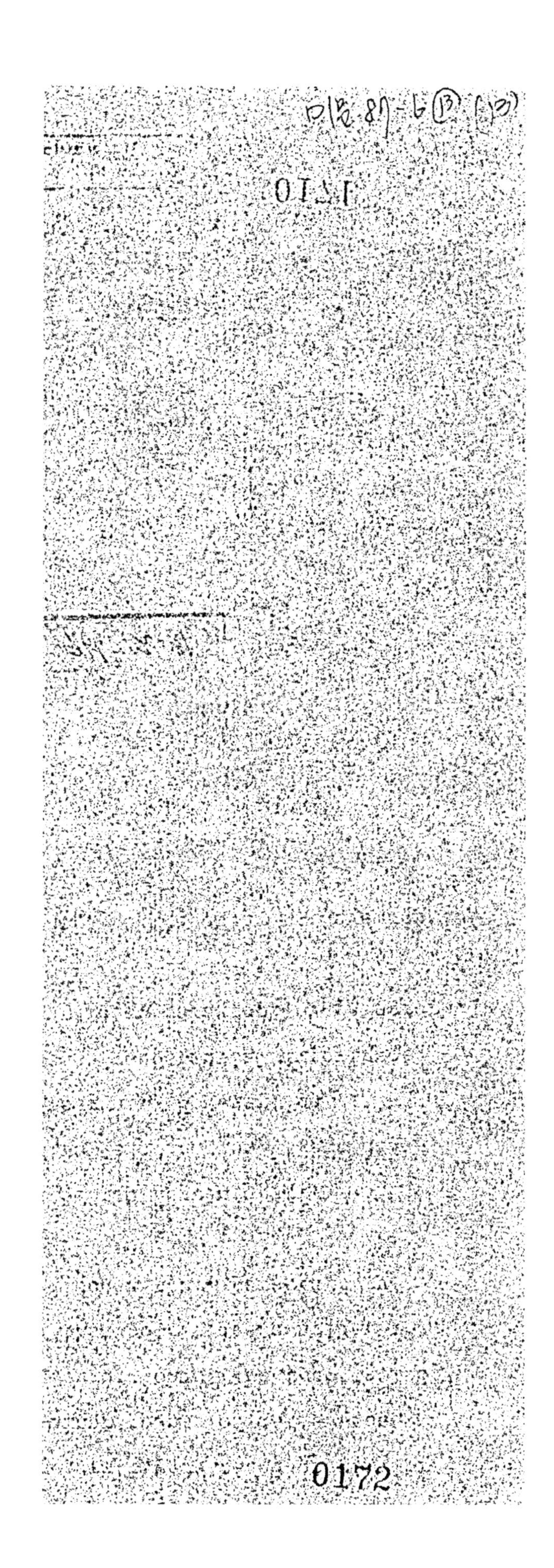
0172

주둔군지위협정 교섭 제7차회의 요약기록

1962. 11. 26.

1. 시일 및 장소 : 1962. 11.26. 하오 2시부터 4시 10분까지

   외무부 회의실

2. 참석자 :

   한국측 :

진 필 식	외무부 정무국장
이 경 호	재무부 세관국장
박 근	외무부 미주과장
이 남 구 대령	국방부 군무과장
박 봉 진	재무부 관세과장
채 의 석(기록및공보관)	외무부 2등서기관
신 정 섭	"
강 석 재 (통역)	외무부 3등서기관
이 창 범	"

   미국측 :

필립 시.하비브	주한미대사관 참사관
제이.디.로버 준장	주한미8군 참모차장
윌리암 제이.포드	주한미대사관 1등서기관
지.지.오코나 대령	주한미8군 참모차장
알.엠.부톤티 대령	주한미해군 참모부장
다불.에이.살프 대령	주한미8군 법무참모
벤자민 에이.후텔 (기록및공보관)	주한미대사관 1등서기관
로버트 에이.루이스	주한미대사관 2등서기관겸영사
알.에이. 버트 중령	주한미군민사참모
켐펜	통역

62-4-83

0173

62-4-10 (10)

0174

3. 회담요지:

가. 미측 참석자 소개

(1) 실질적 토의에 들어가기 전에 "하비브"씨는 미국교섭 대표단의 교체대표로서 "지.티.스드멘" 중령을 교체한 민사참모장교 "다블.에이.버트" 중령을 소개하였다. "하비브"씨는 또한 지난회의에 수차 참석치 못하였던 "켐페"씨가 돌아온것을 환영하였다.

나. 서 문

(2) 그다음 교섭자들은 제출된 서문초안의 검토를 재개하여 실질적 토의에 들어갔다. "하비브"씨는 미국측은 양측 초안을 면밀히 검토하였으며 미국측이 제출한 간결한 내용을 계속 취할것을 바란다고 진술하였다. 그는 근본적으로 서문은 미국군대의 한국 주둔근거에대한 성명이 되어야하며 미국측은 한국측 초안이 길고 복잡하며 어떤점에 있어서는 중복되고 있는반면 미국측 초안은 만족스러운 종류의 성명이라고 믿는다고 말하였다. 양측 초안은 동일한 목적을 달성코저 기도하고 있으나 한국측 초안은 필요 이상으로 복잡하다. "하비브"씨는 그다음 "진"씨에게 미국초안과 비교하여 한국측 초안의 가장 현저한 특징을 말하여 달라고 부탁하였다.

(3) "진"씨는 서문의 중요한 미국측 초안에서 기술되고 있다. 연이나 한국측은 미국군대의 한국 주둔은 유엔 결의와 상호 방위조약 둘다에 의거하고 있는 사실을 서문에 기술하고저 원한다. 따라서 비록 한국측 초안의 표현이 완전한것이 아닐지라도 수정될수 있으며 한국측은 그들이 기초한것과 비슷한 내용을 원한다고 답변하였다. 62-4-84

0175

62-4-18

미문 87-7②

0176

(4) "하비브"씨는 역사적 배경에 대한 언급을 서문에 포함시키자는 한국측의 희망을 인식하며 세밀히 검토 하였다. 한가지 명백히 해둘 필요있는일이있는바 그것은 현재의 교섭은 다만 미국군대에 관한것이며 유엔군에 관한것이 아니다라고 진술하였다. "하비브"씨는 한국측은 지난 토의에서 교섭결과 어떠한 협정이 나타날지라도 유엔군과는 하등의 관련이 없다는점에 합의한바 있다고 지적하였다. 그는 그러한 양해하에 미국측은 서문에서 역사적 배경에관한 언급을 포함시키고저 하는 희망을 즐거이 검토하겠다고 말하였다.

(5) "하비브"씨는 계속하여 한국측 초안에는 미국측 초안에 없는 두가지사항 즉 (ㄱ) 유엔결의에 대한 언급 (ㄴ) 양국간의 상호 이익의 결속을 강화하자는 희망의 피력이 있다고 말하였다. 그는 미국측은 이들 두가지점을 통합하였고 또한 한국측 초안보다 덜복잡하고 새초안을 제출하고저 한다고 말하였다.

(6) "진"씨는 한국측은 교섭되고 있는것은 주한 미국군대의 지위를 포함하는 협정이라는 점에 동의한바 있다. 동 협정은 여타 다른국가의 군대와는 하등관계가 없다. 동 협정은 유엔사령부의 일부로서 복무하고있는 타국가의 군대에는 관련이 없다고 답변하였다. 그는 미국 군대는 그들이 유엔결의의 규정이나 혹은 한미 상호 방위 조약의 규정하에 주둔하고 있든지간에 주둔군 지위협정 의 규정에 따라야한다고 계속하였다. 이점에 관하여 그는 유엔결의와 상호방위조약간에 하등의 차이는 볼수 없으며 따라서 미국군대가 미국군대로서 또는 통합 사령부의 일부로서 주둔하면간에 처우에 있어서 차이가 있어서는 안된다고 말하였다. 62-4-85

0177

62-4-18

0178

(7) "하비브"씨는 주둔군지위협정은 주한미국 군대의 지위에 관계하는것이며 여타 타국가의 군대나 혹은 통합사령부 자체에 관련을 갖지않는다 재천명하였다. 그는 재차 미국교섭단은 유엔 안전보장 이사회 결의 하에 설치된 통합사령부를 대신하여 교섭하도록 허가 된것이 아니라고 진술하였다.

(8) "진"씨는 한국측은 주둔군지위협정은 미국군대를 제외한 통합사령부의 어떤다른 군대에는 적용되지 않는다는 점에 동의한다고 답변하였다. 그는 주둔군 지위협정은 미국군대가 통합사령부의 구성부대이건 아니건간에 미국군대에 적용된다는 것을 반복하였다. "하비브" 씨는 그것이 바로 미국측 초안이 기술한바라고 응답 하였다. 그는 바로 제출된바 있는 미국측 수정안에 관한 한국측의 견해를 문의하였다.

(9) 수정안에 관하여 논평하면서 "진"씨는 미국 군대의 목적과 목표는 미국군의 한국주둔이 유엔결의나 혹은 상호방위조약에 의거하고 있거나 간에 동일한 것이다. 따라서 주둔군지위협정이 이러한 목적과 목표를 달성토록 기하기위하여 통합사령부의 구성 부대로 복무하는 미국군대에 대하여 예외를 둘수없다. 통합사령부의 미국 구성부대에 의하여 사용되고있는 시설 및 토지는 따라서 주둔군지위협정의 규정에 따라야 한다고 진술하였다. "진"씨의 논평에 대한 "강"씨의 통역을 부언하여 "박"박사는 주둔군 지위협정의 기본목적은 유엔결의와 상호 방위조약의 목적 및 목표의달성을 돕는데있다. 따라서 유엔

62-4-86

0179

62-4-18

미분 87-7④

[illegible]

[illegible]

[illegible]

0180

결의나 혹은 상호방위조약에 의거하여 한국에 주둔하는 미국군대에 관하여 차별이 있을수없다고 말하였다.

(10) "하비브"씨는 미국측 서문초안에는 유엔결의나 상호방위조약의 목적과 목표에관하여 하등 언급이 없다. 다만 서문은 주둔군지위협정을 제결의와 조약에 의거하여 대한민국에 주둔하고있는 미국군대를 규제한다고 기술하고 있다고 답변하였다.

(11) "진"씨는 결과적으로 통합사령부의 군대의 지위와 시설 및 토지에관한 대한민국 정부 및 통합사령부간의 협정은 여타 국가의 군대에 적용되며 미국군대에는 적용되지 않는다고 응답하였다. "하비브"씨는 미국측은 한국측의 입장을 이해하며 고려하겠다고 말하였다. "진"씨는 만약 그점에관하여 명백한 양해가 이루어진다면 한국측은 서문의 문장을 최종적으로 작성하는데 하등 애로가 없을것이라 말하였다. 그는 차기회의에서 그토의를 계속하도록 제의하였으며 "하비브"씨는 이에 동의하였다.

관세업무

제 1 항

62-4-87

(12) 지난회의에서 제출된 관세업무 조문 초안에 관하여 "진"씨는 조항별 토의를 제의하였다. "하비브"씨는 이에 동의하였다. 그는 미국측이 제1항초안은 명백한 것이며 미국측은 그이상 더 부언할 이유가없다고 말하였다. "진"씨는 두초안사이에는 근본적인 차이가 없으며 그목적과 요점은 같은것이라고 말하였다.

0181

62-1-18

미불 87-7日

[illegible]

[illegible]

0182

그는 한국측 초안의 둘째 문장을 삭제할것을 제의 하였으며 "하비브"씨는 이에 동의하였다. "하비브" 씨도 첫째문장의 미국측 안의 말씨가 매우 정확하고 상세하다는 견해를 피력하였다. "진"씨는 양측의 초안내용이 기본적으로 동일한것임으로 미국측의 제1항 초안은 한국측으로서 수락할수 있다고 진술하였다.

제 2 항

(13) 제2항에 대하여 "진"씨는"공인된 구매기관 및 비세출 자금기관을 포함한" 이란 구절에대한 설명을 요구하였다. "하비브"씨는 미국측은 제2항의 자기네 초안이 복잡하고 약간 내해한줄알며 따라서 그는 이항의 수정안을 제출코저 한다고 답변하였다. 이때 그는 제 2 항의 새안을 제출하였다. 그는 새안을 간결하며 매우 쉽사리 이해할수 있다고 진술하였다.

(14) "진"씨의 해명 요청에 대답하여 "살프"대령은 미국측 초안에있는 "포함한"이란 말은 공인된 구매기관은 미국군대의 일부임을 뜻한다. 사실상 이는 "포함한" 이란 단어의 사용이 그기관들의 위치를 명백히 하는것 외에는 한국측 초안의 말씨와 틀리지 않는다. 이와같이 미국측 초안의 범위는 한국측 초안의 범위보다 넓은것이 아니라고 지적하였다. 62-6-88

(15) "진"씨는 "공인된 구매기관"이 민간회사를 포함하는지를 질문하였다. "하비브"씨는 그렇치않다고 답변하였다. 그는 민간회사들은 미국군대의 배타적 사용을위하여 "미국군대 이외의 자에 의하여 수입된" 물품에 언급하고 있는 미국측 수정안의 둘째문장에 포함되어있다고 지적하였다.

0183

62-4-18

미문 81-7 ⑥

0184

그는 민간인 계약자에 의한 데미다랍 건축에 사용될 물자의 수입은 그한예가 될수있다. 그러한 물자는 명백히 무세 수입되어야 한다고 말하였다.

(16) "진"씨는 미국측 초안의 둘째문장에 대하여 더이상 토의하기를 바란다고 말하였다. 차기회의에서 이 문장에 대한 토의를 계속하기로 합의하였다.

(17) 증명문제에 관하여 "진"씨는 한국측 초안의 둘째 문장은 "합동위원회에 의하여 결정될 양식에따라 발급된 증명서를....." 이라고 언급함으로써 더욱 정확함에 반하여 수정안의 셋째문장은 "적절한 증명" 을 요구하고 있다고 지적하였다.

(18) "하비브"씨는 지난회의에서 다른 조문의 동일한 문제에관하여 비슷한 토의가 있었음을 상기시켰다. 그는 "적절한 증명"은 적절하기 위해서는 분명히 양측에 수락할만한 것이야 한다. 미국측은 무엇이 "적절한" 것인가를 협정문에서 세밀히 규정할 필요성을 느끼지 않는다고 말하였다. 양측은 이와같은 모든 절차적 사항은 협정에서 상세히 규정하기 보다 합동위원회에 의하여 차후 결정하도록 남겨둘수 있다는데 합의하였다.

제 3 항 62-4-89

(19) "하비브"씨는 제3항의 양초안의 서문문장은 미국측 초안이 "및 기타 수수료"라는 구절을 포함하고 있는 것을 제외하고는 동일하다고 지적하였다. "진"씨는 본질적 차이없는것이라는데 동의하였다. 연이나 "기타 그러한 수수료"가 창고료, 하역료 및 통관업자에 의한 수수료 등과같은 민간회사들이 징수하는 수수료를

0185

0186

포함하는지를 질문하였다. "하비브"씨는 그구절은 다만 정부 수수료에 대하여 말하는것이며 개인회사에 의한 수수료를 말하는것이 아니라고 답변하였다. 이점에관하여 다음회의에서 토의하기로 합의하였다.

(20) "진"씨는 미국측 초안의 세항(a)에 합의한다고 말하였다. "하비브"씨가 그러면 미국측 초안의 둘쨋항의 의사록에 대한 합의를 포함하는가를 문의하자 "진"씨는 합의의사록은 별도 토의할것을 제의하였으며 "하비브"씨는 동의하였다.

(21) "진"씨는 미국측 초안 세항(b)와 한국측 초안 세항(c)간의 유일한 차이는 한국측 초안에 2개월의 시간적 제한을 명백히 하고있는점이라고 지적하였다. 그는 그제한을 3개월로 변경할것을 제의하였다. "하비브"씨는 시간제 제한은 부속품의 수입에관하여 애로를 조성한다. 또한 자동차가 미국으로부터 한국에 도착하는 상당한 시간을 요한다는 사실에서 나타나는 문제도 있다. 이것은 비단 미국군대 구성원에 속하고 자동차에 대한것뿐만 아니라 대사관원의 경험도 또한 그러하다고 진술하였다. "진"씨는 부속품에 관한 애로를 인정한다. 연이나 그는 미국군대 인원들은 1년간의 근무후에 한국을 떠난다고 알고있음으로 자동차에 대한 3개월의 제한은 적절하다고 생각한다고 답변하였. "하비브"씨는 그것은 모든경우에서 같지는 않다. 한국에서의 복무기간에는 특히 군속의 경우에 있어서는 상당한 차이가 있다고 답변하였다. 이문제는 다음회의에서 더욱 토의하기로 합의하였다. 6-4-7 P.O

0187

62-4-18

대음 87-7 ⑧

0188

(22) "진"씨는 한국측은 미국측 초안 세항(c)에 합의한다고 진술하였다.

제 4 항

(23) "하비브"씨는 제 4 항에 대한 두초안은 미국측 초안은 한국측 초안이 "면제"로하고 있는데 반하여 "면제들" 이라고 한것외에 똑같다고 지적하였다. "진"씨는 한국측은 미국측 초안에 동의한다고 진술하였다.

제 5 항

(24) 제5항에관하여 "하비브"씨는 미국측 초안의 서문 문장은 세관검사 면제에대한 한국측 초안의 해당 문장보다 더욱 상세하다고 진술하였다. "진"씨는 한국측은 다음회의에서 이문제를 토의하도록 검토 하겠다고 답변하였다.

(25) "하비브"씨는 세항(a)에서 미국측 초안은 미국군대 인원의 대부분은 조직된 부대로서가 아니라 개인으로서 한국에 들어오고 있으니만큼 "부대"대신에 "구성원" 이란 단어를 사용하였다고 지적하였다. 그는 "부대" 란 단어는 미국군대의 구성을 이루는 병력의 조직된 일단을 의미하는 특수한 의미를갖고 있다고 설명하였다. 그는 세항(a)의 적용구절은 "명령하에"라는 구절이라고 지적하였다.

(26) 이때 2시간 이상 속계하였던 회의를 휴회하기로 결정하였다. 다음회의는 12월 4일 화요일 하오 2시에 개최키로 하였다.

62-4-91

0189

62-4-18 外문 817-7(9)

0190

(27) 합의사항 개요

세관업무 조문의 다음 미국측 초안의 원문이 협정의 최종적 문장으로 포함하도록 합의하였다.

제 1 항

제 3 항 세항 (a)

제 3 항 세항 (c)

제 4 항

62-4-82

0191

6-4-18 (10)　　　　미문 81-7 (10)

0192

SUMMARY RECORD OF THE SEVENTH SESSION
STATUS FORCES NEGOTIATION

November 26, 1962

I. Time and Place: 2:00 to 4:10 p.m. November 26, 1962
at Conference Room of the Ministry of
Foreign Affairs

II. Attendants:

ROK Side:

Mr. Chin, Pil Shik	Director Bureau of Political Affairs Ministry of Foreign Affairs
Col. Lee, Nam Koo	Chief, Military Affairs Section Ministry of National Defense
Mr. Yi, Kyung Ho	Director Bureau of Legal Affairs Ministry of Justice
Mr. Pak, Kun	Chief, America Section Ministry of Foreign Affairs
Mr. Pak, Pong Chin	Chief, Customs Duty Section Ministry of Finance
Mr. Chai, Eui Sok	2nd Secretary Ministry of Foreign Affairs
Mr. Shin, Chung Sup	2nd Secretary Ministry of Foreign Affairs
Mr. Kang, Suk Jae	3rd Secretary Ministry of Foreign Affairs
Mr. Lee, Chang Bum	3rd Secretary Ministry of Foreign Affairs

U.S. Side:

Mr. Philip C. Habib	Counselor of the Embassy for Political Affairs
Brig. Gen. J.D. Miller	Deputy Chief of Staff 8th Army
Mr. William J. Ford	First Secretary of the Embassy
Col. G.G. O'Connor	Deputy Chief of Staff 8th Army

0193

[illegible]

0194

0196

Capt. R.M. Brownlie	Assistance Chief of Staff USN/K
Col. W.A. Solf	Staff Judge Advocate 8th Army
Mr. Benjamin A. Fleck (Rapporteur and Press Officer)	First Secretary of the Embassy
Mr. Robert A. Lewis	Second Secretary and Consul of the Embassy
Lt. Col. R.E. Miller	Staff Officer, JAG 8th Army
Lt. Col. W.A. Burt	J-5
Mr. Campen	Interpreter

Introduction of New U.S. Participant

1. Before beginning substantive discussion Mr. Habib introduced Lt. Col. W.A. Burt, J-5, who has replaced Lt. Col. G.T. Sudermann as an Alternate Member of the U.S. negotiating team. Mr. Habib also welcomed back Mr. Campen, who had not been able to participate in the last several meetings.

Preamble

2. The negotiators then began substantive discussion by resuming their consideration of the tabled drafts of the Preamble. Mr. Habib stated that the U.S. side had carefully considered both drafts and continued to prefer the simple statement that it had submitted. Fundamentally, he said, the Preamble should be a statement of the basis for the presence of the U.S. forces in Korea and the U.S. side believed its draft was a satisfactory statement of this kind, whereas the Korean draft was lengthy, involved, and in some respects repetitive. Both drafts were attempting to accomplish the same purpose but the Korean draft was unduly complex. Mr. Habib then asked Mr. Chin to indicate the most outstanding feature of the Korean draft in comparison with the U.S. draft.

0195

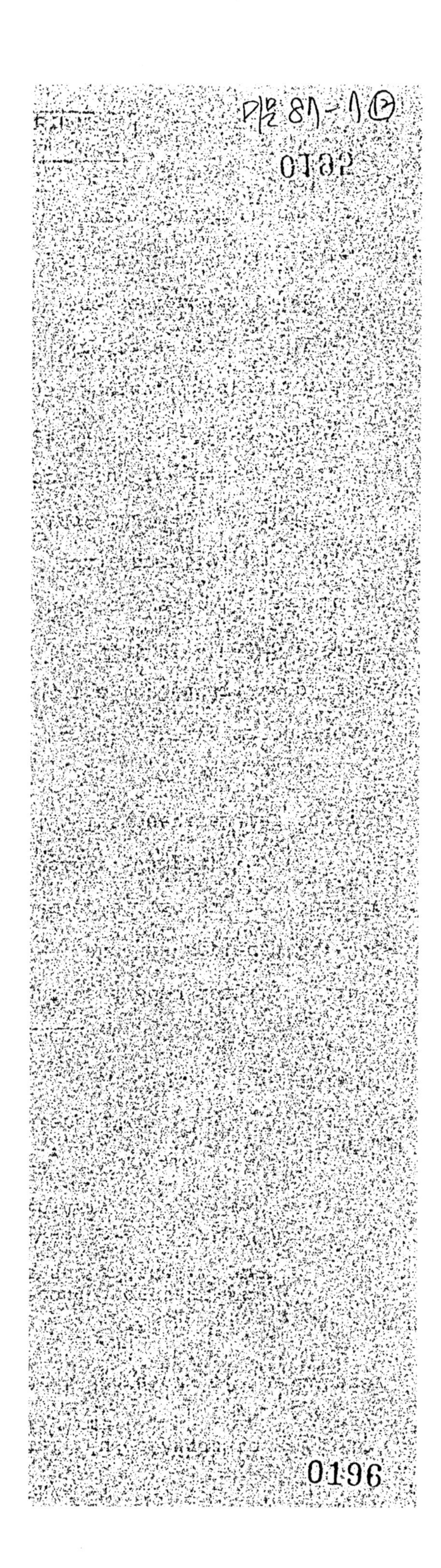

3. Mr. Chin replied that an important purpose of the Preamble was stated in the U.S. draft. However, the Korean side wished to state in the Preamble the fact that the presence of the U.S. forces in Korea is based on both the UN resolutions and the Mutual Defense Treaty. Therefore, even though the wording of the Korean draft was not perfect and could be altered, the Korean side desired a text similar to that which they had drafted.

4. Mr. Habib stated that the U.S. side had recognized and carefully considered the desire of the Korean side to include in the Preamble some reference to the historical background. There was one thing that needed to be absolutely clear -- that the present negotiations were concerned solely with the U.S. forces and not with United Nations forces. Mr. Habib pointed out that the Korean side had agreed in earlierrdiscussions that whatever agreement emerged from the negotiations would have no bearing on the United Nations forces. With that understanding, he said, the U.S. side was willing to take under consideration the desire of the Korean side to include in the Preamble some reference to the historical background.

5. Mr. Habib went on to say that there were two items in the Korean draft which were not found in the U.S. draft: (a) the reference to the United Nations resolutions, and, (b) an expression of the desire to strengthen the bonds of mutual interest between our two countries. The U.S. side, he said, wished to submit a new draft which incorporated these two points but was less complex than the Korean draft. At this point he tabled a revised U.S. draft.

6. Mr. Chin replied that the Korean side agreed that what was being negotiated was an agreement covering the

0197

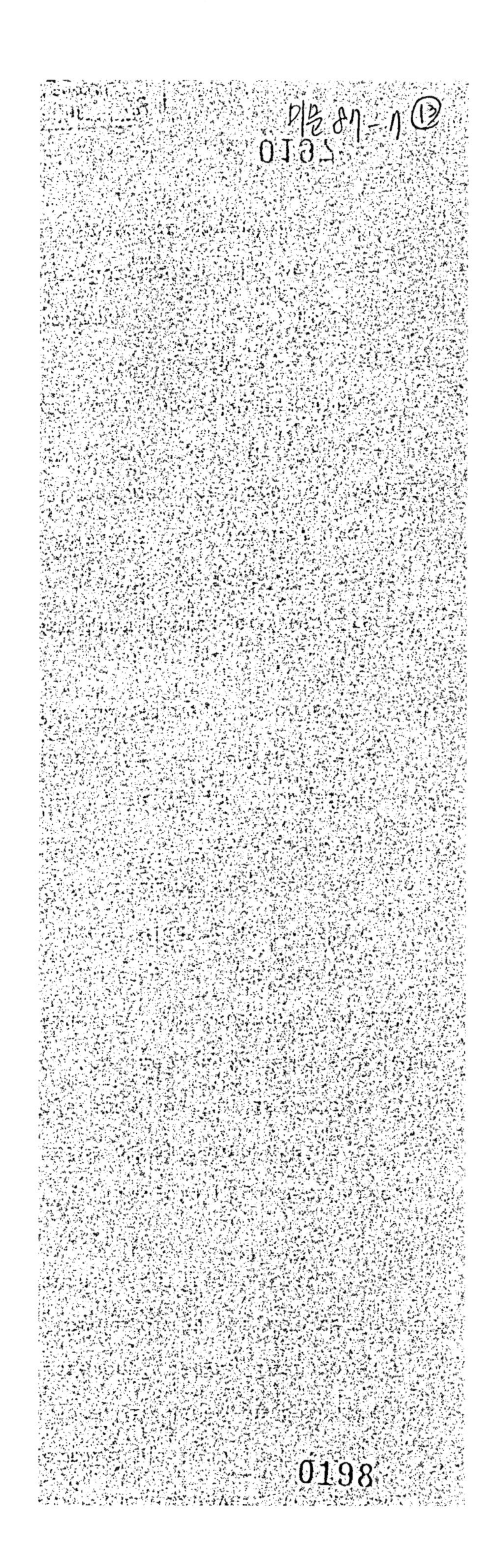
0198

status of U.S. forces in Korea. It had nothing to do with the forces of any other nation. Nor did it have any relevancy to the forces of other countries serving as part of the United Nations Command. The U.S. forces, he continued, will be subject to the provisions of the SOFA whether they are in Korea under the provisions of the UN resolutions or the provisions of the ROK-US Mutual Defense Treaty. In this respect, he said, he could see no difference between the UN Resolutions and the Mutual Defense Treaty. Therefore, there should be no difference in treatment, regardless of whether the U.S. forces were here as U.S. forces or as components of the unified command.

7. Mr. Habib reiterated that the SOFA is concerned with the status of the U.S. armed forces in Korea. It has no relevance to the forces of any other country or to the unified command established under the UN Security Council resolutions.

8. Mr. Chin replied that the Korean side agreed that the SOFA would apply to no other forces in the unified command except the U.S. forces. He repeated that that the SOFA will govern U.S. forces whether or not those forces are components of the unified command. Mr. Habib replied that this was exactly what the U.S. draft stated. He asked for the views of the Korean side on the revised U.S. draft which had just been tabled.

9. Commenting on the revised draft, Mr. Chin stated that the purposes and objectives of the U.S. forces are the same, whether or not the presence of those forces in Korea is based upon the UN resolutions or upon the Mutual Defense Treaty. Therefore, in order to make sure that the SOFA will facilitate those purposes and objectives, there

0199

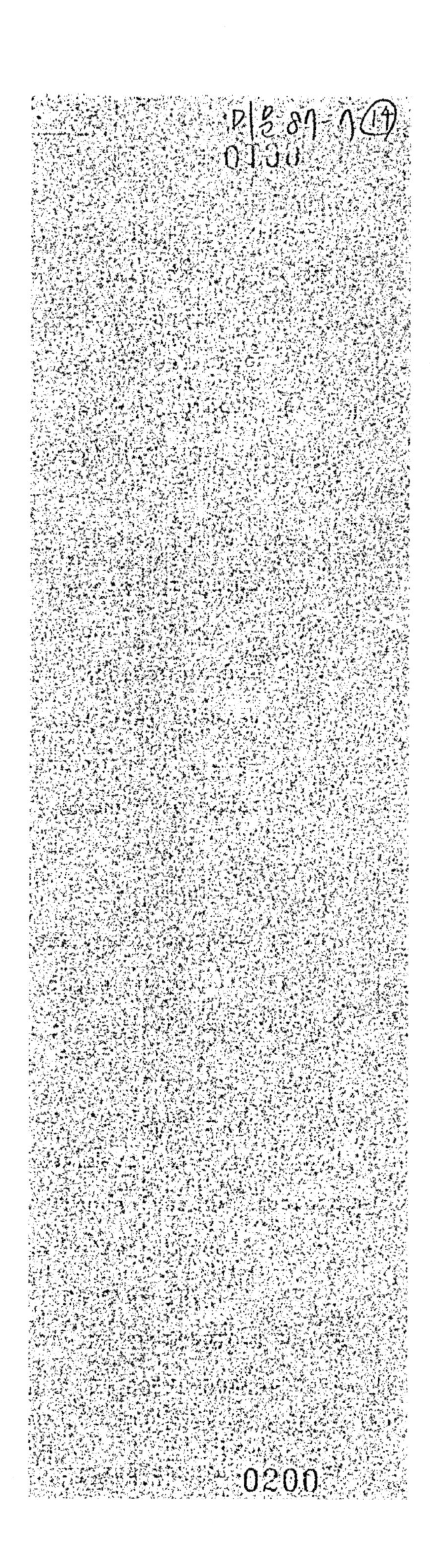

should be no exceptions for U.S. forces serving as components of the unified command. Facilities and areas used by U.S. components of the unified command would therefore come under the provisions of the SOFA. Elaborating on Mr. Kang's interpretation of Mr. Chin's remarks Dr. Pak said that the fundamental objective of the SOFA is to facilitate the fulfillment of the purposes and objectives of the UN resolutions and the Mutual Defense Treaty. Therefore, there should be no discrimination in regard to U.S. forces stationed in Korea under one or the other.

10. Mr. Habib replied that there is nothing in the U.S. draft Preamble regarding the objectives or purposes of either the UN resolution or the Mutual Defense Treaty. The Preamble merely states that the SOFA covers U.S. forces stationed in the Republic of Korea "pursuant to" the resolutions and the Treaty.

11. Mr. Chin replied that consequently, any agreement between the Republic of Korea Government and the unified command concerning the status and facilities and areas of the forces of the unified command will apply to the forces of other nations but not to the U.S. component. Mr. Habib said that the U.S. side understood the position of the Korean side and would take it under consideration. Mr. Chin said that if a clear understanding could be reached on that point, the Korean side would have no difficulty in finalizing the wording of the Preamble. He suggested that the discussion be continued at the next meeting, and Mr. Habib agreed.

Customs and Duties

Paragraph 1

12. Turning to the drafts of the customs and duties article which had been tabled at the previous meeting, Mr. Chin suggested paragraph by paragraph discussion. Mr. Habib

0202

agreed. He stated that the U.S. draft of Paragraph 1 was a clear and unequivocal statement and the U.S. side saw no reason to go beyond it. Mr. Chin said there was no fundamental difference in the two drafts and that the purpose and main points were the same. He suggested that the second sentence of the Korean draft be deleted, to which Mr. Habib agreed. Mr. Habib expressed the view that the phraseology in the U.S. draft of the first sentence was more precise and specific. Mr. Chin stated that the U.S. draft of Paragraph 1 was acceptable to the Korean side in as much as the content of the drafts of both sides is basically the same.

Paragraph 2

13. Turning to Paragraph 2, Mr. Chin asked for an explanation of the phrase "including their authorized procurement agencies and their non-appropriated fund organizations". Mr. Habib replied that the U.S. side realized that their draft of Paragraph 2 was cumbersome and somewhat difficult to understand. He wished, therefore, to submit a revised version of this paragraph. At this point he tabled a new draft of Paragraph 2. He stated that the new version was simpler and more readily understood.

14. In reply to Mr. Chin's request for clarification, Colonel Solf pointed out that the word "including" in the U.S. draft means that the authorized procurement agencies are a part of the U.S. armed forces. In effect this is no different from the wording of the Korean draft, except that use of the word "including" clarifies the position of the agencies. The scope of the U.S. draft is thus no larger than that of the Korean draft.

0203

0503

[illegible]

0204

15. Mr. Chin inquired whether "authorized procurement agencies" included civilian companies. Mr. Habib replied that they did not. He pointed out that civilian companies were covered in the second sentence of the revised U.S. draft which refers to items "imported by others than the United States armed forces" for the exclusive use of the U.S. armed forces. An example, he said, would be the importation by a civilian contractor of materials to be used in the construction of a radar tower. Clearly such materials should enter free of duty.

16. Mr. Chin said that he would like to have further discussion of the second sentence in the U.S. draft. It was agreed to continue discussion of this sentence at the next meeting.

17. Turning to the question of certification Mr. Chin pointed out that the third sentence of the revised U.S. draft called for "appropriate certification" whereas the second sentence of the Korean draft was more precise in referring to "a certificate issued ... in the form to be determined by the Joint Committee".

18. Mr. Habib recalled that in previous meetings a similar discussion had been held regarding the same point in another article. He said that "appropriate certification" obviously has to be acceptable to both sides in order to be appropriate. The U.S. side saw no necessity for spelling out specifically in the agreement what is "appropriate". Both side agreed that all procedural matters such as this might be left for later determination by the Joint Committee, rather than specified in the Agreement.

Paragraph 3

19. Mr. Habib pointed out that the introductory sentence in the two drafts of paragraph 3 was identical, except that the U.S. draft includes the phrase "and other such

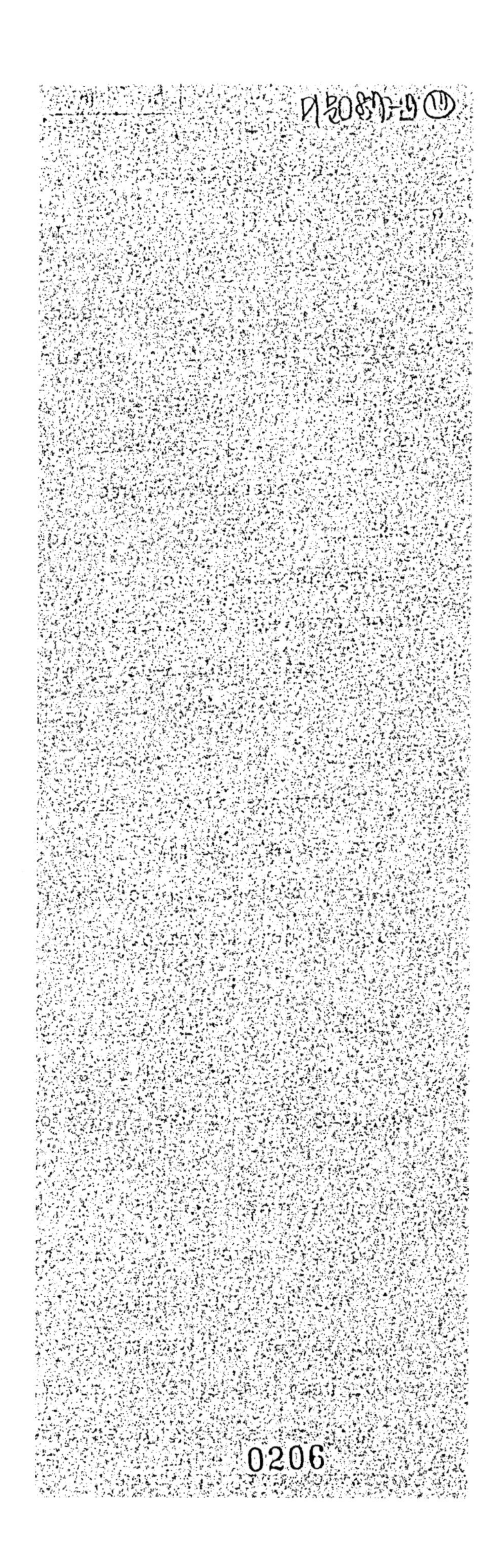

charges" included charges by civilian firms, such as storage charges, unloading charges, charges by customs brokers, etc. Mr. Habib replied that the phrase referred only to governmental charges and not to charges by private companies. It was agreed to discuss this point at the next meeting.

20. Mr. Chin expressed agreement to the U.S. draft of subparagraph (a). When Mr. Habib inquired whether this included agreement to the Agreed Minute #2 in the U.S. draft Mr. Chin suggested that the Agreed Minutes be discussed separately and Mr. Habib agreed.

21. Mr. Chin pointed out that the only difference between the U.S. draft of subparagraph (b) and the Korean draft of subparagraph (c) was that a time limit of two months was specified in the Korean draft. He suggested that the limit be changed to three months. Mr. Habib stated that a time limit created a problem with regard to the importation of spare parts. There was also the problem arising from the fact that it took some time for vehicles to arrive in Korea from the United States. This was not only true of vehicles belonging to members of the U.S. armed forces but had also been the experience of Embassy personnel. Mr. Chin replied that he recognized the difficulty with regard to parts. However, he thought a three month limit on vehicles would be appropriate since he understood that personnel of the U.S. armed forces leave Korea after one year of service here. Mr. Habib replied that this was not true in all cases. There was considerable variation in the lengths of tours of duty here, particularly in the case of members of the civilian component. It was agreed that this matter should be discussed further at the next meeting.

0207

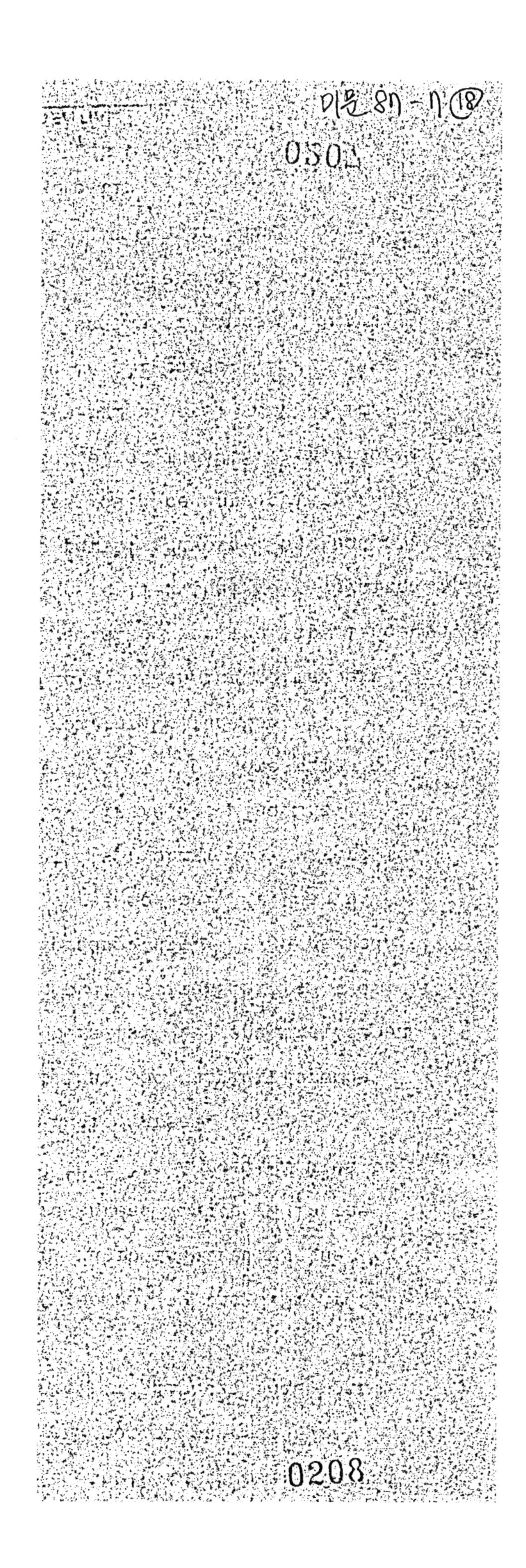
0208

22. Mr. Chin stated that the Korean side agreed to the U.S. draft of subparagraph (c).

Paragraph 4

23. Mr. Habib pointed out that the two drafts of Paragraph 4 were identical, except that the U.S. draft read "exemptions" where the Korean draft read "exemption". Mr. Chin stated that the Korean side agreed to the U.S. draft.

Paragraph 5

24. With respect to paragraph 5, Mr. Habib stated that the introductory sentence in the U.S. draft was a more specific statement than the corresponding sentence in the Korean draft of the exemptions to be granted from customs examination. Mr. Chin replied that the Korean side would study this matter for discussion at the next meeting.

25. Mr. Habib pointed out that in subparagraph (a) the U.S. draft used the word "members" instead of "units", inasmuch as the great bulk of the personnel of the U.S. armed forces entered Korea as individuals and not in organized units. He explained that the word "unit" had a specific connotation, denoting an organized body of troops forming a component of the U.S. forces. He pointed out that the operative phrase in subparagraph (a) was the phrase "under orders".

26. At this point it was decided to adjourn the meeting, which had then been in session for over two hours. The next meeting was scheduled for Tuesday, December 4, at 2:00 p.m.

기본 87-7 (19)

0503

0210

0515

27. Summary of Points of Agreement - The following of the text of the U.S. draft of the customs and duties article were agreed upon for inclusion in the final text of the Agreement:

Paragraph 1

Paragraph 3, subparagraph (a)

Paragraph 3, subparagraph (c)

Paragraph 4

1966,12.31에 예고문에 의거 일반문서로 재분류됨

0211

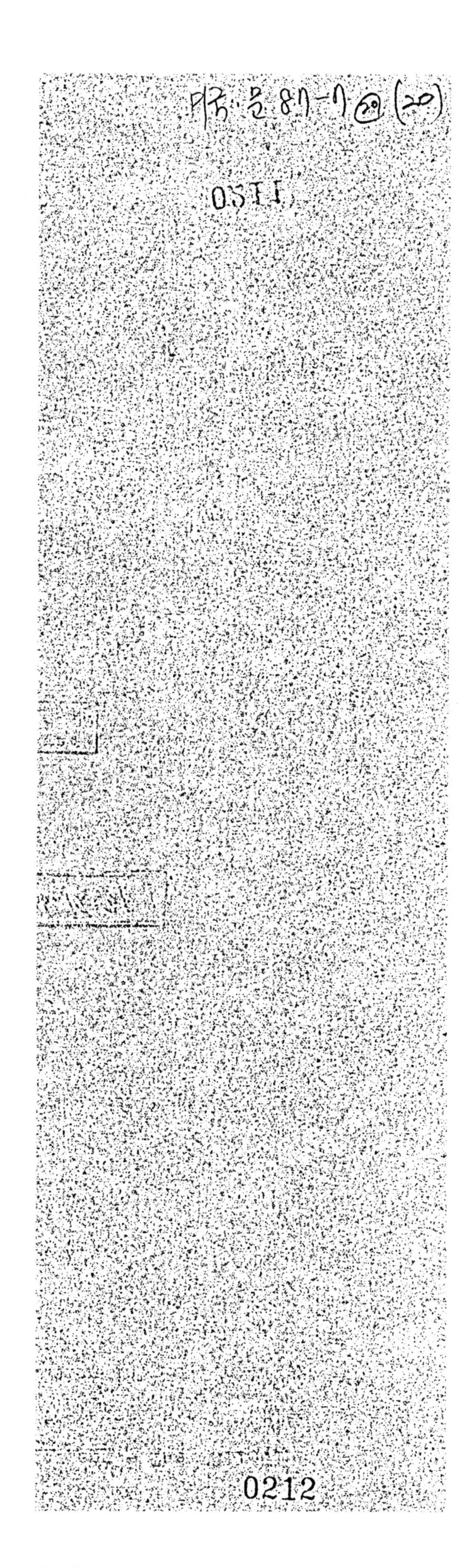
OSTI
0212

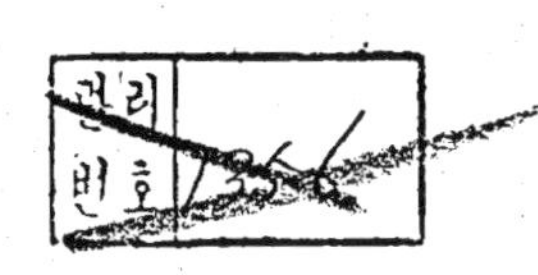

주둔군지위협정 교섭 제8차회의 요약기록

1962. 12. 4.

1. 시일 및 장소 : 1962. 12. 4. 하오 2시 30분부터 4시 35분까지
   중앙청

2. 참석자 :

한국측 :

진 필 식	외무부 정무국장
이 경 호	법무부 법무국장
이 남 구 대령	국방부 군무과장
박 근	외무부 미주과장
오 원 용	외무부 조약과장
신 정 섭	외무부 2등서기관
이 경 훈(기록및공보관)	외무부 2등서기관)
이 창 범	외무부 3등서기관
강 석 재 (통역)	외무부 3등서기관

미국측 :

필립 씨.하비브	주한미대사관 참사관
제이 디.로버준장	주한미8군 참모차장
윌리암 제이.포드	주한미대사관 1등서기관
지.지.오코나 대령	주한미8군 참모차장
알.엠 부톤리 대령	주한미해군 참모부장
다불.에이.쇼프 대령	주한미8군 법무참모
로버트 에이.루이스	주한미대사관 2등서기관겸영사
알.이. 밀러 중령	주한미8군 법무장교
다불.에이.버트 중령	주한미군 민사참모
케니즈 켐펜	통역

62-4-83

0213

62-4-19 (6)

미국.문 87-8(12)

0214

3. 회의목록 :

서 론

(1) "진필식" 한국측 수석 교섭자는 제8차 주둔군지위 교섭회의를 개회하고 서문에관한 토의부터 시작할것을 제의하였다.

서 문

(2) "하비브"씨는 미국측은 지난회의에서 미국측이 제출한 서문 원안을 좋아한다고 진술하면서 실질적 토의에 들어갔다. "하비브"씨는 한국측의요구에 따라 수정안을 미국측이 제출하였으며 이수정안은 관계된 유엔결의에 대한 언급을 포함시키자는 한국측 요망을 참작하였음을 주목하였다.

(3) 미국 군인에대한 주둔군 지위협정의 적용에관한 한국측 질문에 대답하여 미국측은 "합의된 사항의 범위내에서 주둔군지위협정의 규정은 유엔 안전보장이사회 결의나 혹은 상호 방위조약에의거하여 대한민국에 있는동안 미국군대와 그구성원에게 적용한다. 그러나 1950년 1월 26일 조인한 군사고문판협정에서 그지위가 규정되고 있는 미국군대 구성원 및 미국대사관 무관들에게는 적용되지 않는다" 라는 성명을 하였다. 그는 그후 이성명이 지난회의에서 한국측이 주둔군지위협정의 미국군대에 대한 적용에관하여 제기한 질문에 대답이 되었는지를 문의하였다. 또한 미국인에 대한 주둔군지위협정의 적용 문제는 정의 조문에서도 천명되었음이 지적되었다. "진"씨는 한국측은 미국입장을 이해하며 수정안은 수락할만한 것이라고 답변하였다.

(4) 제7차 회의에서 미국측이 제출한 수정안을 수락하기로 합의하였다. 양측은 그와같이 양해하였다. 62-4-PU

0215

2-4-1.

미문 87-8 ③

0216

관세업무

(5) "진"씨는 한국측은 제7차 회의에서 제출된 제2항의 수정안 보다도 제6차회의시에 미국측이 제출한 제2항 원안을 검토 하기 바란다고 진술하면서 관세업무 조문에관한 토의를 시작 하였다. "진"씨는 그는 원안이 더잘 분류되었고 더욱 상세 함으로 원안을 좋아한다고 진술하였다. "하비브"씨는 제2항 의 수정안도 다음 토의를위하여 고려할것이라는 양해하에 제2항의 원안을 토의하는데 합의하였다.

(6) "진"씨는 한국측은 미국측에 제출한 제2항 원안을 수락할 용의가 있다고 진술하였으나 최종문장에 있는 "미국군대로 부터 병참지원을 받고 기타의 한국 주둔군의 사용을위한"이란 구절의 해명을 요구하였다. "하비브"씨는 그구절은 미국으로 부터 병참지원을 받고있는 카튜사 및 다른군대를 언급하며 미국은 명백히 미국에 그지원을 의지하고있는 군대를 지원하기 위하여 들어오는 물자에 대해서는 통관세를 지불할수 없다고 진술하였다. "진"씨는 한국측은 그러한 보급품의 무세통관에 대하여 하등 반대하지 않으나 한국측은 그러한 군대가 어떤 것인지를 명백히 규정하기를 바란다고 진술하면서 그설명에 답하였다. "하비브"씨는 "병참지원을 받는" 이란 적용구절이 그러한 군대가 어떤것인지를 규정하고 있다고 지적하였다. "진"씨는 말씨가 지나치게 융통성이 있으며 한국측은 원문이나 합의의사록에 예를들면 그러한 군대는 통합사령부의 구성부대등" 이라는것을 명백히하는 말을 넣기를 희망한다고 진술하였다. "하비브"씨는 차기회의에서 제의코저하는 말을 제출하여 주도록 한국측에 요청하였으며 그후 고려하겠다고 말하였다. "진" 씨는 이에 동의하였다.

62-4-15

0217

62-4-19

외문 87-8

0218

(7) "진"씨는 미국측이 3(b)항에 관하여 지난토의가 첨가할것이 있는지를 문의하였다. "하비브"씨는 없다고 답변하였다.

(8) 그후 지난회의에서 중단한바 있는 제5항으로 주의를 돌렸다. 한국측은 미국초안의 제5항 서문문장에 동의하였다.

(9) 제5항 (a)에 관하여 "진"씨는 한국측 초안에 있어서의 "부대"에 반하여 미국측 초안에서는 "구성원"으로 명백히하고 있으며 또한 일본의 주둔군지위협정은 부대로 규정하고 있는 사실에 대하여 질문을 제기하였다. "하비브"씨는 병력이 부대로서기보다 오히려 하명받은 개인으로 입국하고 있는 한국의 실정 현실성에 적합토록 구성으로 변경한것이라고 답변하였다. "하비브"씨는 일본의 주둔군지위협정은 사실상 부대보다 군대구성원을 기초로하여 시행되고 있다. 더욱 한미주둔군 지위협정은 현존하는 실제의 사정에의거해야 하며 다른조치에 대한 말은 관련이 없다고 진술하였다. "하비브"씨는 만약 미국측이 부대로 동의한다면 한국에 입국하는 개인 구성원은 세단검사에 복하게될것이라고 진술하였다. 그러자 "진"씨는 미국측은 세관검사면제를 최초 최초입국시와 최종출국시에 적용할 의도가 있는지 혹은 휴가 목적으로 출입국할시도 포함하는지를 질문하였다. "하비브"씨는 면제는 명령하에 한국을 출입국하는 군대 구성원에 적용된다고 말함으로서 답변하였다. "진"씨는 개인적으로 한국에 입국하는 구성원은 관세특혜를 남용할지 모른다는것이 한국측의 입장이라고 진술하였다. "하비브"씨는 제8항에는 남용방지를 위한 적절한 대책이 있다고 진술하였다. "하비브"씨는 이항에관한 한국측이 이문제를 더욱 검토하기 까지 연기하도록 제의하였다. "진"씨는 이에 동의하였다. 62-4-86

0219

62-4-11

[illegible]

0220

(10) 제5항(b)에 관하여 "진"씨는 한국측 초안은 다만 공용 우편물만을 포함하며 미국측 초안에서 하고있는것과 같이 미국 군사우편 계통의 기타 우편물은 포함치 않는다는 점을 주목하였다. "하비브"씨는 그들의 가족과 함께 있지 않는 주한 병사들을 위한 우편물은 중요한 사기에관한 것이며 미국측은 그러한 우편물의 신속하고도 방해되지 않는 배달을 제공할것을 바란다고 답변하였다. "진"씨는 개인 우편물은 신속히 통관될것이라는 보증을 하였으며 한국측 견해로서는 다만 공적 우편물 만이 세관검사를 면제 한다고 진술하였다. 양측은 한국측 입장을 장차 회의에서 토의하기로 합의하였다.

(11) "진"씨는 제5항(c)에 관한 한국측 초안과 미국측 초안에 있어서의 차이점에 대한 설명을 요청하였다. "하비브"씨는 근본적 차이는 한국측 초안은 정부 선하 증권으로 발송된 군사하물에 대한 면제를 규정하고 있는데 반하여 미국측 초안은 미국군대에 탁송된 군사하물에 대한 면제를 규정하고 있는점이다. 미국측 초안에 있어서의 그변경 이유는 단순히 대부분의 군사하물은 이전 과거에 하던것과 같이 정부 선하 증권에 의하여 발송되지 않고 있기때문 이라고 답변하였다. "진"씨는 한국측 견해로서는 미국 군대에 탁송된 하물과 비세출자금 기관에 탁송된 하물간에는 차이가 있다는점에 주의하였다. "진"씨는 한국측은 비세출 자금기관에 탁송된 하물은 세관검사를 받도록하기 원한다고 진술하고 그요청을 그러한 활동을위한 물자의 수입을 단지 적절한 량으로 제한코저 하는 희망과 결부시켰다. 이문제는 앞으로의 회의에서 더욱 토의하기로 합의하였다. 66-11-P7

0221

'62-4-17 [illegible] 미문 07-8 [illegible]

[illegible]

0222

(12) "진"씨는 미국측 초안의 제 6,7 및 8 항은 내용에 있어서 한국측 초안과 일치하며 따라서 미국측 초안의 이들 3개항을 수락한다고 하였다. "하비브"씨는 동의하였다.

(13) "진"씨는 한국측 초안의 제7항(e)를 미국측 초안 제9항(d)로 삽입하고 미국측 초안 제9항(d)를 제9항(e)로 할것을 제의하였다. "진"씨는 만약 그것이 삽입된다면 미국측 초안의 제9항을 수락하는데 동의하였다. "하비브"씨는 이 제안을 고려하여 다음회의에서 답변하기로 동의하였다.

(14) "하비브"씨는 기타사항으로 옮기기 전에 관세조문에 관한 일반적인 성명을 하고저한다. 미국측은 한국정부 당국은 물품의 통관에 있어서 신속히 처리한다는 양해사항을 교섭기록이나 기타 방법으로 통합하기 바란다고 진술하였다. "진"씨는 한국정부 당국은 통관에 있어서 불필요한 지연을 야기시키지 않기위하여 가능한 범위까지 협조할것이라고 진술하며 답변하였다.

(15) "알.엠.부론티" 대령은 선박 및 항공기의 기착 및 민간군사 항공 교통통제에 관한 두개의 조문을 설명하며 조문을 제출하였다.

62-4-98

(16) "박근" 박사는 동일한 문제에관한 두개의 조문을 설명하였다. "박" 박사는 민간군사 항공교통 통제에 관한 한국측 초안은 미국측 초안은 포함치않고 있으나 기상업무를 포함하고 있다는 점을 주목하였다. "하비브"씨는 미국측은 기상 업무에 대해서는 별도 조문을 생각하고 있다고 답변하였다. "박" 박사는 만약 미국측이 필요하다고 생각한다면 한국측은 비록 포함되어 있지만 기상업무를 분리하는데 반대하지 않을것이라고 진술하였다. "하비브"씨는 그제의를 고려하겠다고 동의하였다. 초안을 검토하여 다음회의에서 토의를 계속키로 합의하였다.

196 12.31.에 예고문에 의거 일반문서로 재분류됨

0223

(17) 다음회의는 1962년 1월 14일 하오 2시에 개최하기로 합의하였다.

62-4-19 (6) 미분 87-8 ⑥

[illegible]

0224

JOINT SUMMARY RECORD OF THE 8TH SESSION
STATUS FORCES NEGOTIATION

December 4, 1962

I. Time and Place: 2:30 to 4:35 p.m. December 4, 1962
in the Capitol Building

II. Attendants:

ROK Side:

Mr. Chin, Pil Shik	Director Bureau of Political Affairs Ministry of Foreign Affairs
Mr. Yi, Kyung Ho	Director Bureau of Legal Affairs Ministry of Justice
Mr. Shin, Kwan Sup	Director Bureau of Costums Duty Ministry of Finance
Col. Lee, Nam Koo	Chief, Military Affairs Section Ministry of National Defense
Mr. Pak, Kun	Chief, America Section Ministry of Foreign Affairs
Mr. O, Won Yong	Chief, Treaty Section Ministry of Foreign Affairs
Mr. Shin, Chung Sup	2nd Secretary Ministry of Foreign Affairs
Mr. Lee, Kyung Hoon	2nd Secretary Ministry of Foreign Affairs
Mr. Lee, Chang Bum	3rd Secretary Ministry of Foreign Affairs
Mr. Kang, Suk Jae	3rd Secretary Ministry of Foreign Affairs

U.S. Side:

Mr. Philip C. Habib	Counselor of the Embassy for Political Affairs
Brig. Gen. J.D. Lawlor	Deputy Chief of Staff 8th Army
Mr. William J. Ford	First Secretary of the Embassy

0225

0551

Col. G.G. O'Connor	Deputy Chief of Staff 8th Army
Capt. R.M. Brownlie	Assistant Chief of Staff USN/K
Col. W.A. Solf	Staff Judge Advocate 8th Army
Mr. Robert A. Lewis	Second Secretary and Consul of the Embassy
Lt. Col. R.E. Miller	Staff Officer, JAG 8th Army
Lt. Col. W.A. Burt	J-5
Kenneth Campen	Interpreter

Introduction

1. Mr. Chin, Pil-sik, Korean Chief Negotiator, opened the eighth meeting of the Status of Forces negotiations and suggested beginning with further discussion on the Preable.

Preamble

2. Mr. Habib opened the substantive discussion by stating that the U.S. side preferred the original preamble tabled by the U.S. at a previous meeting. Mr. Habib noted that under Korean urging a revised version had been tabled by the U.S. and that this revision took into account Korean desire to include reference to relevant UN resolutions.

3. In answer to a Korean question on the applicability of SOFA to U.S. Armed Forces personnel, the U.S. side made this statement: "Within the scope of the matters agreed to, the provisions of the SOF will apply to U.S. Armed Forces and their members, while in the Republic of Korea pursuant to the resolutions of the United Nations Security Council or pursuant to the Mutual Defense Treaty.

0226

미문.81-8 (11)

0356

[illegible]

0227

0350

They will not, however, apply to members of the U.S. Armed Forces for whom status is provided in the MAAG Agreement signed on January 26, 1950 and personnel of service attache offices in the Embassy of the United States." He then asked if this statement answered the question raised at the previous meeting by the Korean side regarding the applicability of SOFA to the U.S. Armed Forces. It was also noted that applicability of SOFA to U.S. personnel was set forth in the definitions article. Mr. Chin replied that the Korean side understood the U.S. position and that the revised preamble was acceptable.

4. It was agreed to accept the revised preamble tabled by the U.S. side at the seventh meeting. Both sides so noted.

Customs and Duties

5. Mr. Chin opened the discussion on customs and duties article by stating that the Korean side wished to work from the original draft on paragraph two tabled by the U.S. side at the sixth meeting rather than from the revised draft of paragraph 2 tabled at the seventh meeting. Mr. Chin stated that he preferred the original draft because it is better divided into categories and more detailed. Mr. Habib agreed to discuss paragraph 2 of the original draft with the understanding that the revised paragraph 2 be kept in mind for subsequent discussion.

6. Mr. Chin stated that the Korean side was ready to accept the original paragraph 2 tabled by the U.S. side but be requested clarification of the phrase in the final sentence "for the use of other armed forces in Korea which receive logistical support from the U.S. Armed Forces."

0228

0531

Mr. Habib stated that the phrase referred to Katusas and other armed forces receiving logistical support from the U.S. and that clearly the U.S. should not pay customs duty on materials brought in to support armed forces dependent on U.S. for support. Mr. Chin acknowledged the explanation by stating that the Korean side had no objection to the duty-free entry of such supplies but that the Korean side wished to have spelled out exactly who these forces are. Mr. Habib pointed out that the operative clause "who receive logistical support" defines who these forces are. Mr. Chin stated that the wording is too flexible and that the Korean side desired wording either in the text or in an agreed minute which would specify that such forces were, for example, a "component of the United Command, etc." Mr. Habib requested the Korean side to submit suggested wording at the next meeting, after which it could be considered. Mr. Chin agreed.

7. Mr. Chin asked if the U.S. side had anything to add to previous discussion on paragraph three (b). Mr. Habib replied in the negative.

9. On paragraph five(a), Mr. Chin raised the question of specifying "members" of armed forces in the U.S. draft as opposed to "units" of armed forces in the Korean draft and the fact that the Japanese SOFA provides for units. Mr. Habib replied that the change to members was made to fit the practicality of the situation in Korea where troops arrive as individuals under orders rather than as units. Mr. Habib stated that the implementation of the Japanese SOFA was actually on the basis of members of the armed forces rather than units. Moreover, a U.S.-ROK SOFA should

0230

기문 87-8 ⑨

0530

0231

be based on actual conditions which exist and the wording of other agreements may not be relevant. Mr. Habib stated that if the U.S. side agreed to units, then individual members of the armed forces entering Korean would be subject to customs examination. Mr. Chin then asked if the U.S. side intended exemption to apply to original entry and final departure or did it include departures and entry for leave purposes. Mr. Habib answered by stating that exemption applied to any member of the armed forces entering or leaving Korea under orders. Mr. Chin replied that the Korean position was that members entering Korea as individuals may abuse customs privileges. Mr. Habib stated that there were adequate safeguards in paragraph eight to prevent abuses.

Mr. Habib suggested that the discussion on this paragraph be postponed until the Korean side has studied the matter further. Mr. Chin agreed.

10. On paragraph five(b), Mr. Chin noted that the Korean draft only included official mail and did not include other mail in the U.S. military postal channels as did the U.S. draft. Mr. Habib replied that mail for servicemen in Korea without their families was an important morale factor and that the U.S. side wished to provide for the prompt and unimpeded delivery of such mail. Mr. Chin gave assurance that private mail would be quickly cleared through customs and stated that in the Korean view only official mail should be customs exempt. Both sides agreed to discuss the Korean position at a future meeting.

11. Mr. Chin requested an explanation of the differences in the Korean draft and the U.S. draft on paragraph five(c).

0232

0533

0233

Mr. Habib replied that the basic difference was that the U.S. draft provided for exemption of military cargo consigned to the U.S. Armed Forces wherease the Korean draft provided for exemption on military cargo shipped on a government bill of lading; the reason for the change in the U.S. draft was simply that a large part of the military cargo no longer was shipped on a government bill of lading as had been done in the past. Mr. Chin noted that in the Korean view there was a difference in cargo consigned to the U.S. Armed Forces and cargo consigned to a non-appropriated fund activity. Mr. Chin stated that the Korean side wished to have cargo consigned to non-appropriated fund activities subject to customs examination and related this request to the desire to limit imports of goods for such activities to reasonable amounts only. It was agreed to discuss this subject further at a later meeting.

12. Mr. Chin noted that paragraphs six, seven and eight in the U.S. draft coincide in substance with the Korean draft; therefore, he accepted these three paragraphs of the U.S. draft. Mr. Habib agreed.

13. Mr. Chin requested that paragraph seven(e) of the Korean draft be inserted as paragraph nine(d) of the U.S. draft and that paragraph nine(d) of the U.S. draft be made paragraph nine(e). Mr. Chin agreed to accept paragraph nine of the U.S. draft if this insertion was made. Mr. Habib agreed to consider this proposal and to answer at a subsequent meeting.

14. Mr. Habib stated that he wished to make a general statement on the customs article before turning to other business. The U.S. side would like to have an understanding incorporated in the negotiating record or otherwise to the effect that Korean authorities would act promptly in clearning

0234

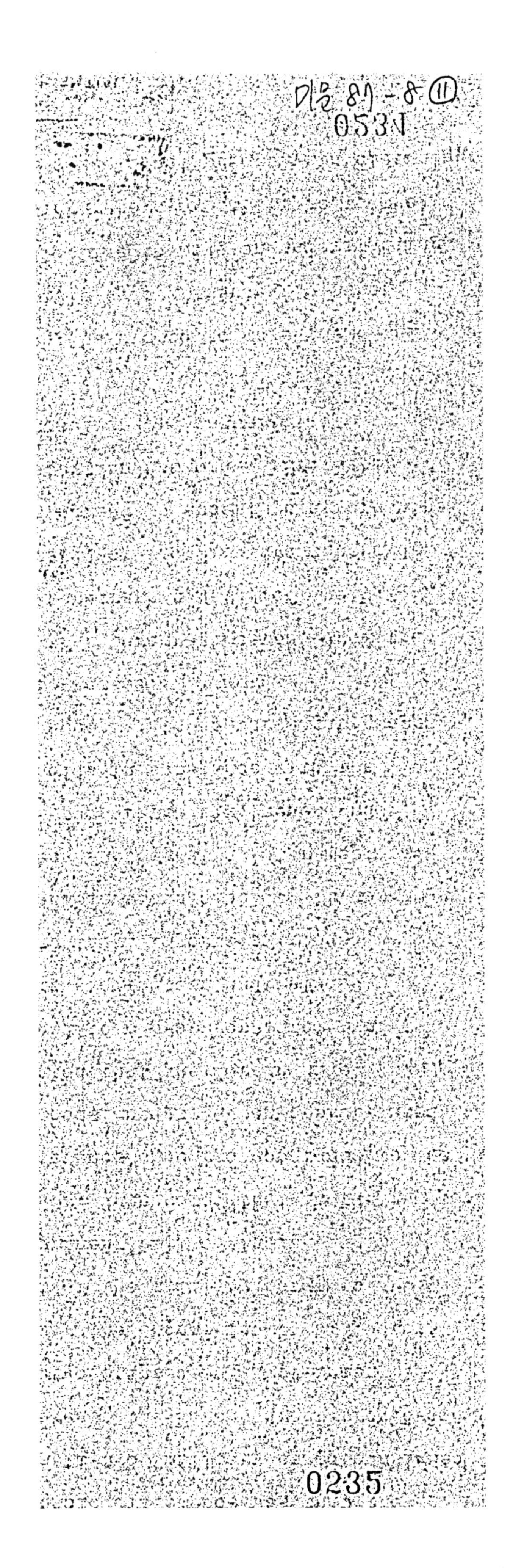
미승 87-8 ⑪
053N
0235

items through customs. Mr. Chin replied by stating that the Korean authorities will cooperate to the extent possible so as not to cause unnecessary delay in clearing items through customs.

0033

15. Captain R.M. Brownlie, USN, introduced two articles dealing with Landing Rights for Vessels and Aircraft and Civil and Military Air Traffic Control. The articles were tabled.

16. Dr. PAK Kun introduced two articles on the same subject. Dr. Pak noted that the Korean draft on Civil and Military Air Traffic Control included meteorological services whereas the U.S. draft did not. Mr. Habib replied that the U.S. side envisaged a separate article on meteorological services. Dr. Pak stated that although included, the Korean side would have no objection to separating meteorological services if the U.S. side found it necessary. Mr. Habib agreed to consider the suggestion. It was agreed to study the drafts further and to continue discussion at a subsequent meeting.

17. It was agreed to hold the next meeting on December 14, 1962 at 1400 hours.

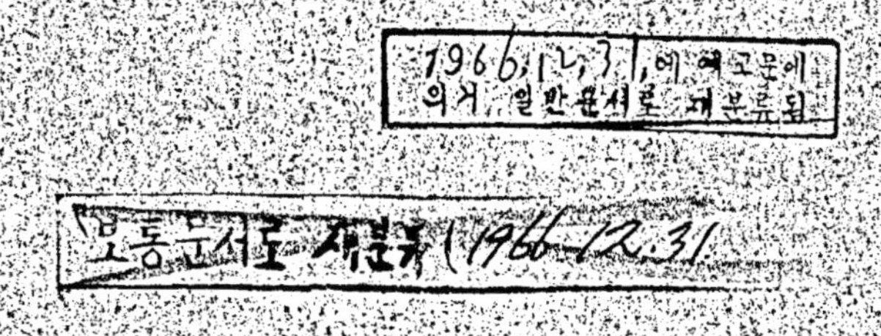

0236

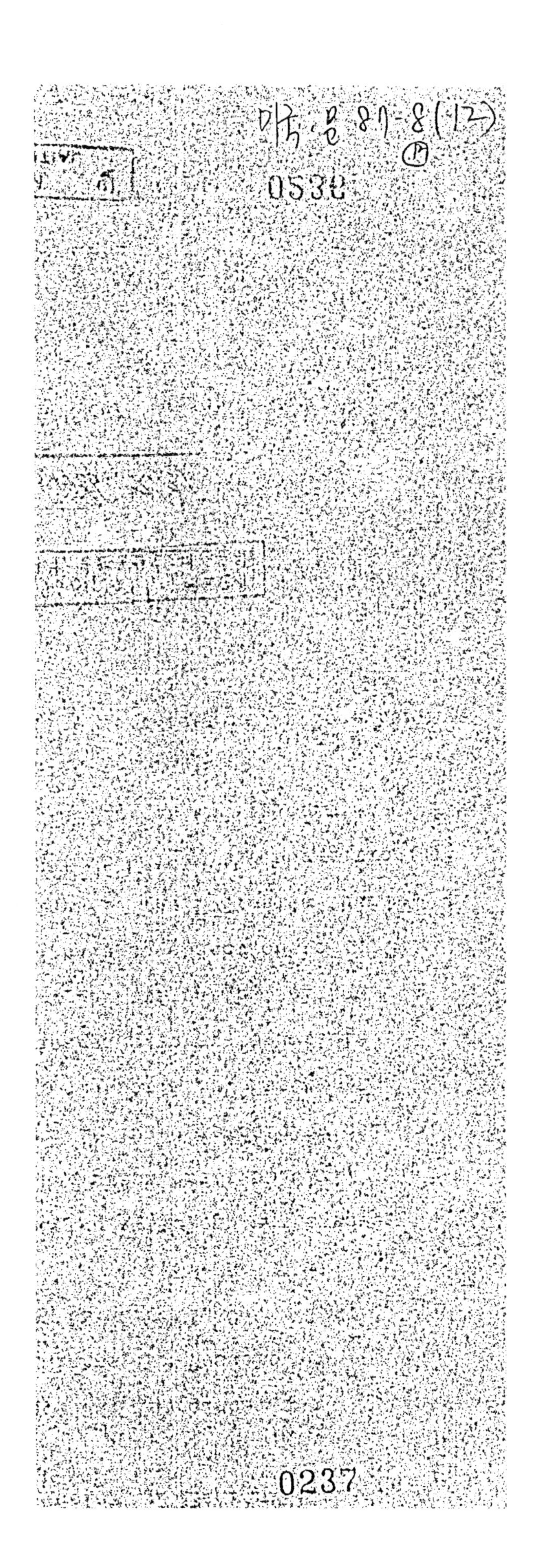

0538
0237

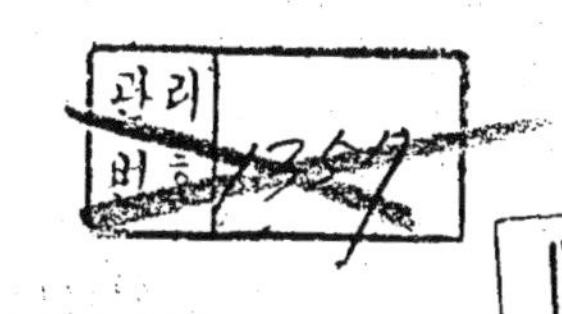

주둔군지위협정 제9차회의 요약기록

1962. 12. 14.

1. 시일 및 장소 : 1962. 12. 14. 하오 2시부터 4시까지
중앙청

2. 참석자 :

한국측 :

진 필 식	외무부 정무국장
이 경 호	법무부 법무국장
신 관 섭	재무부 세관국장
이 남 구 대령	국방부 군무과장
박 근	외무부 미주과장
오 윤 용	외무부 조약과장
지 성 구 (공보)	외무부 공보관
신 정 섭	외무부 2등서기관
이 경 훈 (기록)	"
이 창 범	외무부 3등서기관
강 석 재 (통역)	"

미국측:

62-11-89

필립 시. 하비브	주한미대사관 참사관
제이.디.로며 준장	주한미8군 참모차장
윌리암 제이.포드	주한미대사관 1등서기관
지.지. 오코나 대령	주한미8군 참모차장
알.엠. 부론티 대령	주한미해군 참모부장
다불.에이.솔프 대령	주한미8군 법무참모
벤자민 에이.후멜 (기록및공보)	주한미대사관 1등서기관
로버트 에이.루이스	주한미대사관 2등서기관겸영사
알.이. 밀러 중령	주한미8군 법무장교
다불.에이.버트 중령	주한미군 민사참모

0238

62-4-20 (9) 미원 87-9(20)

0239

3. 회의요록 :

정의 조문

(1) 회의는 정의조문의 토의로서 시작되었다. "진"씨는 한국측은 세항 1(a)의 "그신분이 별도 규정된자를 제외한" 이란 구절은 너무 애매하다고 생각한다고 진술하였다. 그는 따라서 그 구절은 삭제하고 대신에 그가 제출한 합의의사록을 승낙하도록 제안하였다.

(2) "하비브"씨는 미국측은 주둔군지위협정에 부수될 합의의사록의 수를 최소한도로 제한할것이 요망된다고 생각한다고 답변하였다. 그는 합의의사록을 채택하는 대신에 동구절을 원문에 두고 요약기록서에 이구절은 군사고문단 인원과 대사관 무관실 인원에 적용하기를 의도한바를 명시토록 하자고 제의하였다. "진"씨는 양측은 문제점의 본질에 대하여 합의하고 있다. 연이나 한국측은 이구절이 협정의 적용에 대한 예외에 관한것인 만큼 상세히 규정되어야 한다. 모든 예외는 명확히 규정되어야 한다는것이 한국측 견해이다라고 답변하였다.

(3) 그러자 "하비브"씨는 대안으로서 그구절을 그냥두고 합의의사록을 추가적으로 채택할것을 제의하였다. "진"씨는 그가 바로 제출한바 있는 합의의사록은 주둔군지위협정에서 제외될 군인을 명확히 규정하고 있음으로 미국측으로서 수락할 만한것이라고 답변하였다. 그는 이를 인원들은 역시 상호 방위조약 규정으로 부터도 제외된다고 지적하였다.

(4) "하비브"씨는 미국측은 합의의사록의 채택에 동의할것이나 추가적으로 조문자체도 예외가 있다는 사실을 언급해야한다고 생각한다고 진술하였다. 그는 곧 합의의사록의 초안을 제출하였다."진"씨는 미국측 초안을 읽어본후 양초안간에는 실질적 차이가 없다고 진술하였다. 62-4-1~~

0240

0241

"하비브"씨도 이에 동의하였다. 양초안을 다음회의에서 토의하기 위하여 결정하였다.

(5) 세항 1(b)에 대하여 "진"씨는 한가지 차이점은 "군속"이란 말뒤에 "미국국적의" 라는 구절을 삽입하느냐 하지않느냐의 문제이라고 말하였다. 그는 미국측으로서 이점에관하여 더 이상말할것이 있는지를 물었다.

(6) "하비브"씨는 주한미국 군대는 제3국의 국적을 가진사람들을 고용하고 있다고 답변하였다. 그는 그들은 수적으로 작으며 한국에서 쉽사리 구하지못하며 미국군대의 임수수행을 위하여 필요로하는 기술을 제공하고 있다. 따라서 제3국 국적 소유자를 포함케하는다른 방도를 모색해야 할것이라고 말하였다. 그는 제3국 국민은 그들의 직무를 수행하는데 방해되지 아니 한다라는것을 기술하고 다른 세항의 추가를 제의하였다.

(8) "하비브"씨는 만약 제3국 국민이 오직 미국군대의 임무수행을 돕기위한 목적만을 위하여 한국에 있다면 그들은 동일한 목적을 위하여 한국에와있는 기타 민간인과 꼭같은 대우를 받아야 한다고 답변하였다. 그는그다음에 만약 "미국국적의" 라는 구절이 세항 1(b)에 삽입된다면 미국군대가 고용할 미국 국적을 갖지않은자의 신분을 규정할 합의의사록이 추가되어야 한다고 제의하였다. 그는 다른 주둔군지위협정의 경우에서는 그와같은 약간의 조치가 필요하였다. 일본의 경우에 있어서는 각서교환으로 해결을 보았으며 그것은 합동위원회에 의해서 필요한것이라고 시사하였다. 그리하여 "하비브"씨는 합의의사록의 초안과 만약 그합의의사록이 채택되며는 세항 1(b)에 부가될 추가적 문장을 제출하였다. "하비브"씨는 "미국국적의" 라는 구절삽입에 동의함에 부가하여 합의의사록과 추가적 문장을 내어놓고 미국측은 한국측 요청에 타협을

6-4-101

0242

62-4-20

미문 87-9 ③

0243

한것이며 동시에 비차별적인 기초에서 그러한 사태에 대한 실제적 해결책을 제공한것이라고 말하였다. 그는 만약 이들 제의된 변경에 합의한다면 출입국 조문 제6항의 "..... 에 통상 거주하는" 이란 구절을 "..... 의 국민" 이란 구절로 대치하여 변경할 필요가 있다고 지적하였다. "진"씨는 한국측은 다음회의에서 토의하기 위하여 미국측 제안을 고려하겠다고 진술하였다.

(9) 세항 1( )에 관하여 오직 해결을 보지못한 문제는 "기타친척" 이라는 구절에 관한것이라는 점을 지적하면서 "진"씨는 한국측은 이세항의 미국측 초안에 동의하기로 결정하였다고 진술하였다.

합동위원회

(10) 합동위원회 조문에 대하여 "하비브"씨는 미국측은 양 초안을 비교하였으며 제출된대로의 미국측초안이 좋다고 생각한다고 진술하였다. "진"씨는 "별도 규정한 경우를 제외하고" 라는 구절에대한 해명을 요구하였다.

(11) "하비브"씨는 "별도 규정한경우를 제외하고" 라는 구절은 그초안이 후일 회의에서 제출될 다른조문에 언급한 것이라고 설명하였다. 그는 통신문제에 관해서는 대단히 특수하며 고도로 기술적인것으로 특수한 조치와 협정이 있다. 이들 협정과 조치에관한 협의도 또한 대단히 기술적인 성질의 것이다. 따라서 그러한 문제는 합동위원회가 다른 범위에 속할수 없다고 말하였다. "진"씨는 한국측은 다른 관계조문이 제출될때가지 이구절에 관한 견해를 보류하겠다고 진술하였다.

62-4-107

0244

62-4-20

0245

(12) "진"씨는 이제막 토의한 구절을 제외하면 미국측의 조문 초안에 대체적으로 합의하고 있다. 다만 문제가 되고있는 다른점은 제3항에서 "적절한"이나 혹은 "외교적"이라는 구절의 사용이다라고 말하였다. 그는 한국측은 "적절한 계통"이란 합동위원회에서 외교적 계통을 포함한 양측이 합의하는 계통을 의미한다는 양해하에 "적절한"이란 말의 사용에 동의하기로 결정했다고 말하였다. "하비브"씨는 이양해에 동의하였다.

항해 및 항공 통제

(13) 다음 항해보조물 및 항공통제에 관한 조문을 다루면서 "진"씨는 미국측 초안을 통신조직에 관하여 언급하고 있지않다고 말하였다. "하비브"씨는 이문제는 차후 회의에서 제출될 다른 조문의 미국측 초안에서 포함될것이라고 답변하였다. 그는 이문제에 관한 토의는 다른 조문이 제출될때까지 연기하도록 한국측에 촉구하였다.

(14) "진"씨는 한국측 초안 제2항은 미국측 초안의 해당항보다 더욱 적절하다고 논평하였다. "부론티" 대령은 미국측 초안의 말씨가 한국에 현존하는 행정적 및 운영적 실정에 더욱 밀접히 합치한다고 지적하였다. 그는 한국에서 항해 보조시설을 운영하며 유지하고 있는 미국군대는 때때로 이런 성질의 추가적 시설을 필요로 할것이라고 지적하였다. "하비브"씨는 주둔군 지위협정은 미국군대가 항해 보조시설을 설치하여 유지하도록 허용해야 한다. 왜냐하면 미국군대는 이미 그렇게 하고있으며 또한 장차도 추가적인 항해보조 시설을 설치할 필요가 있기때문이다. 미국측 초안은 명시적으로 그렇게 허용하고 있으나 한국측 초안은 다만 암시적으로만 허용하고

62-4-103

0246

62-4-20

대륙 87-9⑤

0247

있다고 지적하였다. 그는 미국측 초안은 이점에관하여
조금 더 명확하다고 첨언하였다.

(15) "진"씨는 미국측 초안 제2항의 "대한민국 영토를 통하여 또한 그영해에서" 라는 구절에 언급하여 미국측 초안이 수립된 보조시설물의위치를 일방적으로 혹은 한국정부 당국과의 협의하여 선정될것인지를 문의하였다.

(16) "부론티" 대령은 먼저 현존 무전신호소와 공항 통제탑의 위치를 인용하면서 답변하였다. 그는 시설의 현대화는 그특징으로서 현재 점유되어 있지않고 장소에 설치할 필요가 있는 매욱 복잡한 장비의 도입을 필요로 할것입니다. 그러한 경우 새로운 장소의 선택은 쌍방의 협의를 기초로하여 결정될것이라고 답변하였다. 그는 적대 행위가 일어날 경우 현재 민간인들에 의하여 운영되고있는 약간의 시설들은 군대에의하여 인계되어야 할것이라고 부언하였다. "하비브" 씨는 기존시설내에 있지않는 지역에 보조시설물을 설치 하는데 관해서는 미국군대와 한국정부간의 협의가 물론 필요할것이라고 부언하였다. 그는 토의중에있는 보조시설물은 공히 미국과 한국군대의 필요에 아바지하는 점을 지적하였다. 그는 또한 미국측 초안 제2항은 위치나 또한 보조시설물이 기존시설내에 설치될 경우에도 불문하고 통고할것을 필요로하고 있다고 교섭자들에 주의를 환기시켰다.

(17) "진"씨는 미국측이 상호협의를 규정하므로서 그항을 보충할 용의가 없는지를 문의하였다. "하비브"씨가 그질문의 해명을 요청하자 "진"씨는 미국측 초안은 "대한민국 영토를 통하여 또한 그영해내에서" 그들의 시설을 위한 허가를 규정하고 있으나 한국측 초안은"미국이 사용중인 시설 및 토지내와 그인접 영해와 그부근에" 설치된 보조시설물에 대한 통제를

62-4-104

0248

62-4-20

외무 87-9 ⓑ

0249

규정하고 있음을 지적하였다. 그는 미국측 초안의 문장이 상호협의를 의미하는지 혹은 미국군대에 의한 일방적인 조치를 의미하는지를 문의하였다. "하비브"씨는 그는 질문을 이해하였으며 미국측은 이조문에관한 다음토의시에 답변하겠다고 진술하였다.

(18) "진"씨는 미국측 초안은 보조시설물은 사용되고있는 제도에 "일반적으로" 일치하여야 한다고 기술하고 있음을 지적하였다. 그는 "일반적으로" 라는말이 필요한지를 물었다. "하비브"씨는이것은 새로운 장비의 약간의 종류는 기히 사용중에 있는 종류와 다소 기술적인 차이가 있을수 있다는 문제이라고 답변하였다.

(19) "진"씨는 그다음 "가능할경우 사전통고를" 이라는 구절에 대하여 문의하였다. "하비브"씨는 실제 운영하는 상태하에서 먼저 조치를하고 뒤에 통고함이 필요할 그와같은 사태가 있을지 모른다. 그러한 사태가 존재하게될 유일한 때는 비상사태 기간일것이다라고 답변하였다. 이조문에 대한 토의는 다음회의에서 계속하기로 합의하였다.

항공기 및 선박의 기착문제

(20) "진"씨는 항공기 및 선박의 기착에관한 조문은 양측안이 내용에있어서 그다지 틀리지 않음으로 미국측 초안을 토대로 토의할것을 제의하였다. 미국측의 동의가 있은다음 "진"씨는 한국측은 미국측 초안의 제 1 및 2항을 수락한다고 진술하였다. 62-4-11 8

(21) 제3항에 언급하면서 "진"씨는 "통상상태하에서" 라는 구절에 대한 해명을 요구하였다. "하비브"씨는 비상사태나 혹은 선박 및 항공기의 성질이 보안이유상 사전통고를 할수없는

0250

62-4-20 [illegible]

[illegible]

0251

경우를 제외하고는 항상 적절한 통고를 할것이라고

답변하였다. 그는 이는 하나의 기준구절이며 예외를

만드는것이 아니고 오히려 비정상적인것이라고 말하였다.

"진"씨는 한국측은 이점에관하여 이조문에대한 다음토의

시에 논평할것이라고 진술하였다.

(22) "하비브"씨는 한국의 고려를위하여 이조문에 관하여 한가지

더 논평하고저 한다고 진술하였다. 그는 주둔군지위협정

에서 면제가 부여되지 아니한 하물이나 여객에 관한 통고를

요청하는 제1항 둘재문장에 언급하였다. 그는 군사고문단

인원 및 대사관 무관부 인원들은 그들의 지위가 별도로

규정되고 있음으로 이문장에의하여 포함되지 않을것이다.

그러나 주둔군지위협정으로부터 면제가 부여되지 아니한

기타 인원들을 포함될것이며 그들의 도착은 한국정부 당국에

통고될것이다라고 진술하였다.

시설 및 토지

(23) 그다음 "살프"대령은 각조항을 간단히 요약하면서 시설 및

토지에관한 네개의 초안을 제출하였다. 그는 미국측은

네재번 조문에 차후 현존하고있는 공익물 협정에 관계될

하나의 조항을 초가할것을 의도하고 있다고 지적 하였다.

(24) 그다음 "이"대령은 한국측을 대표하여 시설 및 토지에관한

조문초안을 제출하였다. 이조문을 제출하면서 "이"대령은

대한민국 정부는 미국군대의 임무수행을 돕기위한 목적으로

미국군대가 사용할 시설 및 토지를 제공하는데 있어 과거에도

협조하였으며 또한 장차에 있어서도 협조할것이라고 말하였다.

그는 계속하여 한국에 현존하는 비정상적 사정에 감하여

한국측 조문초안은 불가피한 최소한도의 보상 미국정부가

62-4-106

0252

62-4-20 기밀 87-9⑧

0253

지불할것을 규정하고 있다고 말하였다. 그는 보상을 소유자의 손실을 경함케할 목적으로 다만 사유재산의 사용에 대한것만에 대하여 지불토록 기도한것이다. 한국측은 주한미국군대의 주둔목적에 대하여 충분한 고려를 하였다. 미국군대는 전쟁에서 막대한 손실을 입었으며 대한민국정부는 그들의 임무수행을 돕기위하여 최선을 다하였다고 말하였다. 초안을 제출하면서 그는 한국측은 성의와 상호 협조정신으로 조문별로 토의할것을 제안한다고 말하였다. "이"대령은 동 초안은 공익물과 용역에관한 조항을 포함치않고 있으며 그것은 별도로 규정될것이라고 시사하였다.

(25) 시설 및 토지에관한 조문초안의 토의는 각측이 초안을 검토하고 상대방의 입장을 이해할수 있도록 다음회의까지 보류하도록 합의하였다.

(26) 다음회의는 의제를 양측수석대표가 협의하여 결정키로 하고 1963. 1. 7. 하오 2시에 개최하기로 합의하였다. 회의는 년말년시의 인사를 교환하고 종료하였다.

(27) 합의 요약사항 : - 다음부분의 미국초안 원문을 협정의 최종원문으로 포함키로 합의보았다:

정의조문 -

세항 1(c)

항공기 및 선박기착 조문 -

제 1 항

제 2 항

62-4-107 (2)

0254

62-4-2 　　　　　　　　　　 미분 87-9-9

0255

JOINT SUMMARY RECORD OF THE 9TH SESSION
STATUS FORCES NEGOTIATION

0524

December 14, 1962

I. Time and Place: 2:00 to 4:00 p.m. December 14, 1962
at the Capitol Building

II. Attendants:

ROK Side:

Mr. Chin, Pil Shik	Director Bureau of Political Affairs Ministry of Foreign Affairs
Mr. Yi, Kyung Ho	Director Bureau of Legal Affairs Ministry of Justice
Mr. Shin, Kwan Sup	Director Bureau of Costums Duty Ministry of Finance
Mr. Pak, Kun	Chief, America Section Ministry of Foreign Affairs
Col. Lee, Nam Koo	Chief, Military Affairs Section Ministry of National Defense
Mr. O, Won Yong	Chief, Treaty Section Ministry of Foreign Affairs
Mr. Chi, Sung Koo	Press Officer Ministry of Foreign Affairs
Mr. Shin, Chung Sup	2nd Secretary Ministry of Foreign Affairs
Mr. Lee, Kyung Hoon	2nd Secretary Ministry of Foreign Affairs
Mr. Lee, Chang Bum	3rd Secretary Ministry of Foreign Affairs
Mr. Kang, Suk Jae	3rd Secretary Ministry of Foreign Affairs

U.S. Side:

Mr. Philip C. Habib	Counselor of the Embassy for Political Affairs
Brig. Gen. J.D. Lawlor	Deputy Chief of Staff 8th Army

0256

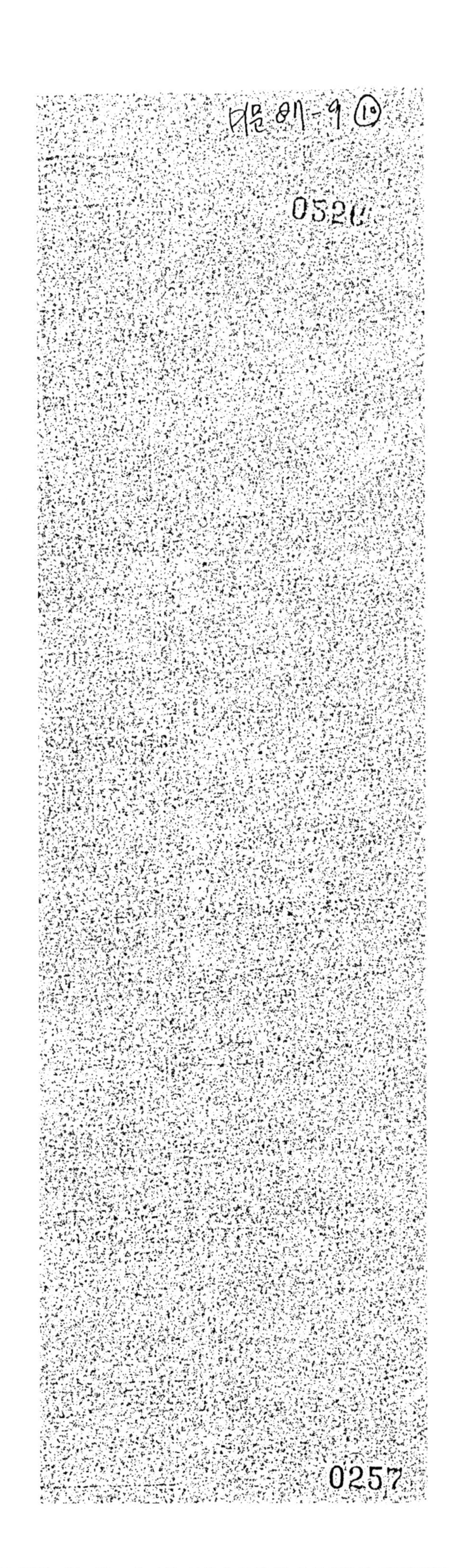

0257

Mr. William J. Ford	First Secretary of the Embassy
Col. G.G. O'Connor	Deputy Chief of Staff 8th Army
Capt. R.M. Brownlie	Assistant Chief of Staff USN/K
Col. W.A. Solf	Staff Judge Advocate 8th Army
Mr. Benjamin A. Fleck (Rapporteur and Press Officer)	First Secretary of the Embassy
Mr. Robert A. Lewis	Second Secretary and Consul of the Embassy
Lt. Col. R.E. Miller	Staff Officer, JAG 8th Army
Lt. Col. W.A. Burt	J-5
Kenneth Campen	Interpreter

0520

Definitions Article

1. The meeting began with consideration of the Definitions Article. Mr. Chin stated that the Korean side believed that the phrase "except for those for whom status has otherwise been provided" in subparagraph 1(a) was too vague. He proposed, therefore, that the phrase be deleted and that in its stead the negotiators approve and Agreed Minute which he thereupon tabled.

2. Mr. Habib replied that the U.S. side believed it desirable to hold to a minimum the number of Agreed Minutes to be attached to the Status of Forces Agreement. He suggested that, instead of adopting an Agreed Minute, the negotiators retain the phrase in the text and agree to let the written record show that this phrase is intended to apply to MAAG personnel and to personnel of the armed forces attache offices of the Embassy. Mr. Chin responded that the two sides were agreed on the substance of the point at issue. However, the Korean side believed that inasmuch as this phrase dealt with an exception to the

0258

application of the agreement, it should be spelled out in detail. It was the view of the Korean side that all exceptions should be clearly defined.

3. Mr. Habib then suggested that, as an alternative, the phrase be retained and an Agreed Minute be adopted in addition. Mr. Chin replied that the Agreed Minute which he had just tabled should be acceptable to the U.S. side since it clearly defined those military personnel who would be excluded from the provisions of the SOFA. He pointed out that these same personnel are also excluded from the provisions of the Mutual Defense Treaty.

4. Mr. Habib stated that the U.S. side would agree to the adoption of an Agreed Minute but believed that, in addition, the article itself should mention the fact that there were exceptions. He thereupon tabled the draft of an Agreed Minute. After perusing the U.S. draft Mr. Chin stated that there was no substantial difference between the two drafts. Mr. Habib agreed. It was decided to study the two drafts for discussion at a subsequent meeting.

5. Turning to subparagraph 1(b), Mr. Chin noted that the only point of difference was whether or not to insert the phrase "of United States nationality" after the words "civilian persons". He asked whether the U.S. side had any further statement to make on this point.

6. Mr. Habib replied that the U.S. armed forces in Korea do employ persons of third country nationality. He said they are few in number and provide skills which are not readily available in Korea but which are necessary for the accomplishment of the mission of the U.S. forces. They are here solely for that purpose and have no other function, he added. Inasmuch as they are in Korea on the same terms as United States nationals, there is no reason

0260

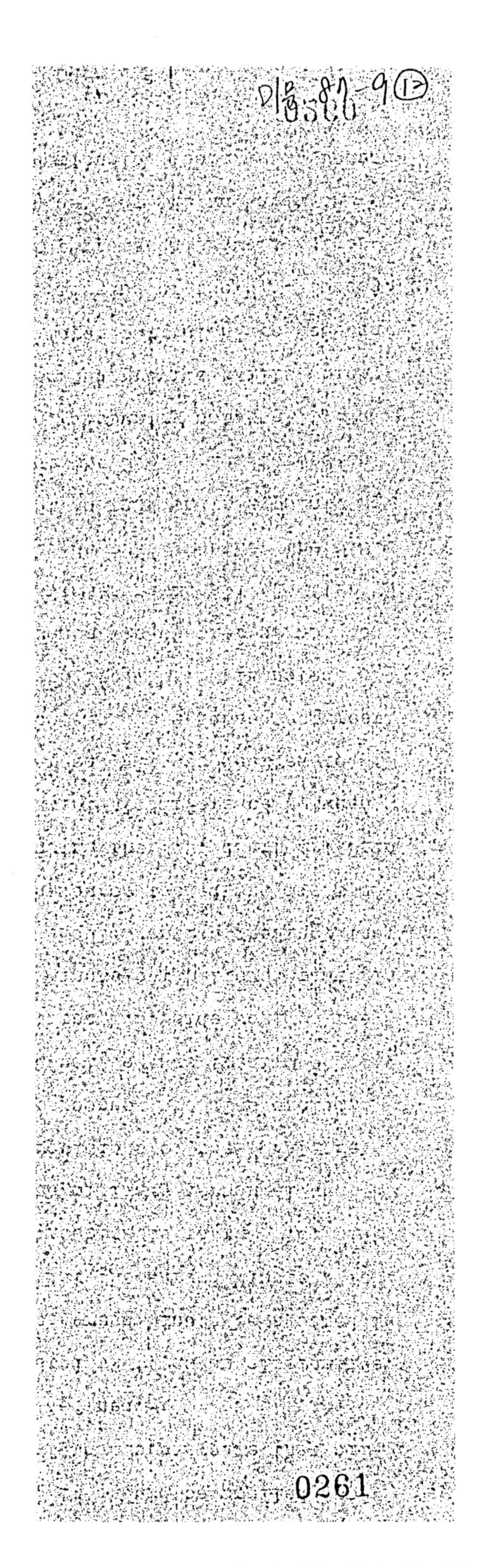
0261

or necessity for discriminating against them. He assured the Korean side that such persons are not hired when the requisite skills which they possess are found to be available in Korea. Therefore, the U.S. side does not believe the insertion of the phrase "of United States nationality" is either necessary or desirable.

7. Mr. Chin stated that the Korean side agreed that the number of third country nationals was relatively samll. However, in the view of the Korean side, the SOFA was meant to apply solely to the U.S. armed forces, and therefore the insertion of the phrase "of United States nationality" was both desirable and necessary. However, the Korean side had no intention of hindering the accomplishment of the mission of the U.S. armed forces. Perhaps, therefore, some other way might be found to cover third country nationals. He suggested the addition of another subparagraph which would state that third country nationals shall not be hindered from the performance of their duties.

8. Mr. Habib replied that if third country nationals are in Korea solely for the purpose of facilitating the accomplishment of the mission of the U.S. armed forces, they should receive the same treatment as other civilians who are in Korea for the same purpose. He then suggested that if the phrase "of United States nationality" were inserted in subparagraph 1(b), an Agreed Minute should be added which would define the status of persons not of U.S. nationality who might be employed by the U.S. armed forces. He indicated that some such arrangement had been found necessary in the case of other status of forces agreements. In the case of Japan, the solution had been an exchange of notes, which had been found necessary by the Joint Committee.

0262

Mr. Habib then tabled the draft of an Agreed Minute and an additional sentence to be added to subparagraph 1(b) if the Agreed Minute were adopted. With the Agreed Minute and the additional sentence, in addition to agreeding to the insertion of the phrase "of United States nationality", Mr. Habib noted, the U.S. side was adquiescing to the request of the Korean side but at the same time was providing a practical solution to the situation on a non-discriminatory basis. He pointed out that if these suggested changes were agreed upon, it would also be necessary to alter Paragraph 6 of the Entry and Exit Article by replacing the phrase "ordinarily resident in" with the phrase "nationals of" Mr. Chin stated that the Korean side would take the U.S. side's proposals under consideration for discussion at a subsequent meeting.

9. Pointing out that the only unreasolved question with respect to subparagraph 1(c) was that concerning the phrase "other relatives", Mr. Chin stated that the Korean side had decided to agree to the U.S. draft of this subparagraph.

Joint Committee

10. Turning to the Joint Committee article, Mr. Habib stated that the U.S. side had compared the two drafts and believed the U.S. draft as tabled to be preferable. Mr. Chin requested clarification of the phrase "except where otherwise provided."

11. Mr. Habib explained that the phrase "except where otherwise provided" referred to another article, the draft of which would be tabled later in the meeting. He said that there are special arrangements and agreements regarding communications which are very special and highly technical.

0264

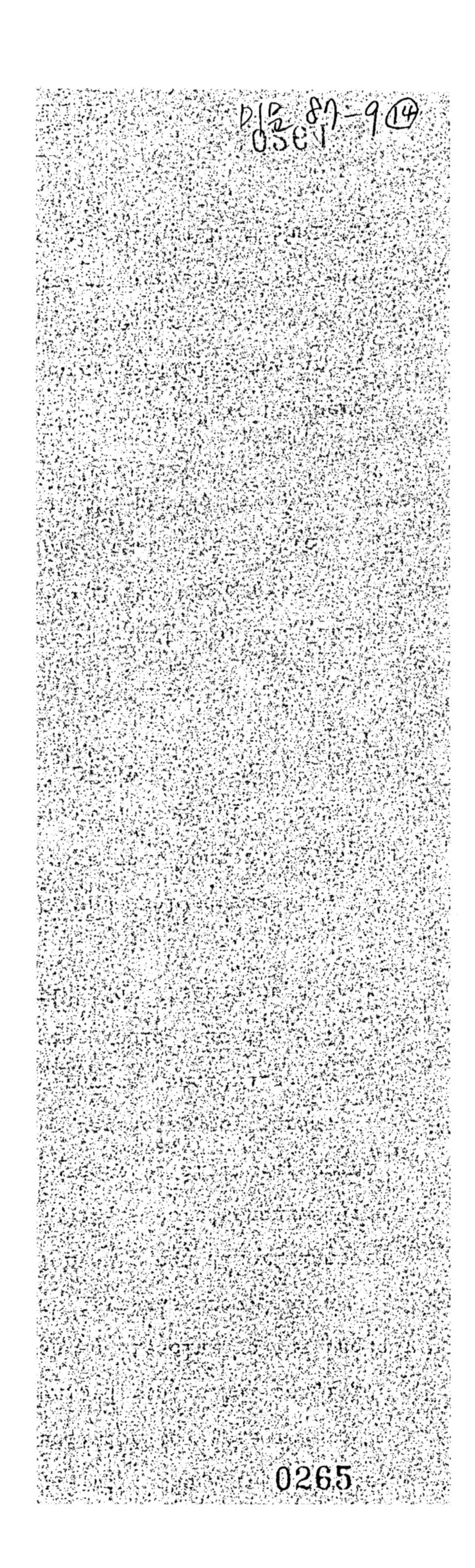

Consultations regarding these agreements and arrangements were also of a very special nature. Therefore, they should not come within the scope of the Joint Committee's labors. Mr. Chin stated the Korean side would reserve its views with regard to this phrase until the other relevant article was tabled.

12. Mr. Chin noted that except for the phrase just discussed, there was general agreement on the U.S. draft of the article. The only other point at issue was the use of "appropriate" or "diplomatic" in paragraph 3. He said the Korean side had decided to agree to the use of the word "appropriate", with the understanding that "appropriate channels" means channels agreed upon by both sides in the Joint Committee, including diplomatic channels. Mr. Habib agreed to this understanding.

Navigation and Air Traffic Control

13. Taking up next the Article dealing with navigational aids and air traffic control, Mr. Chin noted that the U.S. draft makes no mention of communication systems. Mr. Habib replied that this subject was covered in the U.S. draft of another article which would be tabled later in the meeting. He urged the Korean side to defer discussion of this point until the other article had been tabled.

14. Mr. Chin then commented that paragraph 2 of the Korean draft was more appropriate than the corresponding paragraph in the U.S. draft. Captain Brownlie pointed out that the wording of the U.S. draft conforms more closely to the actual administrative and operational situation existing in Korea. He pointed out that the U.S. armed forces, which operate and maintain navigational aids in Korea, will require, from time to time, additional facilities of this nature. Mr. Habib pointed out that the

0266

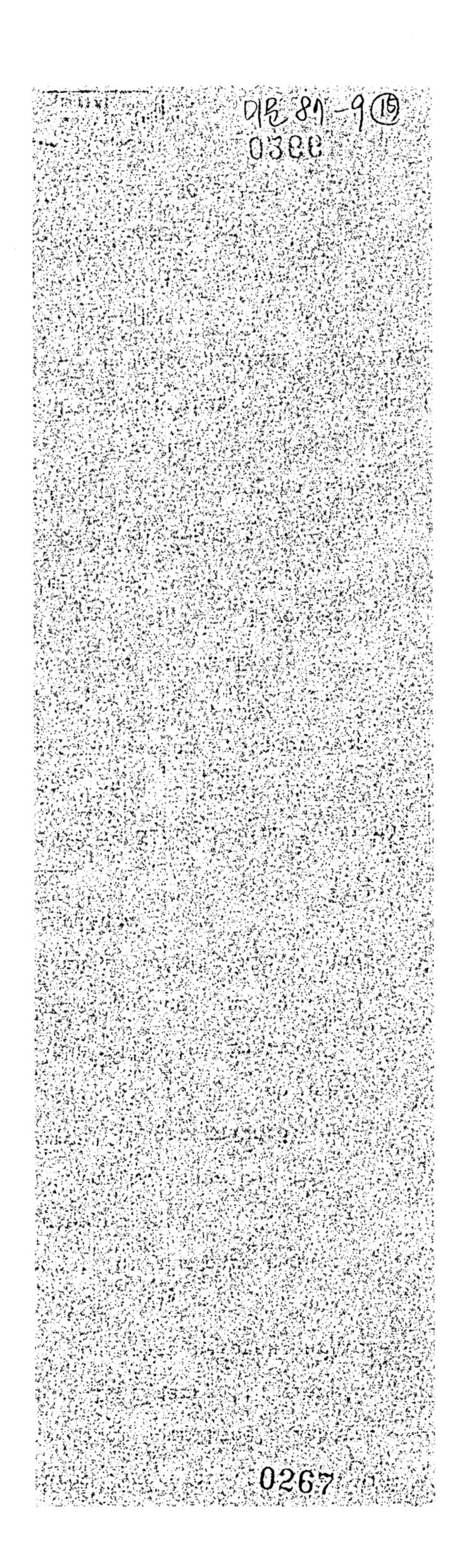

SOFA should authorize the U.S. armed forces to establish and maintain navigational aids, since they are already doing so and will need to establish additional aids in the future. The U.S. draft so authorizes explicitly but the Korean draft does so only implicitly. The U.S. draft, he added, was a little clearer in this respect.

15. Referring to the phrase "throughout the Republic of Korea and in the territorial waters thereof" in paragraph 2 of the U.S. draft, Mr. Chin asked whether the U.S. draft meant that the locations of the aids to be established were to be selected unilaterally or in consultation with Korean authorities.

16. Captain Brownlie replied by first citing the locations of existing radio beacons and airport control towers. He explained that modernization of facilities will require the introduction of more sophisticated equipment, the characteristics of which will require that it be located at stes not now occupied. In such cases, the selection of the new sites would be determined on the basis of bilateral discussion. He added that in case of hostilities, some facilities presently operated by civilians would have to be taken over by the armed forces. Mr. Habib added that consultation between the U.S. armed forces and the ROK Government obviously would be necessary with respect to the establishment of aids in areas not within established facilities. He pointed out that the aids under discussion jointly serve the needs of the U.S. and Korean armed forces. He also reminded the negotiators that paragraph 2 of the U.S. draft requires notification,

0268

regardless of location and even where aids have been established within existing facilities.

17. Mr. Chin inquired whether the U.S. side was prepared to supplement the paragraph by providing for mutual consultation. When Mr. Habib requested clarification of the question, Mr. Chin pointed out that the Korean draft provided for the coordin-tion of aids established "in the facilities and areas in use by the United States and in territorial waters adjacent thereto or in the vicinity thereof", whereas the U.S. draft provided for the authorization for their establishment "throughout the Republic of Korea and in the territorial waters thereof". He asked whether the language of the U.S. draft implied mutual consultation or unilateral action by the U.S. armed forces. Mr. Habib stated that he understood the question and that the U.S. side would respond to it during subsequent discussion of this article.

18. Mr. Chin pointed out that the U.S. draft stated that aids shall conform "generally" to the system in use. He asked if the word "Generally" were necessary. Mr. Habib replied that this was a question of there being possible slight technical differences in certain types of new equipment from the types already in use.

19. Mr. Chin then asked about the phrase "advance notification where practicable". Mr. Habib replied that under actual operating conditions, the situation may be such as to require action first and notification second. The only times when such a situation would exist would be during emergency conditions. It was then agreed to continue discussion of this article at a subsequent meeting.

0270

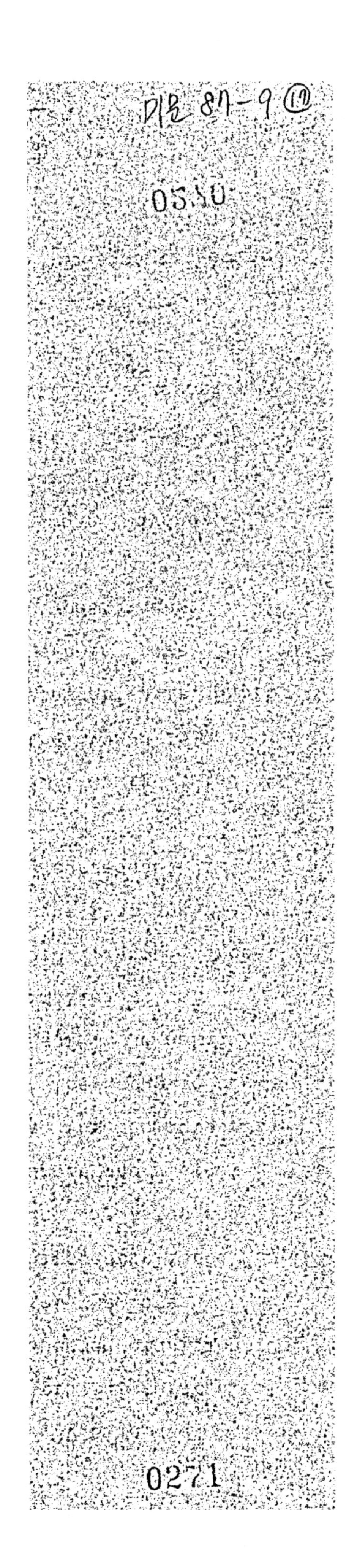
미문 87-9 ⑰
0530
0271

Access by Aircraft and Vessels

0598

20. Mr. Chin suggested that the article on access by aircraft and vessels be discussed on the basis of the U.S. draft since the two drafts do not differ much in substance. Following assent by the U.S. side, Mr. Chin stated that the Korean side accepted paragraph 1 and 2 of the U.S. draft.

21. Referring to paragraph 3, Mr. Chin requested clarification of the phrase "under normal conditions". Mr. Habib replied that appropriate notification would always be made, except in an emergency situation or when the nature of a vessel or aircraft is such that prior notification cannot be made because of security reasons. He said that this was a standard phrase and constituted not an exception but rather an abnormality. Mr. Chin stated that the Korean side would comment on this point during subsequent discussion of this article.

22. Mr. Habib stated th t he would like to make one further comment regarding this article for the consideration of the Korean side. He referred to the second sentence in paragraph 1 calling for notification regarding cargo and passengers not accorded the exemptions of the SOFA. He stated that MAAG personnel and Embassy armed forces attache personnel would not be covered by this sentence, since their status was otherwise provided for. However, any other personnel not entitled to the exemptions of the SOFA would be covered and their arrival would be notified to the Korean authorities.

Facilities and Areas

23. Colonel Solf then tabled four draft articles relating to facilities and areas, briefly summarizing the provisions of each. He pointed out that the U.S. side

0272

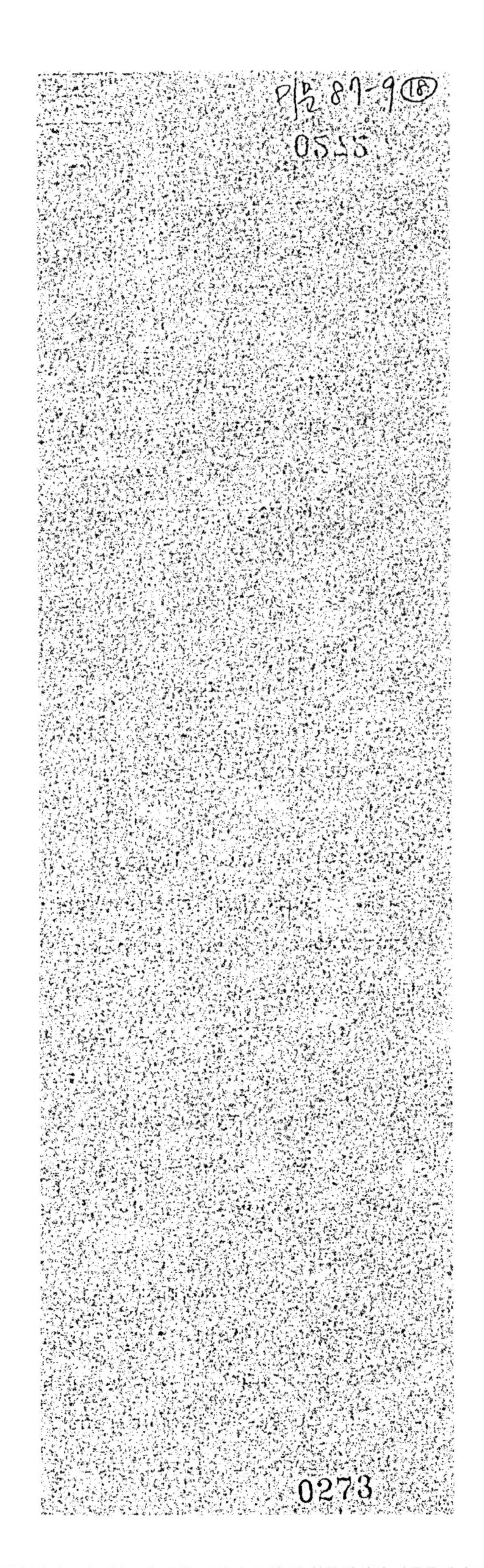

intended to add to the fourth article at a later date a paragraph which would be related to the existing utilities agreement.

24. Colonel Lee then tabled a draft article on facilities and areas for the Korean side. In introducing this article, Col. Lee said that the ROK Government has cooperated in the past and will cooperate in the future in furnishing facilities and areas for use by the U.S. armed forces, for the purposes of facilitating the accomplishment of the mission of those forces. In view of the unusual situation existing in Korea, he continued, the Korean draft article provides for the payment of compensation by the U.S. Government to the least unavoidable extent. It is intended, he went on, that compensation shall be paid only for the use of private property, with a view to alleviating the losses of the owners. The Korean side has given due consideration to the purpose of the presence of the U.S. armed forces in Korea. They have suffered tremendous losses in battle and the ROK Government has done its best to facilitate the achievement of their mission. In tabling this draft, he continued, the Korean side proposed article by article discussion in a spirit of honesty and muutual cooperation. Col. Lee indicated that the draft did not contain provisions regarding public utilities and services, which would be separately provided for.

25. It was agreed to reserve discussion of the draft articles on facilities and areas until the next meeting, thus permitting each side to study the drafts and understand the other side's position.

0532

0274

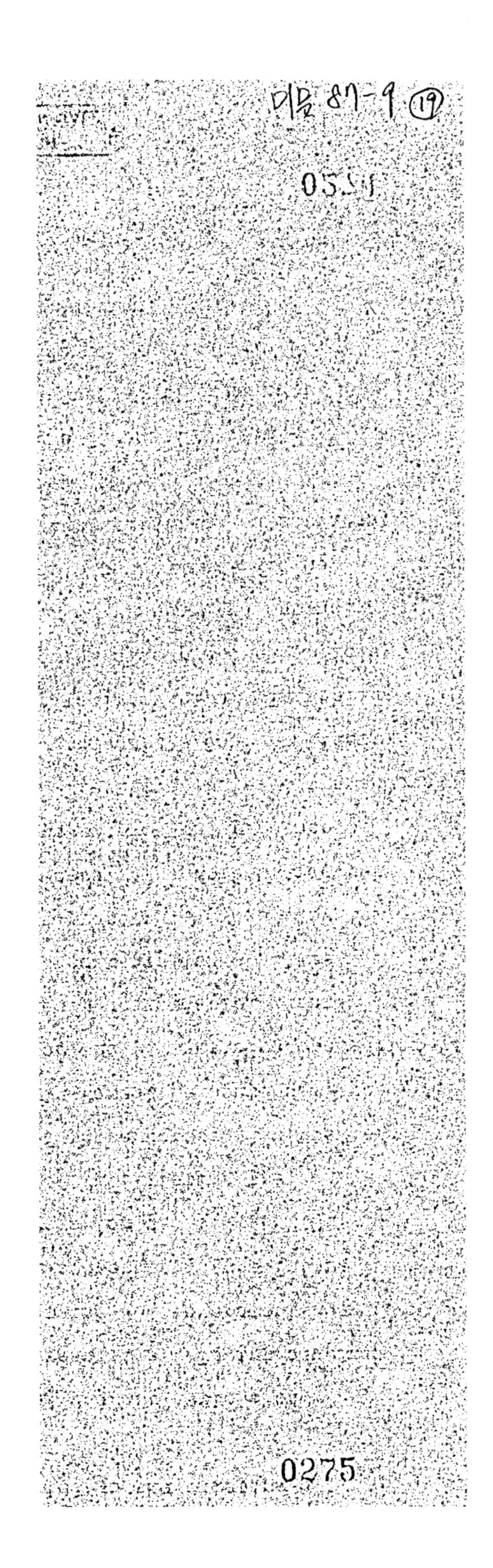
미문 87-9 ⑲
0275

26. It was agreed to hold the next meeting on January 7, 1963, at 2:00 p.m., with the agenda to be decided upon by the two chairmen in consultation. The meeting closed with an exchange of cordial season's greetings.

27. Summary Points of Agreement:- The following portions of the text of the U.S. draft were agreed upon for inclusion in the final text of the Agreement:

Definitions Article-

Subparagraph 1(c)

Access by Aircraft and Vessels Article -

Paragraph 1

Paragraph 2

0279

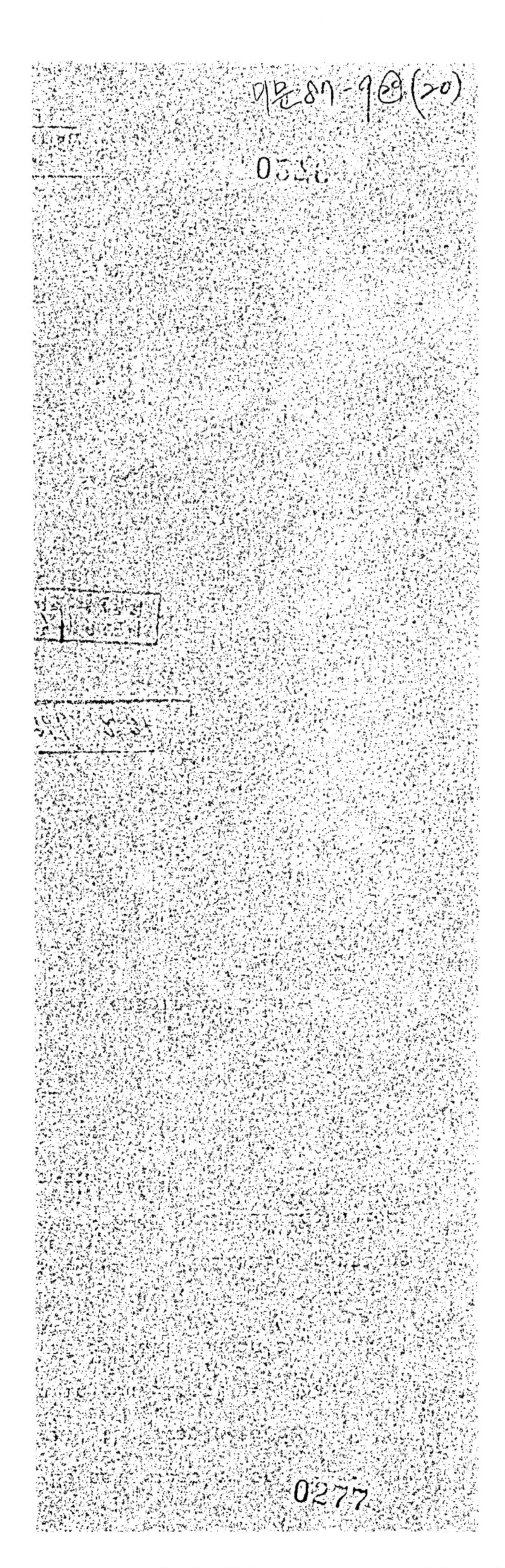

정/리/보/존/문/서/목/록					
기록물종류	문서-일반공문서철	등록번호	948 9621	등록일자	2006-07-27
분류번호	741.12	국가코드	US	주제	
문서철명	한.미국 간의 상호방위조약 제4조에 의한 시설과 구역 및 한국에서의 미국군대의 지위에 관한 협정 (SOFA) 전59권. 1966.7.9 서울에서 서명 : 1967.2.9 발효 (조약 232호) *원본				
생산과	미주과/조약과	생산년도	1952 - 1967	보존기간	영구
담당과(그룹)	조약	조약	서가번호	--	
참조분류					
권차명	V.50 실무교섭회의 합의의사록, 제10-37차, 1963				
내용목차	* 일지 : 1953.8.7 이승만 대통령-Dulles 미국 국무장관 공동성명 - 상호방위조약 발효 후 군대지위협정 교섭 약속 1954.12.2 정부, 주한 UN군의 관세업무협정 체결 제의 1955.1월, 5월 미국, 제의 거절 1955.4.28 정부, 군대지위협정 제의 (한국측 초안 제시) 1957.9.10 Hurter 미국 국무차관 방한 시 각서 수교 (한국측 제의 수락 요구) 1957.11.13, 26 정부, 개별 협정의 단계적 체결 제의 1958.9.18 Dawling 주한미국대사, 형사재판관할권 협정 제외 조건으로 행정협정 체결 의사 전달 1960.3.10 정부, 토지, 시설협정의 우선적 체결 강력 요구 1961.4.10 장면 국무총리-McConaughy 주한미국대사 공동성명으로 교섭 개시 합의 1961.4.15, 4.25 제1, 2차 한.미국 교섭회의 (서울) 1962.3.12 정부, 교섭 재개 촉구 공한 송부 1962.5.14 Burger 주한미국대사, 최규하 장관 면담 시 형사재판관할권 문제 제기 않는 조건으로 교섭 재개 통고 1962.9.6 한.미국 간 공동성명 발표 (9월 중 교섭 재개 합의) 1962.9.20~ 1965.6.7 제1-81차 실무 교섭회의 (서울) 1966.7.8 제82차 실무 교섭회의 (서울) 1966.7.9 서명 1967.2.9 발효 (조약 232호)				

마/이/크/로/필/름/사/항				
촬영연도	*롤 번호	화일 번호	후레임 번호	보관함 번호
2006-11-24	I-06-0072	03	1-366	

0001

관리번호 1358 10次

주둔군지위협정 교섭 제10차회의 요약기록

1963. 1. 7.

1. 시일 및 장소 : 1963. 1. 7. 하오 2시부터 4시 40분 까지
외무부장관 회의실

2. 참석자 :

한국측 :

진필식	외무부 정무국장
이경호	법무부 법무국장
신관섭	재무부 세관국장
박근	외무부 미주과장
오윤용	외무부 조약과장
이남구	국방부 군무과장
이경훈 (기록)	외무부 2등서기관
신정섭	"
지성구 (공보)	외무부 공보관
강석재 (통역)	외무부 3등서기관

미국측 :

필립 씨.하비브	주한미대사관 참사관
제이.디.토머 준장	주한미8군 참모차장
윌리암 제이.호드	주한미대사관 1등서기관
죠.지.오코나 대령	주한미8군참모차장
알.엠 부튼티대령	주한미해군 참모부장
다불.에이.솔프 대령	주한미8군 법무참모
벤자민 에이.후렉 (기록및공보)	주한미대사관 1등서기관
로버트 에이.루이스	주한미대사관2등서기관겸영사

1966, 12, 31 에 예고문에 의거 일반문서로 재분류됨

0002

마이문 87-100 (22)

0003

알.이. 밀러 중령　　주한미8군 법무장교

다볼.에이.버트 중령 주한미군 민사참모

케니즈 캠펠　　통역

3. 회의요록 :

정의조문

(1) "진"씨는 미국측으로서 정의조문에 관하여 추가적인 론평을 할것이 있는지를 문의하면서 회의를 시작하였다. "하비브"씨는 보조문에 대한 지난번 토의를 검토하면서 미국측은 세항 (a)의 "별도 그지위가 규정된자" 라는 구절을 설명하는 합의의사록의삽입에 원측적으로 동의한다고 말하였다. 그는 교섭자들에게 미국측은 그러한 합의의사록 초안을 제출한바 있음을 상기 시켰다. 그는 그다음 교섭자들이 미국측이 제출한 세항(a)와 합의의사록에 합의할것을 제의하였다.

(2) "진"씨는 양측이 제출한 합의의사록 초안에는 다만 적은 차이가 있을뿐이라고 론평하였다. 그는 "별도 그지위가 규정될 자를 제외한"이란 구절을 세항 (a)에서 삭제할것을 제의하였다. 만약 그렇게한다면 그는 한국측은 "......와같은 인원들과 같이 별도 그지위가 규정된자" 란 구절을 합의의사록 초안에서 삭제한다는 조건에서 미국측의 합의의사록 초안을 수락할 용의가있다고 말하였다.

(3) "하비바"씨는 세항과 합의의사록으로부터 다같이 동구절을 삭제한다는것은 지나치게 제한적인 것이라고 답변하였다. 그는 합의의사록의 운영구절은 바로 한국측이 삭제하기를 원하는 구절이다. 문제가 되고 있는점은 기타 인원들이 한국에 있는가 없는가의 문제가 아니다. 문제점은 그들의 지위가 별도 규정되었는지의 여부이라라고 지적하였다.

0004

미군 81-10 ㉠

0005

(4) "진"씨는 현재 한국에 군사고문단 인원 및 대사관 무관부 인원이외에 이조항이 적용될 다른 인원에 있는지를 문의하였다. "하비브"씨는 현재로서는 별도 그지위가 규정된자로서 언급한그들외에 다른 인원은 없다고 답변하였다.

(5) "진"씨는 이규정은 주둔군지위협정의 일반적 규정에 예외를 규정한다. 장차 기타 인원이 있게된다면 기타 인원에관한 예외는 다른 협정에서 규정하게 될것이라고 논평하였다. 그는 그다음에 미국측의 세항(a)와 한국측의 합의의사록의 채택을 제안하였다. "하비브"씨는 미국측은 이제안을 고려하겠다고 답변하였다.

(6) 세항 (b)에 관하여 "진"씨는 한국측은 미국측이 제안한 추가적인 문장을 수락한다고 진술하였다. 그는 미국측이 제출한 합의의사록 초안은 둘째줄에 있는 "쉽사리"란말을 제외하고서는 역시 수락할만 한다고 말하였다. 그는 그 단어의 삭제는 문장의 내용을 변경하는것이 아니라고 시사하였다. "하비브"씨는 미국이나 혹은 한국에서 어떤 기술을 얻을수 있는지의 정도는 실제적 문제이다. 미국측은 "쉽사리"얻을수있는" 이란 말은 현존하는 상태에대한 가장 솔직한 말이라고 생각한다고 답변하였다. "하비브"씨는 한국측에게 미국당국은 제3국 국민을 한국에 많이 입국케할 의사가 없음을 보장하면서 한국측 제안을 고려하겠다고 동의하였다.

출입국관리

(7) "하비브"씨는 정의조문의 세항 (b)에 관하여 충분한 합의가 이루어져서 교섭자들로 하여금 출입국관리 조문 제6항에 있어서 약간의 변경에 합의케되었음을 지적하였다.

0006

미몽 87-10

0007

그는 한국측 교섭자들이 바로 동의한바 있는 추가적 문장과 아울러 세항 (b)의 첫째줄의 "군속"이란 말뒤에 "미국 국적을가진" 이란 말을 삽입하는데 합의하면 출입국 조문 제 6 항에서 "통상 거주하는" 이란말 대신 ".....의 국민들" 이란 말로 대치할 필요가 있다고 지적하였다. "진"씨는 한국측은 출입국 조문에 있어서 이변경에 동의한다고 말하였으며 최종적 원문이 확인되었다.

합동위원회

(8) 합동위원회 조문에관하여 "진"씨는 교섭자들은 제1항 첫째 문장의 "별도 규정된 경우를 제외하고" 라는 구절을 제외하고 미국측 초안에 대체적인 합의에 도달한바 있음을 상기시켰다. "진"씨는 그는 이구절이 미국측이 제출한 시설 및 토지에 관한 둘째번 조문의 제 2(b)항에 의하여 규정될 통신에관한 특별한 조치에 언급하는것으로 이해한다고 말하였다. "하비브"씨는 그것이 맞다고 진술하고 제2(b)항도 또한 그러한 조치에 대하여 언급한다고 지적하였다. "진"씨는 한국측은 이구절을 합동위원회 조문에서 삭제하여야 하고 그규정은 통신에관한 관계조문에 상세히 규정해야 한다고 믿는다고 진술하였다. 그는 합동위원회의 우월성은 주둔군 지위협정에 의하여 완전히 수립해야 하며 예외를 두어서는 안된다. 합동위원회는 주둔군지위 협정의 이행과 관계된 어떠한 문제라도 고려할 권한을 가져야 하며 또한 그기능을 "적절한 당국"에 위임할 권한을 가져야한다고 말하였다.

(9) "하비브"씨는 주둔군지위협정의 일부에서 합동위원회의 기능에대한 예외를두고 합동위원회 기능을 다루는 조문에서 그 예외를 언급하지 않는다는것은 혼동과 오해를 야기시킬것 이라고 답변하였다. 그는 합동위원회의 우월성은 주둔군

0008

미문 811-10(4)

0009

지위협정의 조문으로 완전히 수립되고 있다. 연이나 미국측은 어떠한사항은 합동위원회가 토의하는데 적절하지 않다고 믿는다. 미국측 의견으로서는 합동위원는 시설 및 토지에 관계된 조문에서 규정된 통신조치와 같이 달리 취급하는것이 더욱 좋은 특수사항의 토의에는 적절한 기구가 아니다. 미국측 초안에 의하여 그러한 사항들은 양국정부의 적절한 당국에 의한 상호협의로 합의된 공동조치에 의하여 취급될것이다. 미국측은 합동위원회의 우월성은 충분히 수립되고 있다고 말하였다.

(10) "박근" 박사는 한국측 입장을 재차 말하고저 한다고 진술하였다. 그는 합동위원회는 주둔군지위협정 사항에 관한 집중적이며 일반적이며 또한 포괄적 협의기관이어야 한다. 이원측은 합동위원회에 관한 조문에서 수립되어야 한다. 기술적 사항은 자연히 시설 및 토지조문에서 규정된바와 같이 적절한 당국에 의하여 취급되어야 한다. 한국측은 특별한 규정은 일반적인 규정에 우선해야 한다고 믿는다. 따라서 시설 및 토지조문의 특수규정은 합동위원회 조문의 일반적 규정에 우선할것이다라고 말하였다. "박"박사는 만약 이원측이 명확히 이해된다며는 합동위원회 조문은 예외규정에 의하여 방해되지 않을것이라고 계속하여 말하였다. "진"씨는 만약 시설 및 토지조문의 규정하에 있는 특수한사항에 관하여 적절한 당국에 의하여 합의가 이루어지지 않는다면 그문제는 그다음에 합동위원회에 회부되어야 한다고 추가하였다. 그는 문제는 합동위원회의 융통성을 기하는데 있다고 말하였다.

(11) "하비브"씨는 한국측은 예외를 두는것을 바라면서도 예외를 두었다는것을 합동위원회 조문에서 기술한는것을 바라고 있지 않는것같다고 답변하였다. 그는 미국측안이 훨신 명확하고 간결한 말이라고 말하고 아마 "별도 규정된 경우를

0010

미본 87-10⑤

0011

제외한"이란 구절이 충분히 이해되지못하고 있다. 그는 양측이 합의에 도달치못한채 그들의 입장을 충분히 진술하였음으로 이번회의에서 더이상 토의하는것이 효과있을 것이라는 보지않는다고 시사하였다.

<u>선박 및 항공기의 기착</u>

(12) 선박 및 항공기의 기착에관한 조문에대하여 "진"씨는 한국측은 이미 제 1 및 2항에 동의하였다고 진술하였다. 그는 계속해서 지난번회의시 제3항에관한 미국측의 설명에 기초하여 한국측은 역시 2-항의 미국측 초안을 수락한다고 말하였다. 이렇게하여 이조문에 관한 완전합의가 이루어졌다.

<u>항해보조시설물 및 항공통제</u>

(13) 항해보조시설물에 관한 조문을 토의함에 "하비브"씨는 이조문에관한 지난번 토의시에 한국측은 그러한 보조시설물의 협의없이 혹은 상호합의를 통하여 설치될것인지의 기본적 질문을한바 있음을 회상시켰다. 그는 미국측은 항해보조시설물은 관계조문에서 규정된바와 같이 통제된 기초에서 설치될것이라는 점을 명백히 해두고저 한다. 오직 예외는 보조시설물이 즉시 필요한 비상시나 혹은 임시로 항해보조시설물의 설치를 요하는 특수 전투훈련의 경우에만 있게 될것이다라고 말하였다. 그는 상호협의는 과거에 실시하여 온바이며 장래에있어서 계속 실시될것이라고 지적하였다.

(14) "하비브"씨는 한국측은 또한 미국측 초안의 "대체로 일치할것"이라는 구절에대한 의미를 물문한바 있다고 말하였다. 그는 미국군대에 의하여 필요로하는 장비중에는 현재 한국에서 실시되고있는 항해 보조시설물 제도하에서는 사용할수 없는

0012

미문 87-10⑥

0013

것이 몇종류인다. 이장비에는 주로 표적목격에 사용되는 "쇼란"제도와 장거리 항해를위한 "로란"제도가 포함된다. 그는 이에부가하여 군사 항공기에 의하여 38선에 관련한 자기위치를 측정하는데 사용토록 되어있는 "타칸"제도가 있다. 이제도는 어느것이나 한국의 민간당국에 의하여 사용되고있지 않다고 지적하였다. "하비브"씨는 계속해서 끊임없는 기술적 변화에 비추어 미국측은 "대체로"라는 용어의 사용을 좋아한다고 말하였다.

(15) "진"씨는 상호협의의 이행을 제2항에서 상세히 규정하자고 제의하였다. "하비브"씨는 그것은 제 1 항에서 규정되어 있으며 제1항과 2항은 같은것이라고 답변하였다. 그는 미국측 초안 제 2 항은 미국군대에 항해보조시설물을 설치하고 건설하며 유지하는 권리를 부여한다. 의미에 있어서 두 초안간에는 차이가 거이없다. 연이나 한국측 초안은 기설 시설에 "인접하고 있는" 지역 및 영해를 말하고있다. 이것은 항해 보조시설물의 경우에있어서는 항상 실용적인 것이다라고 답변하였다. "진"씨는 "하비브"씨의 말은 한국측이 제기한 질문에 회답한것이라고 답변했다. 그는 제2항에 있어서 첫재문장에 다음과같은 추가적 구절 즉 "양정부의 적절한 당국간의 합의를 통하여" 를 "그"란말 다음에 추가하도록 제의하였다. "하비브"씨는 미국측은 이제안을 고려하겠다고 말하였다.

시설 및 토지

(16) 지난회의에서 양측이 제출한 시설 및 토지조문 초안에 대하여 "진"씨는 항별토의를 제의하고 "하비브"씨에게 미국측 초안을 설명하여 달라고 요청하였다.

0014

미올 87-10 ⑰

0015

(17) "하비브"씨는 미국측 초안 첫째조문의 제1항 (a)와 한국측 초안 조문의 해당 첫 두항에는 용어사용에 있어서 차이가 있다. 미국측 초안은 "조치"라기 보다 오히려 "협정"이란 말을 쓰고있다. 왜냐하면 그것은 의도하는바를 더욱 정확히 말한다고 믿으며 또한 문서를 포함하게될것이기 때문이다. "체결된"이란 말은 한국측 초안에있어서 "조치"가 "취해졌다" 는것과 같이 "협정"이란말과 함께 사용된것이다. 더욱 실질적 차이점은 미국측 초안에서 "어디 위치하던간에"와 한국측 초안에 나타나있는 "필요한" 이란 용어대신에 "사용된"이란 말을 사용하고 있는점이다 라고 지적하였다. 그는 이특수한 말은 일본과의 주둔군 지위협정의 운영 경험의 결과로 사용된것이다. 미국측은 이것은 경험으로서 나타난바와같이 시설에관계된 설비와가 장비가 항상 전적으로 특수시설내에 위치하고 있지않기 때문에 후자의 협정의 용어보다 진보한것이라 생각한다고 진술하였다. 그는 더욱 문전 주파수는 시설이나 어떠한 정확한 위치에 위치하고 있다고 말할수 없다. "사용된" 이란 단어는 사실을 반영하며 그반면 "필요한"이란 단어는 판단을 의미한다고 지적하였다.

(18) "하비브"씨는 미국측 초안의 제1항 (b)와 한국측 초안 제3항은 약간 틀린다고 지적하면서 그의 분석을 계속하였다. 그는 중복된것 같이 보이는 "이협정의 목적을위하여" 란 구절을 설명하여 달라고 한국측에 요청하였다. 그는 또한 "조사하고 결정한" 이란 구절에관한 설명을 요구하였다. 그는 현재 사용중에 있는 모든토지 및 시설에대한 증발 서류가 있으며 또한 의심할바 없이 합동위원회에 등록

0016

미문 87-10⑧

0017

될것이라는 점을 지적하면서 한국측의 제3항 둘째문장은 그전문장부터 후퇴하고 있다는 의견을 피력하였다. 그는 미국측 초안의 제1항 (a)은 합동위원회에서 체결하게될 이들 시설 및 토지에관한 협정을 규정하고 있다고 지적하였다.

(19) "진"씨는 답변으로서 한국측 "협정"이라기 보다 "조치"라는 용어를 사용하였다. 왜냐하면 후자는 전자보다 광범위한 용어이며 모든것을 포함하여 융통성이 있기때문이다라고 진술하였다. 미국측 초안 첫째조문의 제1항 (a)에 규정되어 있지않는 "본 협정에서 규정된바와 같이"라는 한국측 초안의 구절을 지적하면서 그는 대한민국은 상호방위 조약에 기초해서 뿐만아니라 주둔군지위협정의 관계조항에 의거하여 토지 및 시설의 사용을 허용할것이다라고 논평하였다. 그는 미국측 초안에 논평하면서 이에관련하여 "사용되고있는" 이란 용어사용에 비추어 "어디에 위치" 하면간에"라는 용어의 사용에 대하여 질문하였다. 그는 미국측 초안의 "사용되고 있는"이란 용어와 한국측 초안의 "......의 운영에 필요한" 이란 구절의 사용에관련하여 양측이 차기회의에서 더욱 수락할만한 용어를 만련하기 위하여 양초안의 용어를 비교 검토할것을 제의하였다. 그는 한국측은 "본협정의 목적을 위하여"와 "본협정하에"라는 구절사용을 재고하겠다고 말하였다. 한국측 초안 제2항 둘째번 문장, 특히 "조사하여 결정된"이란 말에관하여 "진"씨는 동항의 첫째번 문장에 의거하는 현존 시설 및 토지에 상태나 범위를 변경코저 의도한바가 아니다. 그 의도는 본협정이 효력발생할때 미국군대에 의하여 사용중인 현존 시설 및 토지를 확인 하는데 있다고 말하였다. 그는 더욱 시설 및 토지의 반환이나

0018

미문 87-10 ①

0019

추가적 제공과같은 사항은 그조문의 관계항에서 적절히 규정될것이라고 말하였다.

(20) "하비브"씨는 미국측 초안의 제2항과 그에 해당하는 한국측 초안의 제6항에 관하여 단하나의 실질적 차이는 미국측 초안에서는 시설의 일부의 반환을 규정하고 있는 점이라고 진술하였다. 그는 이말이 좋다는 견해를 피력하였다. "진"씨는 미국측 초안에있는 "그러한"이란 말의 선행되는것을 상세히 규정해야 할것이라고 론평하였다.

차기회의

(21) 이때 교섭자들은 2시간 반 동안 회의를 계속하였으며 휴회하기로 합의하였다. 차기회의는 1월 16일 하오 2시에 개최하기로 하였다.

합의사항

(22) 가. 출입국 관리조문 (원문 별첨)

나. 선박 및 항공기의 기착조문 (원문 별첨)

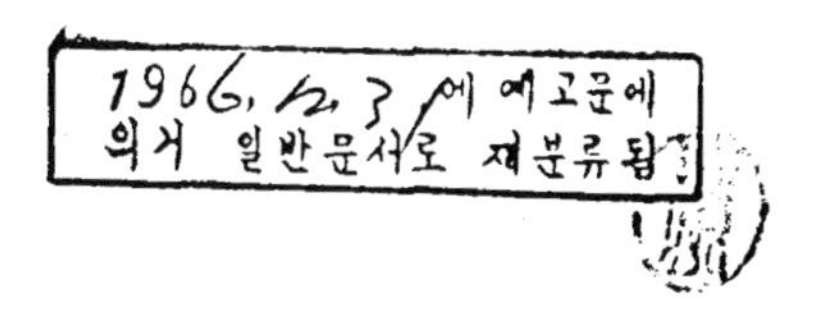

0020

미운 81-10 ⑩

0021

JOINT SUMMARY RECORD OF THE 10TH SESSION
STATUS FORCES NEGOTIATIONS

January 7, 1963

I. Time and Place : 2:00 to 4:40 p.m. January 7, 1963
at the Foreign Minister's
Conference Room

II. Attendants:

ROK Side

Mr. Chin, Pil Shik	Director Bureau of Political Affairs Ministry of Foreign Affairs
Mr. Yi, Kyung Ho	Director Bureau of Legal Affairs Ministry of Justice
Mr. Shin, Kwan Sup	Director Bureau of Costums Duty Ministry of Finance
Mr. Pak, Kun	Chief, American Section Ministry of Foreign Affairs
Mr. O, Won Yong	Chief, Treaty Section Ministry of Foreign Affairs
Col. Lee, Nam Koo	Chief, Military Affairs Section Ministry of National Defense
Mr. Lee, Kyung Hoon	2nd Secretary Ministry of Foreign Affairs
Mr. Shin, Chung Sup	2nd Secretary Ministry of Foreign Affairs
Mr. Chi, Sung Koo	Press Officer Ministry of Foreign Affairs
Mr. Kang, Suk Jae	3rd Secretary Ministry of Foreign Affairs

US Side:

Mr. Philip C. Habib	Counselor of the Embassy for Political Affairs

0022

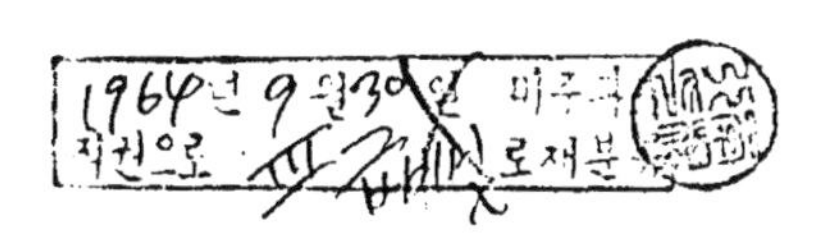

미문 87-10 ⑪

0023

Brig. Gen J.D. Lawlor	Deputy Chief of Staff 8th Army
Mr. William J. Ford	First Secretary of the Embassy
Col. G.G. O'Connor	Deputy Chief of Staff 8th Army
Capt. R.M. Brownlie	Assistant Chief of Staff USN/K
Col. W.A. Solf	Staff Judge Advocate 8th Army
Mr. Benjamin A. Fleck (Rapporteur and Press Officer)	First Secretary of the Embassy
Mr. Robert A. Lewis	Second Secretary and Consul of the Embassy
Lt. Col. R.E. Miller	Staff Officer, JAG 8th Army
Lt. Col. W.A. Burt	J-5
Kenneth Campen	Interpreter

Definitions Article

1. Mr. Chin opened the meeting by asking whether the U.S. side had any additional comments to make regarding the Definitions Article. Reviewing previous discussion of this article, Mr. Habib noted that the U.S. side had agreed in principle to the inclusion of an Agreed Minute explaining the phrase "those for whom status has otherwise been provided" in subparagraph (a). He reminded the negotiators that the U.S. side had tabled the draft of such an Agreed Minute. He then suggested that the negotiators agree to subparagraph (a) and to the Agreed Minute tabled by the U.S. side.

0024

P/B 87-10 ⑫

0025

2. Mr. Chin commented thatthere were only minor differences in the drafts of the Agreed Minute tabled by the two sides. He suggested that the phrase "except for those for whom status has otherwise been provided" be deleted from subparagraph (a). If this were done, he said the Korean side was prepared to accept the U.S. draft of the Agreed Minute, provided the phrase "for whom status has otherwise been provided such as personnel" were deleted from the draft of the Minute.

3. Mr. Habib replied that elimination of the phrase from both the subparagraph and the Agreed Minute would be too restrictive. He pointed out that the operative phrase in the Agreed Minute is the very phrase which the Korean side wished to eliminate. The question at issue is not whether other personnel are present in Korea; the question is whether or not their status has otherwise been provided for.

4. Mr. Chin inquired whether there were now present in Korea any personnel to whom this provision would apply in addition to the MAAG personnel and the personnel of the Embassy's armed forces attache offices. Mr. Habib replied that there are at present no personnel other than those mentioned for whom status has otherwise been provided.

5. Mr. Chin commented that this provision constituted an exception to the general provisions of the SOFA. In the future, exceptions regarding other personnel, if any, would be provided for in other agreements.

0026

미문 87-10 ⑬

0027

He then proposed acceptance of the U.S. draft of subparagraph (a) and the Korean draft of the Agreed Minute. Mr. Habib replied that the U.S. side would consider this proposal.

6. Turning to subparagraph (b), Mr. Chin stated that the Korean side accepted the additional sentecne proposed by the U.S. side. He said the draft Agreed Minute tabled by the U.S. side was also acceptable, with the exception of the word "readily" in the second line. He suggested that deletion of the word would not change the substance of the sentence. Mr. Habib replied that the degree of availability of certain skills in the United States or Korea was a practical question. The U.S. side believed that "readily available" was a more honest definition of the existing situation. Assuring the Korean side that the United States authorities had no intention of flooding Korea with third country nationals, Mr. Habib agreed to take the Korean proposal under eonsideration.

Entry and Exit

7. Mr. Habib pointed out that sufficient agreement had been reached with regard to subparagraph (b) of the Definitions Article to enable the negotiators to agree on a slight change in paragraph 6 of the Entry and Exit Article. He pointed out that agreement to include the words "of U.S. nationality" after the words "civilian persons" in the first line of subparagraph (b), as well as the additional sentence to which the Korean negotiators

0028

미국 87-10⑭

0029

had just agreed, made necessary the substitution in paragraph 6 of the Entry and Exit Article of the words "nationals of" for the words "ordinarily resident in". Mr. Chih stated that the Korean side agreed to this change in the Entry and Exit Article, and the final text was confirmed.

Joint Committee

8. Turning to the Joint Committee Article, Mr. Chin recalled that the negotiators had reached general agreement on the U.S. draft, except for the phrase "except where otherwise provided" in the first sentence of Paragraph 1. Mr. Chin said he understood that this phrase referred to spcial arrangements regarding communications provided for by Paragraph 2(b) of the second Facilities and Areas Article tabled by the U.S. side. Mr. Habib stated that this was correct and pointed out that Paragraph 2(c) also referred to such arrangements. Mr. Chin stated that the Korean side believed that this phrase should be deleted from the Joint Committee Article and that the provisions should be spelled out in the relevant article regarding communications. He said the primacy of the Joint Committee should be fully established by the SOFA and that no exceptions should be made. The Joint Committee should have the power to consider any problems connected with the implementation of the SOFA and should also have the authority to delegate its functions to "appropriate authorities".

0030

미온 87-10 ⑮

0031

9. Mr. Habib replied that to establish an exception to the Joint Committee's functions in one part of the SOFA and then not to mention that exception in the article dealing with the Joint Committee's functions would create confusion and misunderstanding. He said the Joint Committee's primacy was fully established by the terms of the SOFA. However, the U.S. side believed that certain matters were not appropriate for discussion by the Joint Committee. The Committee was not, in the opinion of the U.S. side, a suitable forum for the discussion of certain matters which would better be handled elsewhere, such as the communication arrangements provided for in the article dealing with facilities and areas. According to the U.S. drafts, such matters would be handled by joint arrangements agreed upon in mutual discussion by the appropriate authorities of both governments. The U.S. side believed that the pre-eminence of the Joint Committee was fully established.

10. Dr. Pak Kun stated that he wished to re-state the Korean position. He said the Joint Committee should be the central, general, and comprehensive organ for consultation regarding SOFA matters. This principle should be established in the article dealing with the Joint Committee. Naturally, technical matters should be handled by appropriate authorities, as set forth in the Facilities and Areas Article. The Korean side believed that specific provisions should take precedence over general provisions. Therefore, the specific provisions of the Facilities and Areas Article would take precedence

0032

기문 87-10 ⑯

0033

over the general provisions of the Joint Committee Article. If this principle is clearly understood, Dr. Pak continued, the Joint Committee Article can be left unhampered by exceptions. Mr. Chin added that if agreement were not reached by the appropriate authorities regarding a specific matter under the provisions of the Facilities and Areas Article, the matter should then be referred to the Joint Committee. The point, he said, is to ensure the flexibility of the Joint Committee.

11. Mr. Habib replied that the Korean side appeared willing to make an exception but unwilling to state in the Joint Committee Article that the exception was being made. He stated that the U.S. formula was a much clearer and simpler statement and suggested that perhaps the phrase "except where otherwise provided" was not fully understood. Since both sides had fully stated their positions without reaching agreement, he did not believe further discussion at this meeting would be fruitful.

Access by Vessels and Aircraft

12. Turning to the article concerning access by vessels and aircraft, Mr. Chin stated that the Korean side had already agreed to paragraphs 1 and 2. On the basis of the U.S. side's explanation of Paragraph 3 at the last meeting, he continued, the Korean side accepted the U.S. draft of that paragraph also. This constituted full agreement on this article.

Navigational Aids and Air Traffic Control

13. Taking up the article dealing with navigational aids, Mr. Habib recalled that during the previous

0034

기록 87-10 ⑪

0035

discussion of this article, the Korean side had asked the basic question of whether such aids were to be established without consultation or through mutual agreement. The U.S. side wished to make it clear, he said, that navigational aids would be established on a coordinated basis as provided in the relevant article. The only exceptions would be in the case of an emergency when aide were needed immediately or in the case of special combat exercises requiring the establishment of navigational aids on a temporary basis. He pointed out that mutual consultation has been the practice in the past and will continue to be the practice in the furture.

14. Mr. Habib remarked that the Korean side had also questioned the meaning of the phrase "shall conform generally" in the U.S. draft, He explained that there are some types of equipment required by the U.S. Armed Forces which are not usable under the navigational aid system now in effect in Korea. This equipment includes the SHORAN system, used primarily for pinpoint bombing and the LORAN system for long-range navigation. In addition, he pointed out, there is the TACAN equipment designed for use by military aircraft in positioning themselves relative to the 38th Parallel. None of these systems is in use by the Korean civilian authorities. In ivew of constant technological changes, Mr. Habib continued, the U.S. side prefers use of the term "generally".

15. Mr. Chin suggested that the practice of mutual consultation be spelled out in Paragraph 2. Mr Habib

0036

미분 87-10 (18)

0037

replied that it is spelled out in Paragraph 1 and that Paragraphs 1 and 2 go together. He pointed out that Paragraph 2 of the U.S. draft gives the U.S. Armed Forces the right to establish, construct, and maintain navigational aids. In effect, there is little difference between the two drafts. However, the Korean draft speakes of areas and territorial waters "adjacent to" established facilities. This is not always practicable in the case of navigational aids. Mr. Chin replied that Mr. Habib's statements had answered the questions raised by the Korean side. He suggested that in Paragraph 2 the following additional phrase be added to the first sentence, following the word "thereof": "through agreement between appropriate authorities of the two governments". Mr. Habib said the U.S. side would consider this proposal.

Facilities and Areas

16. Turning to the drafts of the Facilities and Areas Articles which had been tabled by both sides at the previous meeting, Mr. Chin suggested paragraph by paragraph discussion and asked Mr. Habib to explain the U.S. drafts.

17. Mr. Habib noted that in Paragraph 1(a) of the first U.S. draft article and the corresponding first two paragraphs of the Korean draft article there were certain differences in the use of terms. The U.S. draft spoke of "agreements" rather than "arrangements" because the former term was believed to be more accurately descriptive

0038

미문 87-10 ⑲

0039

of what is intended and would include documents. The term "concluded" obviously went with "agreements", just as "arrangements" were "made" in the Korean draft. A more substantive difference was the use in the U.S. draft of the words "wherever located" and "used" instead of the term "necessary" which appeared in the Korean draft. He stated that this particular language had been used as a result of our experience with the operation of the Japanese SOFA. The U.S. side felt that it was an improvement over the language of the latter Agreement, since experience had shown that furnishings and equipment relating to a facility were not always entirely located within that specific facility. Furthermore, he pointed out, a radio frequency is a facility and yet cannot be said to be located at any precise location. The word "used" reflects fact, whereas the word "necessary" limplies judgement.

18. Mr. Habib continued his analysis by pointing out that Paragraph 1(b) of the U.S. draft and Paragraph 3 of the ROK draft differed to some extent. He asked the Korean side to explain their phrase "for the purpose of this Agreement", which appeared to be redundant. He also requested an explanation of the phrase "surveyed and determined". Pointing out that acquisition documents for all of the areas and facilities presently in use are in existence and will undoubtedly be registered with the Joint Committee, he expressed the opinion that the second sentence of the Korean Paragraph 3 detracted from the previous sentence. He pointed out that Paragraph

0040

미문 81-10 (20)

0041

1(a) of the U.S. draft provides for agreements regarding these facilities and areas to be concluded by the Joint Committee.

19. In reply, Mr. Chin stated that the Korean side has used the word "arrangements" rather than "arrangements" because the former was a broader term, more all-inclusive and more flexible than the latter. Pointing out the phrase in the Korean draft "as provided for in this Agreement" which was not provided in Paragraph 1(a) of the first Article, the U.S. draft, he commented that the Republic of Korea will authorize the use of the areas and facilities not only on the basis of the Mutual Defense Treaty, but also in accordance with relevant provisions of the SOF Agreement. Commenting on the U.S. draft, he questioned the use of the word "wherever located" in view of the use of the word "used" in this connection. He suggested that both sides compare and study the wording of the two drafts in connection with the use of the word "used" in the U.S. draft and the phrase "necessary to the operation of" in the Korean draft with a view to working out a more acceptable phrase at the next meeting. He said the Korean side would reconsider the use of the phrase "for the purpose of this Agreement" and "under this Agreement". Regarding the second sentence of Paragraph 2 in the Korean draft, particularly in regard to the words "surveyed and determined", Mr. Chin said that it is not intended to change the status or the scope of the existing facilities and areas which come under the first sentence of the Paragraph. Its intention is to

0042

미문 87-10 (21)

0043

confirm the existing facilities and areas in use by the U.S. armed forces at the time of coming into force of this Agreement. He further said that such matters as the return or the additional provision of the facilities and areas would be appropriately provided for in relevant paragraphs of the Article.

20. Regarding Paragraph 2 of the U.S. draft and the corresponding Paragraph 6 of the Korean draft, Mr. Habib stated that the only substantial difference lay in the provision in the U.S. draft for the return of portions of facilities. He expressed the view that this language was preferable. Mr. Chin commented that the antecedent of the word "such" in the U.S. draft should be spelled out.

Next Meeting

21. At this point, the negotiators having been in continous session for two and one-half hours, it was agreed to adjourn. The next meeting was scheduled for January 16 at 2:00 p.m.

Points of Agreement

22. a. Entry and Exit Article (Text attached)

b. Access by Vessels and Aircraft Article (Text attached)

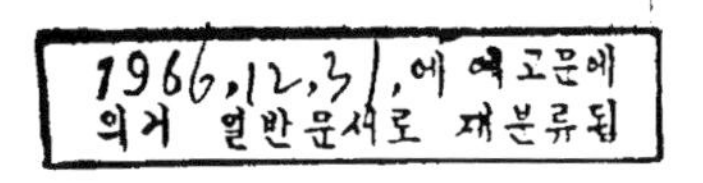

0044

0045

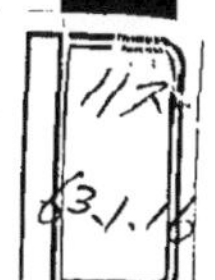

JOINT SUMMARY RECORD OF THE 11TH SESSION
STATUS OF FORCES NEGOTIATIONS

January 16, 1963

1. Time and Place: 2:00 to 4:00 p.m. January 16, 1963 at the Foreign Minister's Conference Room

II. Attendants:

ROK Side:

Mr. Chin, Pil Shik	Director Bureau of Political Affairs Ministry of Foreign Affairs
Mr. Pak, Kun	Chief, America Section Ministry of Foreign Affairs
Mr. O, Won yong	Chief, Treaty Section Ministry of Foreign Affairs
Col. Lee, Nam Koo	Chief, Military Affairs Section Ministry of National Defense
Mr. Chu, Mun Ki	Chief, Legal Affairs Section Ministry of Justice
Mr. Lee, Kyung Hoon	2nd Secretary Ministry of Foreign Affairs
Mr. Shin, Chung Sup	2nd Secretary Ministry of Foreign Affairs
Mr. Chi, Sung Koo	Press Officer Ministry of Foreign Affairs
Mr. Kang Suk Jae	3rd Secretary Ministry of Foreign Affairs

US Side:

Mr. Philip C. Habib	Counslor of the Embassy for Political Affairs
Brig. Gen. J.D. Lawlor	Deputy Chief of Staff 8th Army
Mr. William J. Ford	First Secretary of the Embassy
Col. W. A. Solf	Staff Judge Advocate 8th Army
Mr. Benhamin A. Fleck (Rapporteur and Press officer)	First Secretary of the Embassy

0046

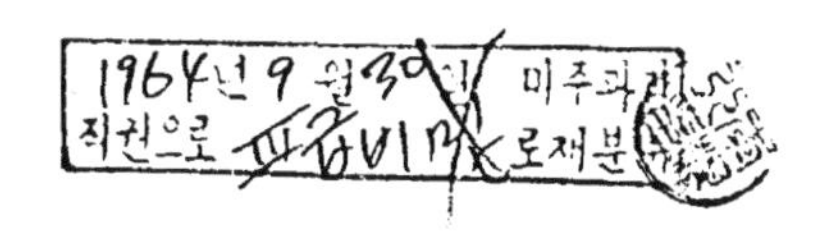

미문 87-11(12)

0047

Mr, Robert A. Lewis	Second Secretary and Consul of the Embassy
Lt. Col. Crawford	Staff Judge Advocate 8th Army
Lt. Col. W. A. Burt	J-5
Kenneth Campen	Interpreter

1. Before beginning substantive discussion, Mr. Habib introduced Colonel Kenneth C. Crawford, of the Staff Judge Advocate's Office, EUSA, who was attending the meeting in place of Lt. Col. R?.E. Miller, Mr. Habib noted the absence of Col. G. G. O'Connor because of illness and of Captain R. M. Brownlie, who was also unable to attend the meeting. Mr. Chin noted the absence of Mr. Yi Kyung-ho and Mr. Shin Kwan-sup. He introduced Mr. Chu Mun-ki, Chief of the Legal Affairs Section in the Ministry of Justice, who was attending in place of Mr. Yi, and Major Ahn Seung Keun from the Ministry of Defense.

Joint Committee

2. In opening substantive discussion, Mr. Chin asked whether the U.S. side had any additional remarks to make concerning the Joint Committee article. Mr. Habib replied that at previous negotiating sessions, the negotiators had reached full agreement on the text of the article, except for the phrase "except where otherwise provided" at the end of the first sentence of paragraph 1 in the U.S. draft. He reminded the negotiators that this phrase had been inserted in anticipation of certain special communications arrangements as provided for under the provisions of the relevenat facilities and areas article. Requesting the Korean side to reconsider its opposition to inclusion of the phrase, Mr.

0048

마른 81-11 ⊖

0049

Habib pointed out that the Joint Committee article was fundamental to the entire SOFA, inasmuch as it established the mechanism for the smooth coordination and effective implementation of the provisions of the Agreement. He urged acceptance of the U. S. draft in keeping with what the U.S. side understood was the desire of both sides to obtain speedy agreement with respect to certain key articles.

3. Mr. Chin replied that the Korean side had carefully considered this matter. He said it was his understanding that the phrase referred solely to paragraph 2(b) of the second facilities and areas draft article tabled by the U.S. side. He inquired whether it also referred to any other draft articles which might be tabled at a later date. Mr. Habib pointed out that the phrase referred to both paragraph 2(b) and 2(c) of the relevant facilites and areas article and stated that it was the understanding of the U. S. side, on the basis of their instructions, that no reference to any other portion of the SOFA was intended or planned.

4. Mr. Chin stated that the provisions of paragraph 2(b) were clearly spelled out but that the reference in paragraph 2(c) to the word "agreements" was vague. He requested an explanation of the word "agreements". Mr. Habib replied that the word referred to any agreements entered into with the Korean authorities by the U.S. authorities. In this connection, he mentioned that one such agreement would be one providing for U.S. notification to the International Frequency Registration Board of frequencies used by the U. S. armed forces in Korea

0050

미원 81-11 ⑥

0051

5. Mr. Chin proposed that the phrase "except where otherwise provided" be retained in the text of the Joint Committee Article and that an Agreed Minute be approved which would explain the reference of this phrase to paragraph 2(b) and 2(c) of the relevant facilities and areas article. Mr. Habib asked whether the Korean side was prepared to table a draft of the Agreed Minute. Mr. Chin suggested that the Agreed Minute read as follows:

> "The exception provided for in the first sentence of paragraph 1 is relevant only to paragraph 2, subparagraphs (b) and (c) of Article _____."

6. Mr. Habib suggested that this explanation be written into the Joint summary record instead of being made an Agreed Minute. However, he agreed to consider the Korean proposal.

Facilities and Areas

7. Turning to the drafts of the facilities and areas artciles, Mr. Chin noted that at the previous meeting views were exchanged on paragraphs 1 and 2 of the U.S. draft article "A" and the corresponding paragraphs (1, 2, 3 and 6) of the Korean draft. He suggested that the negotiators proceed with an examination of paragraphs 3 and 4 of the U.S. draft and the corresponding paragraphs 7 and 8 of the Korean draft.

8. Mr. Habib pointed out that the chief difference between paragraph 3 of the U.S. draft and paragraph 7 of the Korean draft was the provision in the U.S. draft that facilities are to be returned to the Republic of Korea "under such conditions as may be agreed through

0052

미본 87-11 ④

0053

the Joint Committee." He reminded the negotiators that the U. S. armed forces continuously review the possibility of retruning facilities no longer needed. Obsiously, he said, once the return of a facility is decided upon, it would be returned under whatever provisions the Joint Committee agrees to. He asked whether the Korean side had any other procedure or considerations in mind. He also referred to the use of the word "promptly" in the Korean draft and stated that its use was unncessary since any facility being returned would be returned promptly once the Joint Committee agreed on the conditions of its return. Mr. Chin stated that the words "under such conditions as may be agreed through the Joint Committee" were unnecessary, because it is taken for granted that procedural matters concerning the return of facilities and areas no longer needed would be a matter of mutual consultation at the Joint committee. He said the Korean draft did not spell out the details concerning procedural matters connected to the return of facilites becauce the Joint Committee is the body which will implement the provisions of the SOFA. He stated, however, that there was no substantial difference between the two paragraphs. It was agreed that this paragraph presented no difficult problem.

9. Turning to paragraph 4 of the U.S. draft and the corresponding paragraphs 8 and 9 of the Korean draft, Mr. Habib suggested that subparagraph (2) of the U.S. draft was clearer than the Korean paragraph 8. The phrase "and the Government of the Republic of Korea is so advised" is more explicit as to the exact time when the facilites in question would be made available for interim use. The final half of subparagraph (a),

0054

미문 87-11⑤

0055

he continued, tightens up the procedures and provides a cooperative basis for making the facilities available for interim use. Mr. Habib pointed out that the subparagraph serves two basic purposes: (a) it sets a time schedule, and (b) it provides for cooperation and coordination.

10. Mr. Chin stated that there was no substantive difference between the two drafts; the U.S. draft merely elaborated the subject. Since the Joint Committee will always operate in the spirit indicated in the U.S. draft, the Korean side saw no necesssity to elaborate in this article the manner in which the Joint Committee shall perform its functions. He also suggested that the phrase "and the Government of the Republic of Korea is so advised" was unnecessary. Mr. Habib replied that the U.S. side believed the phrase desirable because it would providee the means of avoiding a debate over when any particular facility was to be returned. He said debates at a later date over the meaning of provisions of the Agreement should be avoided whenever possible by making the language of the Agreement as specific as possible. Mr. Chin replied that the two sides were in general agreement. The only disagreement was in how to state the substance of the subparagraph.

11. Mr. Habib noted that paragraph 9 of the Korean draft omitted the words "armed froces" and spoke of a "limited period of time" instead of "limited periods of time". Otherwise, he pointed out that paragraph 9 and subparagraph 4(b) of the U.S. draft are identical.

0056

미묘 81-11⑥

0057

Article "B"

12. Mr. Chin noted that there appeared to be little difference between paragraph 1 of the U.S. draft article "B" and the Korean paragraph 10, except for the sentence in the U.S. draft beginning "in an emergency..". He requested an explanation of this sentence. Mr. Habib replied by stating that this provisions was contained in the SOFA with Japan in the form of a separate Agreed Minute. The U.S. side believed it preferable to embody it in the text of the article rather than in an accompanying Agreed Minute. He said that experience has shown that safety measures are necessary in the vicinity of facilities to protect against subversive activities during emergency situations. He pointed out that during the present condition of armed truce, security is a paramount consideration. He added that the only other difference between the two texts lay in the U. S, wording "United States armed forces" as compared with the Korean wording "Government of the United States". He said that as a practical matter, the armed forces would make any such request on behalf of the United States Government. In addition, he pointed out, both drafts contain the additional requirement of consultation through the Joint Committee. Mr. Chin replied that the Korean side believed that since the request is made to the Government of the Republic of Korea, it should be made by the Government of the United States, thus maintaining a balanced government to government situation. He suggested further consideration of this point.

13. Turning to paragraph 2 of the U.S. draft and paragraph 11 of the Korean draft, Mr. Habib pointed out that subparagraph (2) of the U.S. draft and the first

0058

미문 811-11 ⑦

0059

sentence of the Korean paragraph 11 were identical. The only substantive difference between subparagraph (b) and the second sentence of paragraph 11 was the use in the U.S. draft of the phrase "designated military communications authorities" in constrast to the phrase "appropriate authorities of the two Governments" in the Korean draft. He said that the general subject of paragraph 2 had already been discussed during previous discussions of the Joint Committee Article. However, there was in the Korean draft no equivalent to subparagraph (c), which stated an obligation on the Korean government which the U.S. side believed was a corollary to the obligation placed on the U.S. armed forces by the provisions of subparagraph (a). The U.S. side believed that a mutual obligation existed and should be so stated in the article. With regard to subparagraph (c),Mr. Habib said he wished to remind the negotiators again that one of the agreements envisioned would provide for U.S. notification to the International Frequency Registration Board of frequencies used by the U.S. armed forces in Korea.

14. Mr. Habib pointed out that paragraph 3 of the U.S. draft and paragraph 12 of the Korean draft were identical.

15. Mr. Chin stated that the Korean side fully understood the delegation of authority provided in subparagraph (b) of the U.S. draft. However, they had used the word "appropriate" in paragraph 11 because of its broad, all-inclusive nature (which encompassed the Joint Committee) and because this word had been used elsewhere in the Agreement. Mr. Habib replied that the U.S. side believed a more specific term was

0060

미문 87-11 (8)

0061

desirable in this instance, so as not to involve unnecessarily authorities who had no specific interest or competence in these highly technical classified matters. It was agreed to give further consideration to this question.

Article "C"

16. Mr. Habib pointed out that paragraph 1 of the U.S. draft article "C" was identical with the first sentence of paragraph 13 of the Korean draft. However, the second sentence of paragraph 13 introduced a subject (compensation) which would be discussed in greater detail in connection with U.S. draft article "D". He invited the Korean side to explain their position, if they cared to do so at that juncture. Mr. Chin suggested that discussion of the compensation issue be deferred until the negotiation reached the U.S. draft article "D". Mr. Habib agreed, but pointed out that the point at issue was the provision of facilities and not the source of those facilities. Whether they were originally privately or publicly owned was irrelevant.

17. In reply to Mr. Chin's request for an explanation of paragraph 2 of the U.S. draft, Mr. Habib replied that to state it in simple terms: "What's ours is ours and we can remove it if we wish to do so". Mr. Chin replied that if it were that simple, there was no need to spell it out in the Agreement.

18. Mr. Chin pointed out that paragraph 14 of the Korean draft did not appear in the U.S. draft and could be inserted without difficulty. Mr. Habib replied that the U.S. Government had decided not to request payment of residual value and therefore this provision

0062

미북 87-11 (9)

0063

was omitted from the U.S. draft. He said he agreed in principle to its inclusion but suggested further discussion. However, he indicated the belief of the U.S. side that the words "supply or other materials left thereon" were not relevant and should be omitted. He added that paragraph 3 in the U.S. draft, although it did not appear in the Korean draft, presented no problem and was closely related to paragraph 2.

Article "D"

19. The negotiators then proceeded to discussion of the U.S. draft article "D" and the corresponding paragraphs 4 and 5 of the Korean draft. Mr. Habib said there existed a fundamental difference of opinion regarding the payment of compensation for the use of facilities and areas. He said the views of the U.S. side were well known. The U.S. draft, he continued, states that the United States Government will pay all expenses incident to the maintenance of the U.S. armed forces in Korea except for those to be paid by the Korean Government as provided in paragraph 2. In contrast, paragraph 4 of the Korean draft would place on the U.S. Government the obligation to pay compensation. He reminded the negotiators that early in the negotiations, and also prior to them, the U.S. Government had stated clearly and explicitly its view that no compensation would be paid. There has been no change since then, he said. The United States does not accept, he continued, any distinction in the origin of the facilities. All facilities, he stated, are made available to the U.S. armed forces by the Korean Government. Obviously, however, he continued, the U.S. armed forces are prepared to cooperate to the maximum extent possible

0064

by releasing facilities no longer needed or by accept-

기명 87-11 ⑩

0065

ing alternate facilities offered by the Korean Government. He pointed out that the United States Government has adhered to the principle of no compensation in all of the mutual security negotiations in which it has engaged, on the grounds that the facilities provided are the host country's contribution to the joint effort. There is no reason to deviate from this policy in Korea, he said. He then asked Mr. Chin to state the Korean views.

20. Mr. Chin stated that the Korean side was not unaware of the U. S. position. But, he said, he would like to explain the Korean position from a broader view point rather than on any legal or technical basis. One of the major objectives of the Status of Forces Agreement, he continued, is to further strengthen the friednly relations between the Republic of Korea and the United States. He said that in preparing its draft, the Korean side had fully considered the U.S. position on this matter as well as the objectives of the SOFA, and consequently has limited its request for compensation only to the private property as the minimum necessary compensation. He said that if the U.S. would agree to the Korean proposal it would make a great contribution to an early conclusion of the SOFA and to the attainment of the above objective.

21. Mr. Habib replied that he wished to make clear that the question of compensating private owners was not being debated. The U.S. side agreed that there may be a responsibility to compensate them but held that it was not the responsibility of the United States but of the Government of the Republic of Korea.

0066

미봉 87-11 ⑪

0067

He said it was well known that the United States Government was already making contributions to the Korean Government. The United States is not prepared, he continued, to increase its present contributions in this manner. Mr. Chin requested favorable consideration of the Korean proposal. In reply, Mr. Habib said the U.S. side would give the proposal consideration but not favorable consideration. Mr. Chin stated that this was a difficult matter for both sides and proposed further consideration which might lead to a solution satisfactory to both sides.

22. Mr. Habib then tabled paragraphs 3 and 4 of the U.S. draft of article "D", concerning utilities and services. Mr. Chin stated that the Korean side has also prepared corresponding paragraphs but would not table them unless they differed from the U.S. draft, in which case they would be tabled at the next meeting.

23. Mr. Habib proposed that the facilities and areas draft be divided tentatively in separate articles, along the lines of the U.S. draft, in order to make progress possible. It was agreed that the chairman should meet and decide how to handle this question.

24. The next meeting was scheduled for January 24 at 3 p.m.

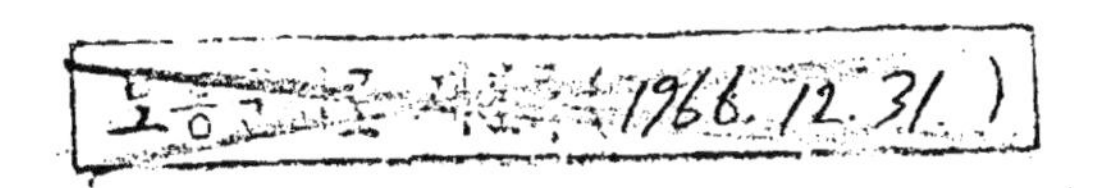

미문 81-11 ⑫ (12)

0069

JOINT SUMMARY RECORD OF THE 12TH SESSION

STATUS OF FORCES NEGOTIATIONS

January 24, 1963

1. Time and Place: 2:00 to 4:00 p.m. January 24, 1963 at the Foreign Minister's Conference Room

II. Attendants:

ROK Side:

Mr. Chin, Pil Shik	Director Bureau of Political Affairs Ministry of Foreign Affairs
Mr. Shin, Kwan Sup	Director Bureau of Costums Duty Ministry of Finance
Mr. Pak, Kun	Chief, America Section Ministry of Foreign Affairs
Mr. O, Won Yong	Chief, Treaty Section Ministry of Foreign Affairs
Col. Lee, Nam Koo	Chief, Military Affairs Section Ministry of National Defense
Mr. Chu, Mun Ki	Chief, Legal Affairs Section Ministry of Justice
Mr. Lee, Kyung Hoon	2nd Secretary Ministry of Foreign Affairs
Mr. Shin, Chung Sup	2nd Secretary Ministry of Foreign Affairs
Mr. Chi, Sung Koo	Press Officer Ministry of Foreign Affairs
Mr. Kang, Suk Jae	3rd Secretary Ministry of Foreign Affairs

US Side:

Brig. Gen. J. D. Lawlor	Deputy Chief of Staff 8th Army
Mr. William J. Ford	First Secretary of the Embassy
Col. G. G. O'Connor	Deputy Chief of Staff 8th Army
Capt. R.M. Brownlie	Assistant Chief of Staff USN/K
Col. W. A. Solf	Staff Judge Advocate 8th Army

0070

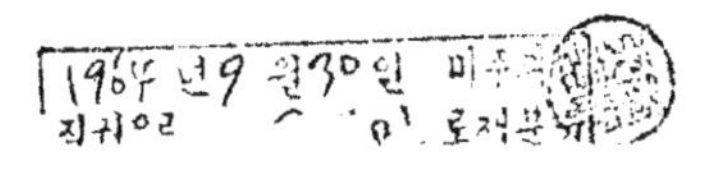

情·음 81-120 (9)

0071

Col. Kenneth C. Crawford	Staff Judge Advocate 8th Army
Mr. Benjamin A. Fleck (Rapporteur and Press Officer)	First Secretary of the Embassy
Mr. Robert A. Lewis	Second Secretary and Consul of the Embassy
Kenneth Campen	Interpreter

Customs

1. In taking up the customs article for discussion, Mr. Chin noted that at the previous discussion, the Korean side had indicated readiness to accept the text of the original paragraph 2 in the U.S. draft, provided a slight modification was made in the phrase "other armed forces". Gen. Lawlor replied that Agreed Minutes 4 and 5 in the U.S. draft would provide certain safeguards against abuses of the provisions of paragraph 2. He said the U.S. side still preferred the revised text of paragraph 2 which it had tabled during the previous discussion because the language had greater clarity. He said there was no substantive difference between the revision and the original text. Mr. Chin replied that although the U.S. side believed the revision to be more precise, the Korean side believed the original text to be clearer and therefore preferred to continue discussion on the basis of the original draft. He then proposed the addition of the words "under the Unified Command" following the phrase "in Korea" inthe final sentence of original draft. He said the addition would not change the meaning and would include Katusas and any other non-U.S. forces serving as part of the Unified Command.

2. Gen. Lawlor replied that the U.S. side would take this apparently minor change under advisement.

0072

미북 87-12 (2)

0073

He said the U.S. side also wished to make a minor change. He then proposed substituting the word "activities" for the word "organizations" and placing the phrase "including their authorized procurement agencies and their non-appropriated fund activities provided for in Article ____" in parentheses. He indicated that the change should be made twice in paragraph 2, once in paragraph 5, sub-paragraph (c), and in the Agreed Minute #3, relating to paragraph 4(c). He indicated that the change was not intended to alter the substance of the phrase but merely to clarify it. Mr. Chin asked whether the change would broaden the scope of the paragraph. Gen. Lawlor replied that it would not. He said the activities under discussion were usually referred to as "activities" and not as "organizations". It was felt that by suing the word "activities", these functions were identified more readily as part of the armed forces, whereas use of the word "organizations" might give the false implication that they were not part of the armed forces. Mr. Chin stated that the Korean side would study the U.S. proposal.

3. Turning to paragraph 3, subparagraph (b), Mr. Chin stated that during the previous discussion, the Korean side had proposed to limit the period during which importation of vehicles and parts would take place. Gen. Lawlor said such a limitation would present a serious problem. He pointed out that privately-owned vehicles might have to be replaced, owing to theft, fair wear and tear, or collision, since in many cases these vehicles were the only means which their owners had of proceeding to and from their residences and places of duty. Imposition of a customs duty on parts

0074

마 87-12③

0075

or vehicles brought in as replacements would, he continued, have a serious adverse effect on morale. He pointed out that the ability of the ROK Government to protect its interests would not be affected, since the disposal of privately-owned vehicles within Korean territory is subject to regulatory and tax regulations. He also reminded the Korean side of other practical difficulties, such as the great distances which these vehicles and parts had to be shipped, the frequent necessity of waiting for the factory to fill an order, and the unexpected delays caused by strikes.

4. Mr. Chin replied that the Korean side had given these matters very careful study. He said the Korean side did not wish to cause any inconvenience to the personnel of the U.S. armed forces. However, the Korean side did feel that a time limit was necessary and suggested that a certain time limit be set, Gen. Lawlor asked what the Korean side feared if there were no time limit. Mr. Chin reiterated his statement that there was no desire to cause any inconvenience to the U.S. personnel and added that a time limit was necessary in order to limit the number of vehicles imported. Gen. Lawlor stated that the U.S. side would consider the Korean position but remined the Korean side that Agreed Minute #5 in the U.S. draft should take care of any problem that might arise.

5. Turning to paragraph 5, Mr. Chin stated that the Korean side was still studying subparagraph (a) of the U.S. draft and would comment at a subsequent meeting. He asked for U.S. comments on subparagraph (b). Gen. Lawlor replied that the speedy delivery of mail to the troops was also a morale factor. He pointed out that

0076

미문 87-12④

0077

the proposed Agreed Minutes would provide safeguards against abuses. He reminded the ROK side that the U.S. authorities were just as interested as the ROK Authorities in seeing to it that no abuses occurred. Mr. Chin reminded the negotiators of the Korean side's previous proposal to insert the word "official" before the word "mail". Gen. Lawlor said the U.S. side had considered this proposal but did not favor it. He pointed out that the subject of discussion was the private mail of individuals. Mr. Chin said that the Korean side did not wish to cause any damage to the morale of the troops, and reminded the U.S. negotiators of his previous assurance that the ROK Government would do its best to ensure speedy delivery of mails. He said the Korean customs officials would always be cooperative. Gen. Lawlor expressed the appreciation of the U.S. side for the considerate attitude of the Korean side and said that the U.S. side would take the Korean position under advisement.

6. Mr. Chin then pointed out that paragraph 3(c), which had already been agreed to by both sides, provided for the importation of "reasonable quantities" of personal effects and household goods through military post offices, free of customs duties. Therefore, he continued, it would be only logical and proper for the Korean customs officers to be given authority under paragraph 5(b) to check the unofficial mail to insure that only reasonable amounts of these items were being shipped in through the military post offices. The provisions of the two paragraphs would then be consistent, he added, Gen. Lawlor stated that the U.S. side would consider this position.

0078

미묵 87-12(E)

0079

7. With regard to subparagraph (c), Mr. Chin stated that there is a differnce between cargo consigned to the U. S. armed fordes and cargo consigned to non-appropriated fund organizations. He said the sources of funds in payment for these two types of cargo were different and stated the belief of the Korean side that the goods consigned to the armed forces were more important for military purposes than goods consigned to non-appropriated fund organizations. Gen. Lawlor replied non-appropriated fund activities were considered to be part of the armed forces. He said it would be very difficult to assign degrees of importance to the various items the U.S. armed forces needed to import into Korea; all such items contribute to the operational efficiency of the troops. He pointedout that non-appropriated fund activities have to do with the mental attitudes and welfare of the soldier. He added that the authorities of the U.S. armed forces police these activities and that if and when abuses are found, corrective action is taken.

8. Mr. Chin replied that he understood the position of the U.S. side. He stated that much of the cargo shipped to the armed forces might be of a classified nature. Naturally, he said, the customs officials would not check this cargo. However, the cargo shipped to the non-appropriated fund organizations would not be classified and therefore it would not be inconvenient to the U.S. armed forces to have the Korean customs officials check it. These officials, Chin, stated, would do their best to cooperate so as not to cause any unnecessary inconvenience.

0080

미문 87-12 ⓑ

0081

Gen. Lawlor pointed out that a great deal of the cargo shipped to the armed forces is of an unclassified nature; hence the categorization was not valid.

9. Mr. Chin then suggested that the phrase and their non-appropriated fund organizations provided for in Articles be deleted from subparagraph (c). He pointed out that the U.S. side had already differentiated cargo shipped to these organization from other types by making specific reference to it in the draft Agreed Minute #1. The Agreed Minute restricts importation of this type of cargo to "reasonable" quantities, and therefore the Korean customs officials should be authorized to examine such cargo to find out if the quantities of cargo are "reasonable".

He said that there was no question of taxation; this was merely a matter of examination. He again stated that the Korean customs officials would be cooperative.

10. Gen. Lawlor replied that the obligation stated in the Agreed Minute #1 was a unilateral obligation on the U.S. armed forces. Mr. Chin said the Korean side believed that the determination of what is a "reasonable" amount should be a mutual determination. In response to Gen. Lawlor's a query as to how such a mutual determination could be arrived at, Mr. Chin said that a "reasonable" amount is a reasonable amount and that the Korean customs officials would cooperate.

11. Mr. Chin noted that paragraphs 6, 7, and 8 had already been agreed to. He reminded the negotiators that the Korean side, in the previous discussion, had

0082

기통 87-12①

0083

suggested the insertion of Paragtaph 7(e) of the Korean draft between Paragraphs 9(c) and 9(d) of the U.S. draft and that the U.S. side had agreed to consider this proposal. He then suggested that the negotiators leave off their discussion of the Agreed Minutes to the customs and duties Article in view of the passage of time, and turn their attention to the remaining items on the agenda. At this point, the negotiators exchanged drafts of the articles dealing with meteorological services, respect for local law, and enrollement and training of reservists. The Korean side also tabled the draft of an article dealing with utilities and services.

Respect for Local Law

12. Mr. Chin commented that the drafts of this article were identical with the exception of minor differences. He asked whether the reference to "persons who are present in the Republic of Korea pursuant to Article____" referred to persons other than those specified in the Definitions Article as being members of the U.S. armed forces. Gen. Lawlor replied that this reference was to an article which had not yet been tabled. Mr. Chin indicated agreement with the U.S. draft article, except for this phrase, which the said the Korean side would take under advisement.

Training of Reservists

13. The differences between the two drafts of this article were noted. Gen. Lawlor pointed out that the

0084

다봉 87-128

0085

U.S. draft included persons who might be present in Korea but not necessarily resident in Korea. Mr. Chin stated that the Korean side would study this point.

14. It was then decided to adjourn the meeting. The next meeting was scheduled for February 5 at 2:00 p.m.

1966.12.31에 예고문에 의거 일반문서로 재분류됨

0086

미문 87-12(9)

0087

JOINT SUMMARY RECORD OF THE 13TH SESSION

STATUS OF FORCES NEGOTIATIONS

February 4, 1963

I. Time and Place: 2:00 to 4:00 p.m. February 4, 1963 at the Foreign Minister's Conference Room

II. Attendants:

ROK Side:

Mr. Shin, Kwan Sup	Director Bureau of Costums Duty Ministry of Finance
Mr. Pak, Kun	Counselor of Embassy
Mr. Koo, Choong Whay	Chief, America Section Ministry of Foreign Affairs
Mr. O, Won Yong	Chief, Treaty Section Ministry of Foreign Affairs
Col. Lee, Nam Koo	Chief, Military Affairs Section Ministry of National Defense
Mr. Lee, Kyung Hoon	2nd Secretary Ministry of Foreign Affairs
Mr. Shin, Chung Sup	2nd Secretary Ministry of Foreign Affairs
Mr. Kang Suk Jae	3rd Secretary Ministry of Foreign Affairs
Mr. Lee, Chang Bum	3rd Secretary Ministry of Foreign Affairs

US Side:

Mr. Philip C. Habib	Counselor of the Embassy for Political Affairs
Brig. Gen. J. D. Lawlor	Deputy Chief of Staff 8th Army

0088

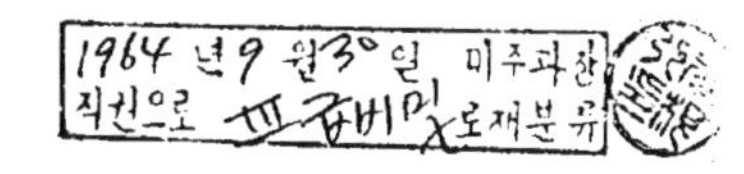

關·문 87-130(11)

0089

Mr. William J. Ford	First Secretary of the Embassy
Col. G. G. O'Connor	Deputy Chief of Staff 8th Army
Capt. R. M. Brownlie	Assistant Chief of Staff USN/K
Col. W. A. Solf	Staff Judge Advocate 8th Army
Mr. Benjamin A. Fleck (Rapporteur and Press Officer)	First Secretary of the Embassy
Mr. Robert A. Lewis	Second Secretary and Consul of the Embassy
Lt. Col. R. E. Miller	Staff Officer, JAG 8th Army
Lt. Col. W. A. Burt	J-5

1. Mr. Shin opened the meeting by noting the absence of the Korean Chief Negotiator, Mr. Chin Pil Shik who was on an official trip abroad. He also noted the absence of Mr. Lee Kyung Ho. Mr. Shin then announced that Dr. Pak Kun, having received transfer orders to the Korean Embassy in Washington, was attending his last negotiating meeting. Mr. Shin introduced Dr. Pak's successor as Chief of the America Section, Ministry of Foreign Affairs, and as a member of the Korean negotiating team, Mr. Koo Choong Whay. Mr. Shin also announced that Mr. Chi Sung Koo had been appointed as Chief of the Southeast Asia Section and, therefore, would no longer participate in the negotiations. Mr. Lee Kyong Hoon will act for the time being, as Press Officer for the Korean side in place of Mr. Chi. Mr. Habib expressed appreciation for the helpful role which Dr. Pak had played on the negotiation and welcomed Mr. Koo.

0090

예동 81-13②

0091

Respect for Local Law

2. Turning to substantive matters, Mr. Habib announced that regrettably he would have to leave the meeting early. He suggested, therefore, that the draft articles concerning respect for local law and training of reservists be taken up for discussion first. Mr. Shin agreed.

3. Mr. Habib reminded the negotiators that at the previous meeting, the Korean side had questioned the meaning of the phrase "the persons who are present in the Republic of Korea pursuant to Article ______. " He said that this phrase had been included in the U.S. draft because the Definitions Article does not include invited contractors. This phrase refers to the draft article dealing with invited contractors. The U.S. draft of the respect for law article, therefore, was more comprehensive than the Korean draft, for it added invited contractors to the list of people called upon to respect Korean law and to refrain from political activity in Korea.

4. Mr. Shin asked whether the phrase included the dependents and the employees of invited contractors. Mr. Habib replied in the affirmative. He said it included all persons who were in the Republic of Korea pursuant to the invited contractors article. Mr. Shin then stated that the Korean side wished to reserve its position until the invited contractors article was tabled. Mr. Habib replied that this was satisfactory to the U.S. side. He asked whether he was correct in concluding that the respect for local law article was generally acceptable to the Korean side if the terms of the invited contractors

0092

미문 87-13 ②

0033

article were as he had explained them. Mr. Shin replied that because of the reference to employees of invited contractors, the Korean side wished to discuss this article when the invited contractors article was tabled.

Enrollment and Training of Reservists

5. Discussion of the article dealing with reservists centered around the difference between persons "residing in" Korea in the Korean draft and persons "who are in" Korea in the U.S. draft. Mr. Habib pointed out that there are Americans present in Korea who are not residents of the country. As examples, he mentioned Embassy personnel and civilian employees of the U.S. armed forces. He said that the phraseology of the U.S. draft would permit such people to undertake training here in Korea in order to maintain their reserve status. Mr. Shin replied that under the provisions of the U.S. draft, persons who have not established legal residence in Korea might be called to reserve training. In such case, the Korean immigration authorities might have difficulty keeping track of them. The Korean side, he said, wished that this provision would not cause any confusion or difficulties for the immigration authorities.

6. Mr. Habib referred the negotiators to the entry and exit article, already agreed to which provides that members of the civilian component are not eligible for permanent residence. He said that both the Korean and U.S. drafts of the article under discussion provide for training for residents; the U.S. draft also provided for non-residents.

0034

미몰 87-13 ④

0095

He suggested that this provision would have no effect on the Korean entry and exit procedures and would not cause any problem with regard to control of alien residents.

7. Dr. Pak said that there would be no confusion regarding the reserve training of members of the civilian component and the Embassy staff. However, the ROK Government might have difficulty enforcing its alien entry, exit and registration law if temporary visitors or invited guests of the Government were enrolled for such training. Mr. Habib replied that the Korean side was creating a problem where none existed. Such persons who were enrolled for reserve training would still have to comply with Korean law. The Korean side agreed to consider the matter further.

8. Mr. Habib mentioned one additional point of difference between the two drafts. He said that the U.S. draft called for enrollment in "forces" rather than in "reserve organizations". He said this wording was proposed because it reflected the actual situation in Korea, in which reservists were trained in existing units of the armed forces, rather than in separate reserve organizations. Mr. Habib then expressed his regret that another pressing engagement made it necessary for him to leave the meeting at this point.

Customs and Duties

9. Turning to the customs article, Mr. Shin repeated the previous suggestion of the Korean side that paragraph 7(e) of the Korean draft be inserted after subparagraph (c) of paragraph 9 in the U.S. draft. General Lawlor replied

0096

미분 87-13⑤

0037

that the U.S side would consider this proposal. He suggested that the Agreed Minutes of the U.S. draft be discussed. Mr. Ford stated that the word "organizations" in Agreed Minute #1 should be changed to "activities", in line with the change proposed by the U.S. side at the previous meeting. Mr. Shin replied that the Korean side would discuss this proposed change in conjunction with discussion of the other proposed changes. Mr. Ford asked if the Korean side had any comments regarding Agreed Minute #1.

10. Mr. Shin replied that, in accordance with their previous comments, the Korean side believed that the meaning of "to the extent reasonably required" should be the subject of mutual determination by both Korean and U.S. authorities. With that understanding, and subject to further discussion of the proposed change of "organizations" to "activities", he said the Korean side agreed to the text of Agreed Minute #1. Mr. Ford replied that the U.S. side was not prepared to agree to mutual determination of what is reasonably required but would consider the Korean position.

11. Turning to Agreed Minute #2, Mr. Shin proposed the insertion of the words "reasonable quantities of" between the word "duty" and the word "their". The second sentence of the Minute would then read as follows: "In this connection, members of the United States armed forces or civilian component and their dependents may import free of duty reasonable quantities of their personal and household effects during a period of six months from the date of their first arrival." Mr. Ford replied that the U.S. side would consider this proposal.

0098

미문 87-13⑥

0039

12. General Lawlor asked if the Korean side was proposing that "reasonable quantities" were to be mutually determined even for members of the U.S. armed forces. Mr. Shin replied that inasmuch as the Korean side wished to closely define "reasonable quantities" in regard to goods shipped to non-appropriated fund organizations, they also wished to place a similar restriction on personal and household effects. Since such effects will be permitted entry free of duty, he added, it was desired to place a limitation on the amounts permitted to enter.

13. General Lawlor asked how the Korean side proposed to determine what was a "reasonable" amount. Mr. Shin replied that it was their desire to avoid the importation of excessive amounts, over and above those normally required. Mr. Ford pointed out that this Agreed Minute refers to paragraph 3(a) of the article, which had already been agreed to. He said the Minute was intended to deal with the question of the period during which importation could be made. He pointed out that it was not intended to deal with quantitative restrictions.

14. Dr. Pak said he wished to answer General Lawlor's question regarding the determination of what is reasonable. He said the Korean side intended no inconvenience to the owners or unreasonable restriction on the amount of such goods to be imported. However, if an individual should import an extraordinarily large amount, the Korean side anticipated no difficulty in reaching agreement that this would be unreasonable. Therefore, the additional language proposed by the Korean side would cause no difficulty or unreasonable restriction.

0100

마음 87-13 ⑪

0101

15. Mr. Ford replied that the article provides for policing of its provisions by both sides. There is also a specific reference to abuses or infringement in Agreed Minute #5. He asserted that these would give all necessary protection to Korean interests and would still provide to the U.S. armed forces sufficient freedom to carry out their mission in Korea.

16. Mr. Shin stated that the provision in paragraph 8 of the article for mutual cooperation is vague and not specifically spelled out. He said that it was necessary to provide in the Agreed Minute standards of what is or is not an abuse of the provisions of the article. General Lawlor replied that the Korean side was unduly worried about abuses. However, the U.S. side would consider the Korean proposal.

17. Mr. Shin agreed with Mr. Ford's remark that the determination of what constitues a "reasonable quantity" would be handled by the Joint Committee. When Mr. Ford then asked him why it was necessary to put it in the Agreed Minute, Mr. Shin replied that the Joint Committee had to have some standard. Mr. Fleck pointed out that the term "reasonable quantity" was hardly a precise standard and would have to be defined by the Joint Committee any way. Mr. Shin stated that the U.S. side seemed unduly concerned about the insertion of the proposed phrase.

18. General Lawlor stated that the U.S. side is aware of the problems connected with the importation of these items. He said the armed forces regulations are constantly

0102

마른 81-13⑧

0103

and stringently enforced. He assured the Korean side that they would continue to be so enforced, without the insertion of the language proposed by the Korean side.

19. Dr, Pak then summarized the Korean position. He said the Korean side appreciated the extreme care and concern shown by the armed forces authorities in dealing with these matters. Since the U.S. side assuared that unreasonable quantities of goods were not imported in practice, the insertion of the proposed phrase would not inconvenience anyone. It would be only a preventive measure. The question of defining what is "reasonable" is no problem; when the Joint Committee takes it up, sound judgment and common sense will prevail.

20. Turning to Agreed Minute #3, Mr. Shin observed that no agreement had yet been reached on the text of paragraph 5(c) to which this Minute refers. He proposed that the language be changed to read as follows: "including their authorized procurement agencies but excluding their non-appropriated fund organizations provided for in Article ____". He said this change would be consistent with the position previously stated by the Korean side with regard to paragraph 5(c).

21. General Lawlor stated that there had been no change in the U.S. position on this question. He repeated his comment of the previous meeting that the differentiation which the Korean side was attempting to make between goods imported for the use of the armed forces and goods imported for the non-appropriated fund activities was not a valid

0104

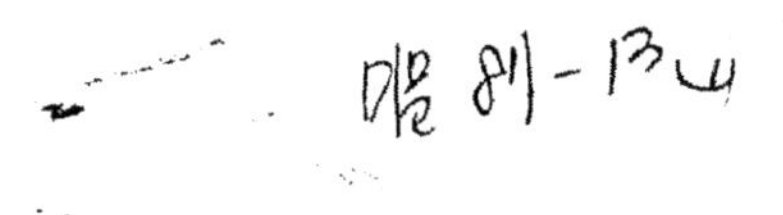

0105

differentiation. He said that many of the items imported for the non-appropriated fund activities were just as important as weapons since they contributed materially to the morale of troops who are thousands of miles from home.

22. Mr. Shin replied that Mr. Chin had previously stated specifically that customs examination of such goods was not intended to inconvenience or hurt the morale of the U.S. armed forces. As the representative on the Korean negotiating team of the Korean customs authorities, Mr. Shin said he again wished to assure the U.S. side that the Korean customs authorities do not intend to cause the U.S. armed forces any unnecessary inconvenience or hinder the completion of their mission.

23. With regard to Agreed Minute #4, Mr. Ford said he wished to make it clear that this Minute was aimed at the importation of harmful substances such as drugs. Mr. Shin acknowledged the clarification and stated that the Korean side agreed to the text of Agreed Minutes #4 and #5 of the U.S. draft.

24. Turning to Agreed Minute #6, Mr. Shin expressed appreciation for the assistance which would be rendered by the U.S. armed forces under the provisions of paragraph 9(b) and this Minute. However, he said, since the U.S. armed forces would in no case act in violation of U.S. laws or service regulations, the Korean side proposed the deletion of the phrase "authorized by United States law and service regulations". He said the meaning of the Minute would be clear without this phrase. Col. Solf replied

0106

대응 87-13 ⑩

0107

that the U.S. side had included the phrase because it wished to make clear that the U.S. armed forces would not and could not take any actions in violation of U.S. laws and service regulations.

25. Mr. Shin stated that cooperation between the U.S. armed forces and the Korean authorities had been good to date. However, the Korean side feared a conflict between Korean regulations and U.S. regulations. Including such specific language in the Agreed Minute might cause undue arguments in the future. Col. Solf replied that the U.S. language was drafted with the intention of avoiding the creation of false assumptions by the Korean authorities at some future date. As an example, he mentioned the fact that the U.S. armed forces cannot try any person over whom they do not have jurisdiction. Retaining the present language of the Minute will prevent arguments in the future, he stated. Mr. Shin said that retaining this language might result in less cooperation by the U.S. armed forces than is now being extended. Dr. Pak added that the phrase "Within their power" was clear enough to the Korean side. General Lawlor brought the discussion to a close by stating that the U.S. side would take the Korean proposal under consideration.

26. It was agreed to hold the next meeting on February 14 at 2:00 p.m.

미울 81-⑬ (11)

0109

JOINT SUMMARY RECORD OF THE 14TH SESSION

STATUS OF FORCES NEGOTIATIONS

February 14, 1963

1. Time and Place: 2:00 to 4:40 p.m. February 14, 1963 at the Conference Room of the Economic Planning Board.

2. Attendants:

ROK Side:

Mr. Chin, Pil Shik	Director Bureau of Political Affairs Ministry of Foreign Affairs
Mr. Shin, Kwan Sup	Director Bureau of Costums Duty Ministry of Finance
Mr. Koo, Choong Whay	Chief, America Section Ministry of Foreign Affairs
Mr. O. Won Yong	Chief, Treaty Section Ministry of Foreign Affairs
Col. Lee, Nam Koo	Chief, Military Affairs Section Ministry of National Affairs
Mr. Chu, Mun Ki	chief, Legal Affairs Section Ministry of Justice
Mr. Lee, Kyung Hoon	2nd Secretary Ministry of Foreign Affairs
Mr. Shin, Chung Sup	2nd Secretary Ministry of Foreign Affairs
Mr. Kang, Suk Jae	3rd Secretary Ministry of Foreign Affairs
Mr. Lee, Chang Bum	3rd Secretary Ministry of Foreign Affairs

US Side:

Brig. Gen. J. D. Lawlor	Deputy Chief of Staff 8th Army
Mr. William J. Ford	First Secretary of the Embassy

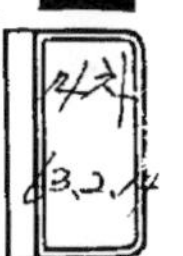

0110

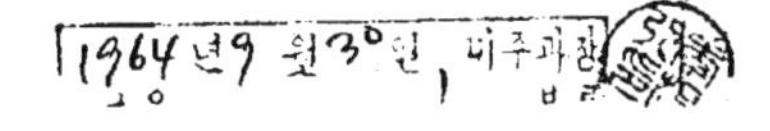

외정 81-140 (16)

0111

Col. G. G. O'Connor	Deputy Chief of Staff 8th Army
Capt. R.M. Brownlie	Assistant Chief of Staff USN/K
Col. W. A. Solf	Staff Judge Advocate 8th Army
Mr. Benjamin A. Fleck (Rapporteur and Press Officer)	First Secretary of the Embassy
Mr. Robert A. Lewis	Second Secretary and Consul of the Embassy
Lt. Col. R.E. Miller	Staff Officer, JAG 8th Army
Lt. Col. W. A. Burt	J-5
Kenneth Campen	Interpreter

Utilities & Services

1. Lt. Col. Miller began the substant discussion by reminding the negotiators that the U.S. side had tabled at the eleventh meeting a draft dealing with utilities and services as part of the U.S. draft article "D". At that time, Mr. Chin had stated that the Korean side would table its corresponding draft at ta later meeting only if there were differences between the two drafts. At the twelfth meeting, the Korean side did table its draft. Lt. Col. Miller suggested, therefore, that the Korean side give its views regarding the differences between the two drafts. He also suggested subparagraph by subparagraph discussion.

2. Pointing out typographic mistake in the Korean draft, Mr. Chin stated that the phrase "however produced" was to be deleted from paragraph 1.

3. Turning to a comparision of the U.S. paragraph 3(a) and the Korean paragraph 1, Mr. Chin requested clarification of the term "political subdivisions thereof" in the U.S. draft. Lt. Col. Miller explained that this referred to municpal, county, and other

0112

기호 87-14②

0113

subordinate administrative offices, such as the Special Cities of Seoul and Pusan, with which the U. S. Armed forces may have dealings from time to time. This language had been included in the U.S. draft in order to insure that the U.S. forces would be able to use utilities controlled or regulated by these subordinate offices. Mr. Chin stated that these subordinate administrations were included in the overall term "Government of Korea" and it was unnecessary, therefore, to refer to them specifically. However, if the U.S. side felt that such reference was desirable, they might be mentioned in an Agreed Minute.

4. Lt. Col. Miller pointed out that the U.S. draft makes clear that the U.S. armed forces could use either publicly- or privately-owned utilities. He suggested that an Agreed Minute would unnecessarily complicate this portion of the Agreement, inasmuch as the language could be included in the Article without complicating or confusing its terms. He said the U.S. side considered an Agreed Minute to be unnecessary and preferred to retain this reference in the body of the article. General Lawlor added that the U.S. armed forces might have to pay utility bills directly to these subordinate administrative offices and therefore this reference should be retained.

5. Mr. Chin stated that there was no substantial difference in content in the two drafts but only in language. Lt. Col. Miller replied that the U.S. side had tried to spell everything out and not leave anything to implication. Mr. Chin stated that absolutely necessary language must be included but suggested that unnecessary words should be avoided. He pointed out that privately-owned utilities-not regulated by the

0114

미본87-14④

0115

ROKG would not be covered by the phrase "publicly or privately owned" in the U.S. draft. Mr. Chin expressed the view that the phrase "belonging to, or controlled or regulated by the Government of the Republic of Korea" in the Korean draft was a better formulation. He further pointed out that this phrase in the Korean draft would be broad enough to cover the meaning and implication of the phrase "whether publicly or privately owned, which are controlled or regulated by the Government of the Republic of Korea" in the U.S. draft. He then suggested that the phrase used in the Korean draft be inserted in place of the corresponding phrase in the U.S. draft. Lt. Col. Miller stated that the U.S. draft is more specific but said the U.S. side would consider the proposal.

6. Mr. Chin pointed out that the definition of utilities and services was identical in both drafts, except for the phrase "however produced", which remained in the U.S. draft. Lt. Col. Miller pointed out that the proposed Agreed Minute #2 of the U.S. draft referred to the existing Utilities Claims Settlement Agreement and stated that the latter Agreement will remain in full force and effect. He also emphasized that the definition of utilities and services in the draft article was taken from the Utilities Claims Settlement Agreement which included the term "however produced". He added that use of the Claims Settlement Agreement definition in its entirety was deemed more desirable because it would obviate questions which might later be raised concerning reasons why the SOFA Article definition was different. Mr. Chin replied that inasmuch as drafts

0116

0117

contain no substantial difference, smoother wording would be better in the formulation. Lt. Col. Miller said the U.S. side recognized this but desired to include a specific reference, in the Agreed Minute, to the fact that the existing utilities agreement would continue in force.

7. Mr. Chin requested an explanation of the remainder of paragraph 3 (a) in the U.S. draft which was not included in the Korean draft. Lt. Col. Miller explained that everything discussed so far had concerned utilities and services provided by the ROKG. However, there were some utilities which the U.S. armed forces themselves had to operate. The nature and extent of these utilities would vary from time to time. The purpose of the language in the U.S. draft is to make clear that the U.S. armed forces have the right to operate such utilities in addition to those which are furnished by the ROKG.

8. Mr. Chin said this would create problems, particularly in the field of transportation, such as the operation of military trains by the U.S. armed forces on the Korean railways system. Lt. Col. Miller replied that the most probable areas were the military communications network, the provision of alternate power sources, and the operation of various types of military transportation facilities. He pointed out that the U.S. armed forces are presently using Korean facilities under the terms of the Utilities Claims Settlement Agreement. He said the U.S. draft would not permit the expropriation of Korean facilities but would permit the U.S. armed forces to operate their own. Mr. Chin

0118

0119

again referred to the operationof military trains on the Korean railways and inquired whether, in such a case, the U.S. armed forces would consult with the Ministry of Transportation. Lt. Col. Miller replied that this would be necessary and that the Joint Committee also would undoubtedly be involved. General Lawlor agreed.

9. Mr. Chin stated that this point was another question of language. He suggested for the consideration of the U.S. side the following alternative language for the third sentence of paragraph 3 (a) of the U.S. draft:

> "The operation by the U.S. armed forces of military transportation, communications, power, and other utilities and services shall be to the extent which is deemed necessary for the operations of the U.S. armed forces and which is not inconsistent with operation by the Republic of Korea of such utilities and services."

Mr. Chin emphasized the necessity of ensuring that operation of such utilities by the U.S. armed forces would not interfere with Korean operation of the same utilities. Therefore, the systems and practices of the U.S. armed forces must be consistent with those used by the Korean authorities concerned.

10. General Lawlor stated that under current procedures, whenever the U.S. armed fordes run military trains, they are operated in a manner consistent with the Korean practices. Lt. Col. Miller pointed out that the U.S. armed forces might also wish to operate other types of utilities which are completely self-contained and unrelated to any existing Korean utilities. General

0120

Lawlor mentioned that the U.S. armed forces may wish to operate their own bus lines from time to time. Mr. Chin said that vehicles operated by the U.S. armed forces should obey all Korean traffic laws and regulations. General Lawlor agreed. Mr. Chin said if operations are continued on the same basis as at present, there will be no problems.

11. Turning to paragraph 3(b) of the U.S. draft, Mr. Chin pointed out that the subject of the draft was the priorities and conditions under which utilities furnished by the ROKG were to be used by the U.S. armed forces. He said the corresponding Korean draft provided for "conditions no less favorable than those that may be applicable from time to time to the ministries and agencies of the Government of the Republic of Korea". He said the conditions applicable to the Government were the most proper conditions. He then asked the U.S. side to explain their draft.

12. Lt. Col. Miller replied that the U.S. draft differs from the Korean draft in two major respects: (1) it includes mention of rates and tariffs, and (2) it provides that the U.S. armed forces would pay rates equivalant to those paid by the most favored user. He pointed out that this provision would provide additional guidance for the negotiation of utilities agreements under the Utilities and Claims Settlement Agreement. Mr. Chin said the Korean side would have no objection to the inclusion of "rates and tariffs" in the article. However, the most reasonable conditions are those which are accorded to the ministries and agencies of the ROKG.

13. Lt. Col. Miller stated that U.S. armed forces in other countries have had unfortunated experiences in

0122

미용87-140

0123

the past by relying on provisions similar to those contained in the Korean draft. he said the language of the U.S. draft would avoid misunderstandings such as have arisen elsewhere. Mr. Chin said that it would be reasonable for the U.S. armed forces to receive the same treatment as that accorded ministries and agencies of the ROK Government. He said cases such as those referred to by Lt. Col. Miller were exceptional. General Lawlor explained that in some cases in other countries, the U.S. armed forces have been forced to pay rates higher than those paid by other users because of manipulated "government"rates. Also, there have been cases in which different agencies of the same government have been charged different rates. In such a case, the question arises as to which rate shall be paid by the U.S. armed forces. Mr. Chin replied that such things could never happen in Korea. General Lawlor acknowledged that the U.S. armed forces have not had that kind of experience in Korea.

14. Mr. Chin explained that according to the existing system, the government pays a reasonable rate and there is only one rate charged to all government agencies. General Lawlor pointed out that in a mixed economy such as that existing in the Republic of Korea, it is often difficut to distinguish the line between government agencies and private organizations. Lt. Col. Miller added that all the U.S. armed forces were asking for was to be charged the lowest rate, whether that was the rate charged to government agencies or not. Mr. Chin said the U.S. side would understand the Korean side's

0124

미문 87-14⑧

0125

position if it examined the treatment accorded to agencies of the ROK Government to date. General Lawlor replied that no criticism was intended of the treatment which has been given to the U.S. armed forces.

15. Mr. Chin stated that the increase of rates was a very important matter which would affect the interest of the entire population. It was utterly unthinkable that the Korean authority would manipulate such an important matter of increasing rates, without due regard to the effect on the interest of the entire population but only with the purpose of charging higher rates to the U.S. armed forces. The U.S. side would not but make the representations to the Korean authorities and also refer the matter to the Joint Committee, should such an unthinkable case take place. General Lawlor agreed but pointed out that the U.S. armed forces would be in a poor bargaining position because of their urgent and continuing need for the utilities and services. Mr. Chin stated that we are discussing the SOFA under the circumstances which are prevailing at present. If the situation be drastically changed after the conclusion of the SOFA, it will bring about the problem on the principle of "change of situation" in international law.

16. Moving on to the second sentence of paragraph 3 (b) of the U.S. draft, Mr. Chin said it appeared that the intent of the U.S. draft was to prevent discrimination against the U.S. armed forces. Treatment equal to that accorded the ROK Government is not discrimination against the U.S. armed forces. Treatment equal to that accorded the ROK Government is not discrimination, he said. Furthermore, it is taken for granted that

0126

마음 87-149

0127

the ROK Government will do everything in its power to prevent any such discrimination. He suggested that the language of the U.S. draft was somewhat degrading and proposed deletion of that sentence. General Lawlor replied that this sentence also was connected with the position of the U.S. armed forces as customers and it had been included in the draft to ensure that the U.S. armed forces would be given favorable treatment. He said the U.S. side would consider the position of the Korean side.

17. Regarding the third sentence of paragraph 3(b) of the U.S. draft, Mr. Chin stated that in emergency situations, the U.S. and Korean armed forces would receive equal treatment. Lt. Col. Miller pointed out that the SOFA has to be tailored to the needs of specific situations. This sentence constitutes recognition of the fact that the Republic of Korea is a potential combat area. There is thus more chance of an emergency arising here than in many other places. This language is meant to ensure that in such an emergency, the U.S. armed forces would not be limited to the usual or normal arrangements with regard to utilities and services. The exact nature of the emergency cannot be predicted.

18. Mr. Chin replied that the Korean side was well aware of Lt. Col. Miller's explanation and had been considering the situation. He said that a separate article, to bee discussed later, would define steps to be taken in the event of the most serious emergency which could arise. He did not think it necessary or desirable to refer to emergency actions in every article

0128

미문 811-14 (10)

0129

of the SOFA. Even if it were not spelled out in this article, he said, the treatment accorded to the U.S. armed forces in the event of emergency would be equivalent to that accorded to the ROK armed forces in such event. He suggested that the sentence be deleted.

19. General Lawlor stated that the point of the sentence was that a commander of military forces must be sure that he is able to move, shoot, and communicate in the event of an emergency. That is why the sentence was included in the draft. Lt. Col. Miller added that certain agencies of the Korean Government might need more assistance during an emergency than others and the U.S. armed fordes might need more assistance than any ROK Government agency. The purpose of this clause is not to assure that the U.S. armed forces get as many as or more utilities and services than any ROK Government agency but that they have some assurance of getting what they require. If such assistance were not forthcoming, the U.S. armed forces might not be able to accomplish their mission.

20. Mr. Chin said the Korean side would study the remarks of the U.S. side concerning this matter. He said apparently there were differences in the ways of thinking of the two sides. He said the Korean side placed ethics and morality on a higher plane than the law. He said it was taken for granted, morally and by common sense, that the Korean Government would extend the utmost possible cooperation in time of emergency. He said the Korean side did not disagree with the substance of the U.S. draft but thought inclusion of this

0130

미문87-14⑪

0131

appreciation for Mr. Chin's remarks.

21. Turning to paragraph 4 of the U.S. draft and paragraph 2(a) of the Korean draft, Mr. Chin expressed the opinion that the Korean draft was more inclusive than the U.S. draft and asked for the comments of the U.S. side. Lt. Col. Miller replied that the U.S. draft was not limited to utilities but refers to accounting arrangements arising out of the SOFA as a whole. He pointed out that payments could be made between authorities of the two governments, as provided for in the Korean draft, or between other agencies or persons. He said this paragraph must also be considered in conjunction with the proposed Agreed Minute #2 in the U.S. draft, which would continue the existing Utilities Claims Settlement Agreement in effect. Referring to paragraph 2 (b) of the Korean draft, he pointed out that the existing arrangements are renegotiated from time to time. Therefore, the relevant language must be kept flexible. He asked the Korean side to clarify their subparagraph (b). Mr. Chin stated that the Korean side would study this point and suggested further discusssion at a subsequent meeting. Lt. Col. Miller pointed out that there would be some arrangements which could not be negotiated until the SOFA comes into effect. There are also some existing agreements which may have to be revised. Mr. Chin said the Korean side understood this point and would discuss it at the next meeting.

22. Mr. Chin then asked the U.S. side to explain its proposed Agreed Minute #1. Lt. Col. Miller explained that an increase in utilities rates would mean an

0132

미문 87-14 ⑰

0133

increase in the expenditure of appropriated funds and a corresponding decrease in the amount of such funds which could be spent on other activities of the U.S. armed forces in Korea. A change in priorities would similarly affect the military posture of those forces. Therefore, this Agreed Minute is intended to provide the two governments with an opportunity to present their respective views before rates were increased or priorities changed.

23. Mr. Chin commented that the U. S. armed forces are given the same priority as ROK Government agencies. According to the U.S. draft, if the U.S. armed forces priority were lowered, which would not happen, prior consultation with the armed froces would surely take place. Similarly, prior consultation must take place before any change in rates, in the U.S. draft. He said that if the sepcial rates accorded the U.S. armed forces applied only to those forces, prior consultation would be a simple matter. However, the rates accorded the U.S. armed forces are the same as those accorded generally to agencies of the ROK Government. An increase in the rates would require scrupulous deliberation and highly technical actions by the ROK Government. Prior consultation, under these circumstances, would be very difficult. The interests of the entire population would be affected. The ROK Government would try to cooperate with the U.S. Government in order to prevent unnecessary inconvenience but it would be extremely difficult for the ROK Government to commit itself to prior consultation. Mr.Chin reiterated that since a change of rates was a matter primarily affecting the interest of the entire population of Korea, such a change would be handled

0134

기본87-14 ⑬

0135

very prudently by the Korean Government. He thus said taht, in a word, such a change would generally be taken up as a matter to be dealt with and decided on the base of domestic considerations.

24. General Lawlor pointed out that we were not suggesting a commitment to obtain US Government agreement but only prior consultation. Lt. Col. Miller added that much advance planning would be required on the part of the U.S. armed forces also. Mr. Chin said the Korean people would not be given the opportunity of prior consultation. In reply, General Lawlor pointed out that the U.S. armed forces were the guests of the ROK Government and would have to do a lot of advance planning if any increase in rates were contemplated.

25. Mr. Chin suggested that the U.S. proposed Agreed Minute #1 be deleted. General Lawlor observed that a change in rates might be amde at a low administratife level. Mr. Chin replied that an increase in rates would be made only after very careful study. General Lawlor observed that the relationship between the U.S. armed forces and the ROK Government was very close. He reminded the negotiators that although a marriage was customarily entered into for other than legal reasons, the legal safeguards written into the marriage contract provide a sound basis for the smooth functioning of the marriage.

Enrollment and Training of Reservists

26. Turning to the draft article on the enrollment and training of reservists, Col. Solf reminded the negotiators that at the previous meeting the Korean

0136

side had expressed certain doubts concerning the U.S. draft. Mr. Habib had made certain explanations which the Korean side had agreed to consider, concerning the Korean side's fear that the U.S. draft might circumvent the Korean alien registration laws. Col. Solf asked if the Korean side had given further consideration to this question.

27. Mr. Chin asked whether it was the intention of the U.S. armed forces to draft temporary visitors to Korea for reserve training. Col. Solf replied that it was extremely unlikely that a tourist in Korea would be involved in reserve training. He said this was not contemplated under any of the existing reserve procedures. Mr. Chin said the phrase "United States citizens who are in the Republic of Korea" included all U.S. citizens. Col. Solf said that this was possible. However, assuming that a tourist is enrolled for reserve training before the expiration of the 30-day period in which he is required to register with the Korean authorities, the Joint Committee would be expected to work out satisfactory procedures to take care of this problem. He pointed out that the only people exempt from the requirement to register were members of the U.S. armed forces on active duty, and other classes enumerated in the definitions article.

28. Mr. Chin said the Korean side had no objection to reserve training for anyone actually residing in Korea. But the Korean side believed the enrollment of temporary visitors to be unreasonable. Col. Solf pointed out that use of the term "resident" had been avoided in the U.S. draft because of the provisions of

0138

미문 811-14 ⑮

0139

the Entry and Exit Article, which debarred members of the U.S. armed forces, the civilain component, and their dependents from acquiring the status of permanent residents or establishing a domicile.

29. Mr. Chin then suggested the addition to the U.S. draft of the phrase "except for ordinary tourists". Col. Solf said the U.S. side would take this under consideration but assured the Korean side that the enrollment of ordinary tourists for reserve training was an extremely rare occurence. He called the attention of the Korean side to the provisions of the U.S. draft of the Definitions Article, and of paragraphs 2 and 5 of the Entry and Exit Article. He said those provisions should resolve the doubts of the Korean side, inasmuch as reservists not on active duty were in no way exempt from Korean Entry Exit or registration Laws.

30. At this point, drafts were exchanged of the article governing foreign exchange.

31. The next meeting was scheduled for February 25 at 2:00 p.m.

미국·조 87-14 (16) (5)

0141

JOINT SUMMARY RECORD OF THE 15TH SESSION
STATUS OF FORCES NEGOTIATIONS

February 25, 1963

1. Time and Place: 2:00 to 3:30 p.m. February 25, 1963 at the Foreign Minister's Conference Room

2. Attendants:

ROK Side:

Mr. Chin, Pil Shik	Coordinator for Planning and Program
Mr. Whang, Ho Eul	Director Bureau of Political Affairs Ministry of Foreign Affairs
Mr. Koo, Choong Whay	Chief, America Section Ministry of Foreign Affairs
Col. Lee, Nam Koo	Chief, Military Affairs Section Ministry of National Defense
Mr. Chu, Mun Ki	Chief, Legal Affairs Section Ministry of Justice
Mr. Lee, Kyung Hoon	2nd Secretary Ministry of Foreign Affairs
Mr. Shin, Chung Sup	2nd Secretary Ministry of Foreign Affairs
Mr. Kang, Suk Jae	3rd Secretary Ministry of Foreign Affairs
Mr. Lee, Chang Bum	3rd Secretary Ministry of Foreign Affairs

US Side:

Mr. Philip C. Habib	Counselor of the Embassy for Political Affairs
Mr. William J. Ford	First Secretary of the Embassy
Col. G. G. O'Connor	Deputy Chief of Staff 8th Army
Capt. R. M. Brownlie	Assistant Chief of Staff USN/K
Col. W. A. Solf	Staff Judge Advocate 8th Army

0142

Mr. Banjamin A. Fleck (Rapporteur and Press Officer)	First Secretary of the Embassy
Mr. Robert A. Lewis	Second Secretary and Consul of the Embassy
Lt. Col. R. E. Miller	Staff Officer, JAG 8th Army
Lt. Col. W. A. Burt	J-5

1. Mr. Chin opened the meeting by introducing Mr. Whang Ho Eul, Mr. Chin's successor as Director of the Bureau of Political Affairs in the Ministry of Foreign Affairs. Mr. Habib congratulated Mr. Chin and Mr. Whang on their promotions and welcomed Mr. Whang to the SOFA negotiations as an old friend.

Foreign Exchange Controls

2. Beginning the substantive discussion, the negotiators took up the article dealing with foreign exchange controls. Mr. Chin stated that the drafts exchanged at the previous meeting were practically identical. He said the Korean side would accept the U.S. draft of the article if the U.S. side would accept the Korean draft of the Agreed Minute. Mr. Habib replied that the only difference occurrred in the final sentence of the Agreed Minute. He asked the Korean side to explain what was meant by the term "basic rate of exchange" in the Korean draft.

3. Mr. Chin replied that the term "basic rate of exchange" referred to the current situation in the Republic of Korea, where there is now in effect a single rate of exchange. Mr. Habib stated that such a definition was not really suitable to an agreement of the kind which was being negotiated, which was intended to endure for a lengthy period and for that reason

0144

[illegible] 87-15 ②

0145

should include a more precise definition of the exchange rate. Mr. Ford added that even in the present situation, differences of opinion might arise over what constituted the "basic" rate of exchange. He pointed out that the present "basic" rate is 125 won to the dollar. However, there is in addition a certificate rate of 5 won, as well as a service charge of 5 won. The question might therefore be raised whether the basic rate was 125 to 1, 129.5 to 1, or 130 to 1. He explained that the U.S. draft of the Agreed Minute was based on the language of the comprehensive aid agreement of February 8, 1961.

4. Mr. Chin replied that the Korean side had not seen the U.S. draft of the Agreed Minute. It was then discovered that the text of the Agreed Minute had been omitted inadvertently from the text of the article tabled by the U.S. side at the 14th meeting. Mr. Habib expressed the opinion that the Korean draft of the Agreed Minute was not entirely suitable. He said the U.S. side would submit alternativel language at the next meeting. Pending agreement on the Agreed Minute, he suggested that both sides agree to the U.S. draft of the article. Mr. Chin agreed.

Enrollment and Training of Reservists

5. Turning to the article on enrollment and training of reservists, Mr. Chin recalled that at the previous meeting, the Korean side had suggested the addition to the U.S. draft of the phrase "except for ordinary tourists". He asked for comment by the U.S. side.

0146

비문87-15③

0147

6. Colonel Solf reminded the negotiators that at the previous meeting, the U.S. side had invited the attention of the Korean side to the provisions of other articles of the SOFA as follows:

a. Definitions Article - subparagraph (a):

"Members of the United States armed forces" means the personnel on active duty belonging to the land, sea or air armed services of the United States of America when in the territory of the Republic of Korea except for those for whom status has otherwise been provided."

b. Entry & Exit Article - paragraph 2:

"Members of the United States armed forces shall be exempt from Korean passport and visa laws and regulations. Members of the United States armed forces, the civilian component, and their dependents shall be exempt from Korean laws and regulations on the registration and control of aliens, but shall not be considered as acquiring any right to permanent residence or domicile in the territory of the Republic of Korea."

c. Entry & Exit Article - paragraph 5:

"If the status of any person brought into the Republic of Korea under paragraph 1 of this Article is altered so that he would no longer be entitled to such admission,the United States authorities shall notify the Korean authorities and shall, if such person be required by the Korean authorities to leave the Republic of Korea, assure that transportation from the Republic of Korea will be provided within a reasonable time at no cost to the Government of the Republic of Korea."

7. Colonel Solf stated that the U.S. side could again assure the Korean side that a reservist entering Korea who is not on active duty is not exempt from any Korean entry or registration procedures. While in Korea as a reservist not on active duty, he acquires no special privileges or immunities. Colonel Solf added that the U.S. side was also prepared to assure the Korean side that the U.S. armed forces have no intention to

0148

미등87-15④

0149

order ordinary tourists to active duty without the consent of the tourists. If, under unusual circumstances, a reservist were to enter on active duty from tourist status, Colonel Solf continued, the U.S. armed forces would work out procedures to notify the Korean authorities of the tourist's change of status. Colonel Solf then asked the Korean side if it would agree to the U.S. draft, on the basis of the preceding assurances and explanation. Mr. Habib commented that the problem raised by the Korean side was taken care of by other articles of the SOFA, as just explained by Colonel Solf. Therefore, it would be much simpler to accept the U.S. draft as tabled.

8. Mr. Chin stated that some confustion appeared to have arisen concerning the position of the Korean side. He said the Korean side did not intend to emphasize the question of enforcing Korean entry, exit, and registration regulations. What the Korean side was concerned about, he said, was the possibility of tourists being drafted for reserve training. He expressed concern over the possibility that American students or other American tourists might feel such measures to be unreasonable.

9. Mr. Habib replied that there was no intention of drafting tourists for reserve training against their will. He pointed out again that enforcement of the entry and exit regulations was provided for in other articles and that if the status of a tourist changed, the Korean authorities would be notified. But the fact that an American is a tourist does no change the fact that he is a United States citizen.

0150

미문 87-15 (5)

0151

The negotiating record, Mr. Habib continued, would include the statement just made by Colonel Solf, which would serve as a guide to the Joint Committee, should the matter ever come up, which he doubted very much. He said the U.S. side greatly appreciated the solicitude shown by the Korean side for the rights of U.S. citizens but, in fact, this point would never cause any problem. No such problem has ever arisen in connection with any other SOFA.

10. Mr. Chin then summed up the Korean position by stating that the point at issue was whether tourists who might stay in the country for lengthy periods could be enrolled for reserve training without their consent. He indicated that the use of the term "residing in" had been used in this sense in the Korean draft, rather than in the strictly legal sense of permanent residence. Colonel Solf had previously said that the drafting of tourists for reserve training would be extermely rare, Mr. Chin continued. Mr. Chin had then suggested the addition of the phrase "except for ordinary tourists". Now Colonel Solf had stated that there was no intention to draft such people for reserve training against their will. On the basis of U.S. side's assurances and explanation, Mr. Chin said, the Korean side agreed to the U.S. draft of the article.

11. Mr. Habib pointed out that a toruist can remain in the Republic of Korea as a tourist for no longer than thirty days. He then suggested that the negotiating redord include the statments just made by Colonel Solf and Mr. Chin. Mr. Chin agreed.

0152

미문 81-15⑥

0153

Joint Committee

12. Turning to the Joint Committee article, Mr. Chin asked if the U.S. side had considered the Agreed Minute proposed by the Korean side at the 11th meeting. Mr. Habib replied that the Korean side had indicated it would accept the text of the U.S. draft of the article, provided the U.S. side accepted an Agreed Minute regarding as follows:

> "The exception provided for in the first sentence of paragraph 1 is relevant only to paragraph 2, subparagraphs (b) and (c) of Article _____".

Mr. Habib stated that the U.S. side accepted the above Agreed Minute. Full agreement was thereupon reached on the Article and Agreed Minute.

Definitions Article

13. Turning to the Definitions Article, Mr. Chin recalled that at previous meetings agreement had been reached on all portions except for Agreed Minutes #1 and #2.

14. With regard to the Korean proposal to delete the word "readily" from the U.S. draft of Agreed Minute #2, Mr. Habib remarked that the word was one of explanation rather than limitation. He said there was no intention that this word provide an occasion for abuse. Without it, the sentence had little meaning, since one could always argue that any skill needed by the U.S. armed forces was "available" in either the United States or Korea. But the practical test was whether such skills were "readily" available or not.

0154

미문 07-15(17)

0155

15. Mr. Chin replied that the Korean side fully understood the situation which Mr. Habib had explained. He agreed that "readily" can be interpreted either broadly or narrowly. He suggested instead the use of the phrase "practically not available". Mr. Habib said the proposed phrase did not sound very good in English. He then suggested that the negotiating record show that discussion of this point indicated that the word "available" means available in a practical sense. If this were agreeable to the Korean side, the U.S. side would agree to deletion of the word "readily". Mr. Chin agreed.

16. With regard to Agreed Minute #1, Mr. Habib stated that the U.S. side had considered the draft previously submitted by the Korean side. He said the U.S. side wished to propose alternative language, reflecting the actual situation and the views of the Korean side. A revised draft of Agreed Minute #1 was thereupon tabled by the U.S. side.

17. After reading the U.S. draft, Mr. Chin suggested that the word "include" be changed to the phrase "refers only to", since the exception actually applies only to those for whom status has already otherwise been provided. Mr. Habib replied that it was for that very reason that the U.S. language should be acceptable to the Korean side. The Korean side had previously objected to the phrase "such as". The U.S. side had now met that criticism. He added that the reference to personnel "attached to" the United States Embassy included

0156

예문 87-1-⑧

0157

both attache personnel and the Marine Guards. He pointed out that the Korean language did not include the Marine Guards. At this point, the Korean side tabled its revised draft of the Agreed Minute #1, and Mr. Chin stated that the both sides would give comparative study to both drafts. Mr. Chin stated that the Korean side preferred its proposed revised draft, but would agree to the U.S. draft of the Agreed Minute #1, provided the phrase "refers only to" were substituted for the word "include". The U.S. side agreed to take this proposal under consideration. It was agreed that the revised text of the U.S. draft of the article and Agreed Minute #2 was acceptable to both sides.

Navigational Aids

18. Turning to the draft article dealing with air traffic control and navigational aids, Captain Brownlie stated that it was the understanding of the U.S. side that the Korean side had indicated a readiness to accept the U.S. draft, provided the phrase "throughout the Republic of Korea and in the territorial waters thereof" in paragraph 2 were further amplified to provide for mutual consultation prior to the establishment or construction of navigational aids. In order to satisfy the Korean requirements in this regard, he said, the U.S. side wished to table an Agreed Minute as an alternative to the additional language suggested by the Korean side. Having tabled the draft Agreed Minute, Captain Brownlie pointed out that paragraph 1 of the first of four articles

0158

on Facilities and Areas previously tabled by the U.S. side, to which this Agreed Minute makes reference, reads, in part, as follows:

> "... Agreements as to specific facilities and areas shall be concluded by the two governments through the Joint Committee".

19. Mr. Chin expressed appreciation to the U.S. side for having taken the previous Korean suggestion under consideration. He said the Korean side would study the proposed Agreed Minute and make known its views at the next meeting.

20. In adjourning the meeting, Mr. Chin noted that the negotiators had made considerable progress that day. The next meeting was scheduled for March 8 at 2:00 p.m.

21. <u>Points of Agreement:</u>

a. U.S. draft of Foreign Exchange Controls Article (Agreed Minute peinding)

b. U.S. draft of Enrollment & Training of Reservists Article

c. U.S. draft of Joint Committee Article Korean draft of Agreed Minute

d. U.S. draft (as revised) of Definitions Article & Agreed Minute #2 (Agreed Minute #1 pending)

0160

외고문서 비밀해제: 주한미군지위협정(SOFA) 19
주한미군지위협정(SOFA) 서명 및 발효 19

초판인쇄 2024년 03월 15일
초판발행 2024년 03월 15일

지은이 한국학술정보(주)
펴낸이 채종준
펴낸곳 한국학술정보(주)
주 소 경기도 파주시 회동길 230(문발동)
전 화 031-908-3181(대표)
팩 스 031-908-3189
홈페이지 http://ebook.kstudy.com
E-mail 출판사업부 publish@kstudy.com
등 록 제일산-115호(2000. 6. 19)

ISBN 979-11-7217-030-1 94340
979-11-7217-011-0 94340 (set)

책에 대한 더 나은 생각, 끊임없는 고민, 독자를 생각하는 마음으로 보다 좋은 책을 만들어갑니다.